Peter Arkad'evich Stolypin

Premier Peter Stolypin and his wife, Olga Borisovna.

Peter Arkad'evich Stolypin
Practical Politics in Late Tsarist Russia

Mary Schaeffer Conroy

Peter Arkad'evich Stolypin, Russian minister of internal affairs and chairman of Tsar Nicholas II's Council of Ministers from 1906 to 1911—when Stolypin was assassinated—was one of the chief figures in the Russian government during a critical period in its history. A modernizer whose ideas and dreams for the future were well based in practicality, he nevertheless was unable to stem the revolutionary tide in Russia. Stolypin has long been a controversial figure, perhaps largely because most of the records of his private statements have been buried in various archives. Dr. Conroy has rectified that situation, analyzing, for example, the statesman's comments in private meetings of the Council of Ministers, reports, personal correspondence, and unpublished orders, as well as the reminiscences of his colleagues, friends, and family. The result is a fascinating view not only of a man, but of government in late Tsarist Russia.

Dr. Conroy has taught at Kansas State University and the University of Illinois, Chicago Circle, and currently teaches Russian history at the University of Colorado, Denver.

Peter Arkad'evich Stolypin

Practical Politics
in Late Tsarist Russia

Mary Schaeffer Conroy

Westview Press
Boulder, Colorado

To my husband, Tom, my daughters, and my parents

Copyright 1976 by Westview Press

Published 1976 in the United States of America by
    Westview Press, Inc.
    1898 Flatiron Court
    Boulder, Colorado 80301
    Frederick A. Praeger, Publisher and Editorial Director

Library of Congress Cataloging in Publication Data

Conroy, Mary S.   1937-
    Peter Arkad'evich Stolypin: practical politics
in late tsarist Russia.

    Bibliography: p. 195
    Includes index.
    1. Stolypin, Peter Arkad'evich, 1862-1911.
2. Russia—Politics and government—1894-1917.
DK254.S595C66   947.08'092'4   [B]   76-48070
ISBN 0-89158-143-X

Table of Contents

Foreword

As Minister of Internal Affairs and Chairman of the Council of Ministers from 1906 until his assassination in 1911, Peter Arkad'evich Stolypin was concerned with vital sectors of Russia's domestic affairs. It was a crucial period in Russian history. Russia was still suffering from the upheaval of 1905. Terrorists still committed outrages. Improvement in the condition of the peasants, Jews, Old Believers and sectarians, the establishment of universal primary education, reform of the local administrative apparatus, and changes in the zemstvos were long overdue. National minorities were restive. Russia had begun to experiment with a representative parliament; thus, Stolypin had to work with a new type of government with which everyone was inexperienced. In addition to these problem areas, over which he had special jurisdiction, Stolypin had to contend with encumbrances which had restricted past chief administrators hoping to effect change in Russia—the attitude of the Tsar, the ultimate authority in Russia, opposition from other ministers, and the obstructionism of reactionary or hostile groups. In many ways Stolypin's administration was a test case as to whether Russia could revitalize herself and whether a parliament could take root.

Stolypin has long been a controversial figure and no full-length biography of him exists. Most historians praise his agrarian reforms and his attempt to remedy the position of the Jews in one major project, but other ministerial proposals on the Jews and on reform of the local administrative apparatus have not been thoroughly analyzed. Most historians criticize Stolypin's nationality policies without, in my opinion, having subjected them to impartial scrutiny. Stolypin's attitude toward the new parliament has not been fully explored. His repressive policies have only been sketched. My primary aim has been to present a three-dimensional study of Stolypin, to ascertain his ideas and general outlook, and secondarily to give better understanding of the milieu in which he worked and in which democracy was supposed to flourish.

In some ways Stolypin is a difficult subject to appraise. Not only did he leave no memoirs or treatises in which his beliefs or feelings were comprehensively and categorically recorded, as a practical administrator he was of necessity somewhat ambiguous and inconsistent in both word and deed. His principles and general outlook therefore must be distilled from reports and orders to administrative officials, remarks to colleagues or outsiders like the British ambassador or British observers, from official correspondence and memoranda, and from extant projects and proposals. Particularly fascinating are the summaries of the meetings of the Council of Ministers contained in the Special Journal of the Council, for here one sees the ministry in operation behind the scenes—the give and take that occurred in the ministers' meetings. Stolypin's actions must be evaluated, of course. His often impressive speeches to the State Council and State Duma have sometimes been helpful. However, I have avoided relying on them too heavily on the assumption that like most politicians, Stolypin's public pronouncements not only were written by others, but were intended for rhetorical or psychological effect.

With the support of Foreign Area fellowships and a University of Illinois faculty fellowship and research grant, research for this book was conducted chiefly in the Valtionarkisto (Finnish National Archive), with its complete collection of materials on Finnish-Russian relations during Stolypin's term of office, among the British Foreign Office records of the Public Records Office, London, in the Hoover Library, Stanford, California, which contains the Special Journal of the Council of Ministers (*Osobyi zhurnal soveta ministrov*), Stolypin's proposals on land reform, reform of the local administrative apparatus and local self-government bodies, and documents on the police, and in the Russian Archive, Columbia University, with its rich fund of unpublished memoirs and letters by Stolypin's colleagues and contemporaries. I wish to thank the staffs of these archives, especially Mr. Markku Järvinen of the Valtionarkisto. I am grateful to Prince A. V. Obolensky, who resided in Stockholm, and especially to Stolypin's daughter, Mrs. Maria von Bock, who resides in San Francisco, for supplying me with personal information about Stolypin and the Stolypin family.

I have used the Library of Congress system of transliteration with some modification: "iu" and "ia" have been rendered "yu" and "ya"; "e" never appears "ë"; soft and hard signs have generally been omitted. The Russian letters in Finnish achival references have been transliterated. Dates are old style except those given in British diplomatic reports.

I wish to thank Professors Robert F. Byrnes, Edward C. Thaden, and George Baranny for the encouragement, advice, and help they have given me over the years. I owe a debt of gratitude to my daughters, Alexandra and Margaret, for their patience, and to my parents Edward and Blanche Schaeffer and my husband Tom, whose interest and unflagging enthusiasm made this book possible.

Chapter 1:
The Making of a
Practical Man

Peter Arkad'evich Stolypin emerged from that charmed circle, the affluent Russian nobility before the First World War. Traced to the sixteenth century, Stolypin's family bequeathed him wealth, good social connections, and a tradition of respectable state service and enlightened thinking. Stolypin's immediate family owned estates in southeastern European Russia, in Penza and Saratov provinces; in the central region around Moscow; and in the northwestern provinces (now the Lithuanian SSR). His great-uncle, Arkadii Alekseevich Stolypin, had served as Privy Councilor and Senator under Alexander I. He also had been an author and a friend of Michael Speransky. Arkadii Alekseevich's sister, Stolypin's great-aunt, Elizabeth Arseneva, was Michael Lermontov's grandmother. Arkadii Alekseevich's eldest son had been ambassador to Würtemberg and the Netherlands.[1] His youngest son, Dmitrii, was an amateur philosopher and a writer on the peasant question. Dmitrii's philosophy was woolly, but his ideas on agrarian matters, which he published from the 1870s onward, were far-sighted and practical. In an article entitled "Arendnye khutora" (Leased Farmsteads), which appeared in 1892, he asserted that the *obshchina* or communal form of peasant tenure was the greatest obstacle to increased peasant productivity and prosperity and he advocated individually owned, separated farmsteads.[2] Stolypin himself espoused these ideas from the late 1890s, but he arrived at his conclusions from personal observation and experience rather than because of Dmitrii's influence.

Stolypin's father, Arkadii Dmitrievich, made the army his career, reaching the rank of general. He fought in the Crimean War and, following it, took a position as aide-de-camp to Prince Michael Gorchakov, Viceroy of Warsaw, whose daughter he married. From 1861 to 1865 he served under M. N. Muraviev, Governor General of Vilensk. The future Chairman of the Council of Ministers and Minister of Internal Affairs, Peter Arkad'evich, was born during this period, on April 17, 1862, in Dresden, where his mother was visiting relatives.

In 1865 Arkadii retired to his estates, returning to active service for the Russo-Turkish War of 1877-78. At the conclusion of the war he was appointed Governor General of Eastern Rumelia. The late 1880s found Arkadii and his wife living, according to their nephew Baron Alexander Meyendorff, in Petersburg in an ugly flat filled with ugly furniture. In 1892 he was appointed to the honorary post of commandant of the Kremlin palace, where he served until his death in 1899.

Arkadii Dmitrievich was a bon vivant, popular at dinner parties because of his facility for small talk. But he also cherished scholarly and artistic ambitions. In his youth he reputedly invented a paraffin gas lamp. He played the violin and composed music, sculptured and exhibited his statutes, dabbled in theology, and wrote a play and a history entitled *Khronika Genrikha Latysha, kak podspor'e k izuchen-iyu Severo-Zapadnago kraya* (The Chronicle of Heinrich Latysha, as an Aid to the Study of the History of the Northwest Krai) which was published in Vilna in 1867. The play, which Arkadii wrote while aide-de-camp to Muraviev, was refused passage by the censor-author Goncharov, on the grounds that it was "too patriotic." It characterized Russians as all-virtuous and Poles as villains, an explosive plot for a border region with a significant Polish population. On the other hand, Arkadii was not anti-Semitic and was tolerant in religious matters. Several of his close friends joined the Uniate church. Vladimir Soloviev, upon the invitation of Arkadii Dmitrievich's son Alexander, lectured in Arkadii's Petersburg flat on several occasions on the subject of the union of the Orthodox and Roman Catholic churches.[3]

Arkadii Dmitrievich also was a friend of Leo Tolstoy. He had first met him during the Crimean campaign and visited and corresponded with him afterward. Alexander Arkad'evich was a friend of Tolstoy's eldest son, Sergei, and after Stolypin became Chairman of the Council of Ministers, Tolstoy wrote Alexander and Stolypin, criticizing Stolypin's agrarian policy and asking aid for a peasant falsely arrested. Stolypin ignored the agrarian matter, but acceded to the request for the peasant.[4] Stolypin's mother, Natalya, who died in 1889, apparently was an intelligent and well-educated woman who also was acquainted with some of the most prominent people of her time, including Gogol.[5]

Stolypin's childhood and youth were similar to that of other privileged Russians. He spent his winters at Kolnoberzhe in Kovno, one of the northwest provinces. This estate, which had been acquired by Stolypin's father as payment for a gambling debt, was one of the family's favorites. Summers were spent in Switzerland, although Stolypin was required to travel third class lest he become spoiled.[6]

We know little about Stolypin's early education, except that he had at his disposal the advantages of a wealthy family. The library at Kolnoberzhe reputedly contained 10,000 volumes, most of which had been brought from the Moscow estate of Srednikovo where Lermontov had been raised and which Stolypin's father had inherited.[7] Stolypin had an English governess and French and German tutors. He studied German and French at the gymnasium in Vilna[8] and in later life continued to read these languages fluently.[9]

In 1881 Stolypin entered St. Petersburg University, and in 1884, while still a student, he married Olga Borisovna Neidhardt, the fiancée of his elder brother who had been killed in a duel. According to Stolypin's daughter, Maria Bock, Stolypin's right arm had been paralyzed in 1883 as a result of a duel with the same man who had killed his brother. This prevented him from entering military service and forced him, when writing, to prop up his injured arm with his left hand and to use a goose quill pen.[10]

The Neidhardts were an old Muscovite family. Olga Borisovna's father was a *Pochetnyi Opekun,* or "honor guardian," an office which involved supervision of foundling hospitals, orphan asylums, and certain schools. The family was related to General Suvorov. Olga Borisovna's sister married S. D. Sazonov, secretary of the Russian embassy in London in 1898, later Minister of Foreign Affairs. Olga Borisovna's brother Dmitrii served as prefect of Odessa from 1903 to 1905. He was compromised by his inept handling of disorder and a pogrom in the city in October 1905, but his close connection with Tsar Nicholas II probably was responsible, to a certain extent, for Stolypin's appointment as Minister of Internal Affairs.[11]

Whether because of his early marriage and fatherhood, or as a reaction to his father and younger brother, Stolypin appears to have been a serious and practical young man. He studied in the faculty of natural science at the University of St. Petersburg and wrote a thesis, for which he was graduated with distinction, on tobacco growing in southern Russia.[12] He had no misadventures with the police, as did his brother Alexander, who flirted with liberalism and later became a journalist for *Novoe vremya,* at one point incurring the wrath of Nicholas II for his articles. Alexander also had inherited his father's literary pretentions; he and his friends the Obolenskys and Bobrinskys founded a literary discussion circle which notables such as Soloviev sometimes attended. Stolypin, on the contrary, was conservative even in his literary taste. He liked Aleksei Tolstoy, but one of his favorite poets was the rather mediocre A. N. Apukhtin, popular in Petersburg society and a frequent visitor to Stolypin's home.[13]

After leaving the university in 1885, Stolypin served four years in the statistical department of the Ministry of State Domains. In 1889 he was appointed *uezd* marshal of the nobility in Kovno *guberniya* and moved to the family estate of Kolnoberzhe with his wife and infant daugher Maria to take up this position. Stolypin remained in Kovno thirteen years, serving first as *uezd* marshal and later as provincial marshal of the nobility.

The time which he spent in Kovno proved to be a formative period in Stolypin's life. His position of *uezd* marshal catapulted him from the bureaucratic atmosphere of St. Petersburg into the center of vital issues: agriculture and the peasant problem, the growing urban proletariat, and the position of minorities within the empire. It developed his practicality and realistic outlook which were, perhaps, his most outstanding characteristics.

Kovno in the 1890s had a population of 1,544,564. Until the partitions of Poland in the eighteenth century the area had constituted part of Lithuania-Poland. The majority of the peasants were Lithuanian with a sprinkling of White and Little Russians. The majority of landowners were Poles. Jews, who formed over 13 percent of the population, were concentrated in the towns. Great Russians, the majority of whom were peasants, amounted to less than 5 percent of the population.[14] Kovno was a fairly prosperous agricultural region. The chief crops were cereals and potatoes, there was a flourishing milk and cheese industry, and horse breeding and animal husbandry had made great progress.[15] Stolypin was more than a gentleman farmer on his own estate. He personally supervised the sowing and harvesting, the fruit orchards, reforestation projects, and stock breeding. He was especially fond of horses.[16]

As *uezd* marshal, Stolypin was in charge of the affairs of the nobility within the district. But the *uezd* marshal also served as chairman of the congress of *mirovye posredniki*, or "arbitrators of the peace," and this brought Stolypin into proximity with the peasantry. Like their counterparts in central European Russia, the peasants in Kovno retained the communal form of landholding after their emancipation from serfdom in the middle of the nineteenth century. The commune or *obshchina* had both administrative and economic functions.[17] The type of commune which existed in Kovno and the other western provinces was hereditary. Except for the plot around his hut the peasant held his land in scattered strips. However, these parcels were not reapportioned and redistributed periodically as they were in the communes which predominated in European Russia. Furthermore, the peasants in Kovno had received larger allotments and were required to pay lower redemption fees as a result of the government's campaign against the Polish landowners. Nevertheless, ownership of scattered strips rather than compact plots of land, a common crop cycle, *servitut* or "right-of-passage" for farmers and animals through farm land, and the correlative prohibition on enclosures precluded efficient cultivation and resulted in low productivity.

Although it was replaced in the central Russian provinces in 1874 by a District Gathering for Peasant Affairs, the congress of *mirovye posredniki* remained an institution in the western provinces and the Caucasus. The *mirovye posredniki* facilitated land agreements between landowners and peasants after the emancipation, composed regulatory deeds, determined the size of allotments (these differed throughout the empire depending upon the quality of land, etc.), analyzed all suits and complaints regarding land relationships, and supervised the sale of peasant allotments. They also supervised peasant self-government, determined the boundaries of *volost'* communities (the *volost'* was a rural unit comprising several peasant communes), and approved the *volost' starshina* or "elder." In cases of misconduct on the part of the officials of peasant self-government, the *mirovye posredniki* were permitted to impose fines up to five rubles and arrest up to seven days, to dismiss officials from office, and to instigate judicial proceedings. As chairman of the congress of *mirovye posredniki*, Stolypin authorized the distribution of peasant allotments, decided complaints against peasant officials, and judged cases of unlawful activity, such as hindering peasants from leaving the commune. Finally, as *uezd* marshal of nobility he was responsible for calling up peasant recruits for the army.[18]

By his own admission, Stolypin's views on the peasant question were developed during the years he served as marshal of nobility and chairman of the congress of *mirovye posredniki.*[19] In Kovno, a few peasants had received full allotments and were quite prosperous. Furthermore, the communal form of organization showed signs of disintegration. There were no cases of land purchase by the entire peasant community and very few by groups of peasants. Most purchases were made by individual peasants.[20] Some peasant families had broken away from the commune and were settled on *khutora,* or individually owned, separated farmsteads. The institution of the *khutor* had taken firmer root in the neighboring German state of Prussia.[21] Stolypin visited Prussia frequently and was delighted with the industriousness and prosperity of the yeoman farmers, as compared with the communal peasants.[22] He gradually came to the conclusion that the major solution to the agrarian problem was to establish the peasants on separate, individually owned farmsteads.

The industrial workers, comprising, of course, a much smaller percentage of the population than the peasants did, also began to engage Stolypin's attention in Kovno, and he initiated the construction of a *narodnyi dom,* a combination doss house and recreational center for the workers and municipal populace of Kovno. His long-range plans for Russian workers were more far-reaching. As in the case of the peasantry, Stolypin's views on the industrial worker were drawn from German models. He greatly admired the German worker and stated that Russia must raise its workers to an equal level of economic and intellectual attainment.[23]

It is interesting to note, in view of charges that later in his career Stolypin was a great Russian chauvinist, that in Kovno Stolypin was on good terms with the Poles.[24] To further harmonious relations among the nationalities, as well as to promote agriculture, Stolypin founded an agricultural society with fairly advanced features. Implements and machinery were procured and produce sold on a cooperative basis; membership included peasants as well as landowners, Poles as well as Russians.[25]

Stolypin looked back to the days in Kovno as the happiest in his life. His work was challenging and satisfying, and he was well liked and respected. Kovno was on the way from Petersburg to Berlin and many actors visited with the Stolypin family while en route. Stolypin enjoyed a pleasant home life. In the evenings, the family played cards or Olga Borisovna read novels and poetry aloud. Stolypin took great interest in his daughter Maria's school work and painting, a hobby with which he had amused himself before his arm become paralyzed. The family also traveled abroad. They were near Berlin, where Stolypin was undergoing treatment for his arm, in May 1902 when he received the news that he had been appointed Governor of Grodno.[26]

Stolypin had been recommended for the post by Alexander Tyshkevich, member of the State Council, who had been impressed by Stolypin's energetic work in the agricultural society and by his ability to get along with non-Russian nationalities.[27] Stolypin remained in Grodno only ten months, but it was an important episode in his career.

Grodno was another of the empire's northwestern provinces and economic and social conditions were similar to those in Kovno. Predominantly agricultural, Grodno, in 1897, had a population of 1,603,409 Ukrainians or Little Russians and White or Belorussians constituted the great majority of the population. Great Russians amounted to only a little more than 4 percent. Poles amounted to little more than 10 percent, but they constituted the bulk of the large landowners. Jews comprised over 17 percent of the population.[28]

As Governor of Grodno, Stolypin was the youngest governor in Russia. However, he was not entirely independent, for Grodno, together with the provinces of Kovno and Vilensk, was under the authority of the Governor General of Vilensk. This man, interestingly enough, was Prince P. D. Sviatopolk-Mirsky, who later preceded Stolypin as Minister of Internal Affairs and who inaugurated many of the reforms which Stolypin translated into reality. Stolypin found the subordination chafing, even though his superior was mild-mannered.[29]

Stolypin proved to be as energetic in Grodno as he had been in Kovno. Soon after his arrival he closed a Polish club on the grounds that it was insurrectionary.[30] However, this did not seem to damage the Poles' feeling toward Stolypin. As in Kovno, they apparently liked and respected him and he counted several Poles as his close friends. One was the Roman Catholic Bishop Ropp.[31] Another was a member of the aristocratic Czartoryski family, whose garden bordered the gubernatorial mansion and who often visited the Stolypin household.[32]

During his tenure in Grodno, Stolypin founded an official newspaper which was to influence the populace in a "socio-religious direction."[33] This sort of moralistic dogmatism surfaced periodically in Stolypin's later activity, but without more information on Stolypin's psychological outlook in regard to this venture it is difficult to assess its relevancy.

The most significant activity which Stolypin undertook in Grodno was one thrust upon him by the government. As governor, he served as chairman of the provincial Committee on the Needs of Agricultural Industry, one of a network of committees which functioned in forty-eight provinces under the auspices of the Ministry of Finance during the winter of 1902-1903.

By the beginning of the twentieth century, shortage of land or poor use of land and high taxes and redemption payments had reduced much of the peasantry to an impoverished state. There had been famine before, but the 1902 crop failure and famine were particularly severe and caused widespread peasant disturbances in the Ukraine, the central agricultural region, and along the Volga River. Peasants seized and burned estates and murdered landowners, policemen, and other local officials. In Georgia, peasant protest against poverty and exploitation became a direct uprising against the government. The government surpressed these disorders with military troops, but in addition it inaugurated a positive program to revitalize the agrarian sector of the economy. Officials in both the Ministry of Finance and the Ministry of Internal Affairs began devising projects and planning legislation which would improve agriculture and the position of the peasantry.[34] The Ministry of Internal Affairs worked within the administration. The Ministry of Finance sent questionnaires to *uezd* and provincial committees composed of administrative officials, landowners, and, where they existed, members of local self-governing institutions. The topics for discussion included agricultural experimentation, dissemination and implementation of new agricultural techniques, the granting of land-exploitation credit, the consolidation of peasant land, and improved methods of transporting agricultural produce to market.[35]

The meetings of the Grodno committee on local agricultural industry, the reports of which were sent back to Petersburg to be reviewed, collated, and it was hoped, acted upon, gave Stolypin a chance to publicize and bring to the attention of central governmental authorities the ideas which he had developed during the past decade. In these reports, Stolypin appeared progressive, resolute, and politically astute.

The main issue under discussion was, of course, the means of improving agriculture in general and the condition of the peasantry in particular. Stolypin spoke in favor of the application of scientific farming techniques, government aid for purchase of land and machinery, and cooperative societies like the one he had established in Kovno as important methods of improving agricultural industry.[36] But he stressed that the fundamental remedy was consolidation of peasant land and with it, the abolition of *servitut*, the three-field system of cultivation, and generally archaic farming methods. Without this change in land tenure, making possible more rational farming, Stolypin warned, not only could there be "no serious improvement of agriculture," but the end would be "economic crisis and the complete destruction of the country."[37] In addition to its economic repercussions, Stolypin realized the political implications of agricultural reform, noting that the landless proletariat were ripe candidates for socialistic propaganda.[38] He invited a landowner from Kovno, where the *khutor* system was more prevalent, to describe to the committee the procedures for enabling the peasants to become owners of *khutora*.[39]

It ought to be noted that sizable numbers of the committeemen agreed with the need for consolidation.[40] In addition, however, Stolypin stamped his special personality on his contribution to the proceedings. He stressed that consolidation was so urgent that it ought to be implemented under the auspices of the central government, with force, if necessary, and not left to popular initiative or even to popular acceptance—a theory he was to espouse throughout his career with regard to all reforms which he considered vital.[41]

Although the chief concern of the committee was the peasant, the government also desired local opinion on the industrial worker. A monetary crisis which had occurred in Europe in 1899 had spread to Russia, causing a depression which reached its lowest point in 1902. Lockouts and unemployment resulted in a wave of strikes, each involving several thousand workers. The workers' grievances were economic but in some instances revolutionary groups intervened, giving the strikes a political character. Stalin, for example, organized strikes in Batum in 1902. In November of that year, workers in the main railway shops in Rostov-on-the-Don, striking for a ten-hour day and betterment of working conditions, were guided by the Don committee of the Russian Social Democratic Labor Party. The committee rallied huge meetings (supposedly amounting to 30,000 workers each) which ended in armed conflict between the Don cossacks and the assembled workers. In 1902, Lenin praised the political significance of the Rostov strike in an article in *Iskra*.[42]

There is no evidence that Stolypin was familiar with this article, but he was aware that workers' grievances could be exploited by revolutionary groups. As in Kovno, he cited Germany for Russia's model, suggesting that workers' insurance, which was widespread in Germany, could prevent the spread of socialism.[43]

Stolypin strongly advocated not only the development of agronomic programs,[44] but universal, compulsory general education, a reform which Russia greatly needed in view of the 1897 census' revelation that only one person in five was literate. In response to one Prince Chetvertinskii, who criticized education as unnecessary and dangerous insofar as it led to the growth of socialistic and anarchistic ideas, Stolypin delivered a stirring defense of education which prefigured the eloquent oratory of his later career. He claimed that it was "impossible to fear learning and education—impossible to fear the light," and stressed that "education of the people correctly and intelligently embarked upon" could never lead to anarchy. As an example he pointed again to Germany, which enjoyed universal education and yet was the epitome of a peaceful and patriotic country, and contrasted this situation with that in Italy, where popular education was weak but which was a breeding place of anarchists.[45] Stolypin also shrewdly noted the unifying aspect of general education in a multinational country and the ideological use to which it might be put, declaring that the "true purpose" and "chief problem" of the school was "teaching the state language and bringing up the Russian citizen." He admitted, however, that universal, compulsory education was not possible in the near future, given the conditions which then existed in Russia.[46]

A final point which Stolypin emphasized was greater decentralization in the socioeconomic sphere—the increased role which local individuals and institutions ought to play in Russia's economic development. Although agents of the central government might be competent, he noted, local persons were more cognizant of local needs.[47]

The views which Stolypin expressed on the peasant question, education, and the importance of local government remained unchanged throughout his career, and these issues became fundamental parts of his later program. Two other issues—reorganization of *volost'* government and the introduction of zemstvos into the western provinces—which also became key parts of his later program, he astutely dismissed from the agenda of the Grodno meetings on the grounds that they were "political" in tone and therefore outside the scope of the committee.[48]

Stolypin's impeccable behavior, as well as his creative ideas, probably impressed the Tsar and his advisors, for in the spring of 1903 he was appointed Governor of Saratov *guberniya*. Since Saratov was larger than Grodno and not under a governor general, the appointment was considered a flattering promotion.[49]

Economic conditions in Saratov were far different from those in the northwest provinces. In 1905 Saratov had a population of 2,405,829. Ninety percent of the population were peasants, the majority of whom owned their land communally. Small and middle-income farmers were a feeble contingent. Vast tracts of land, containing much of the best soil, were in the hands of a few wealthy landowners. At the end of the nineteenth century, 893 large landowners owned 500 or more dessiatines apiece and owned a total of more than 2,000,000 dessiatines. At the other end of the scale, 336,000 peasants held only 3,000,000 dessiatines of land. The average peasant plot equalled 11 dessiatines. Sixty percent of the total number of peasant landholders had only 6 dessiatines each.[50] The scarcity and poor quality of peasant land was serious, and the situation was worsened by periodic droughts.

Saratov also had a sizable industrial proletariat. Conditions were poor, pay was low, and working hours were long. Although a law of 1897 limited the working day to eleven and one-half hours, it does not seem to have been enforced. According to contemporary accounts, hours in the *lesopilnykh* ("sawmill") factories were twelve to fourteen hours per day, hours of handicraft workers were as high as sixteen to seventeen hours per day, and in 1899 workers in tobacco factories labored fourteen hours per day.[51] These conditions were exploited by revolutionary agitators.[52]

The potentially explosive agrarian and industrial situation in Saratov was aggravated by the war and revolution which racked the country as a whole in 1904 and 1905. The war against Japan broke out in 1904; its unpopularity was increased by one Russian defeat after another, culminating in the surrender of Port Arthur in December 1904, the fall of Mukden in March 1905, and the disintegration of Russia's Baltic fleet in the straits of Tsushima in May 1905. In September, Russia signed the Treaty of Portsmouth. It was not severe, but loss of some far eastern territory and the realization that Russia had been defeated by a fledgling, Asiatic power was humiliating. In addition the war weakened the country militarily and economically and flagrantly displayed the ineptitude of the government. Although there had been dissatisfaction among liberals and leftists for some time, revolution erupted with full force in the fall of 1905. A general strike paralyzed the country in October. In the countryside, peasants went on a rampage of vandalism and incendiarism.

As a result of a particularly bad harvest in 1905, Saratov was hardest hit of all the provinces. Revolutionary turmoil caused 9,500,000 rubles worth of damage—30 percent of the total losses suffered in all the internal provinces.[53] Stolypin's daughter Maria, returning by train from Kolnoberzhe, saw flaming manors dotting the countryside. On one occasion, the railroad strike forced Stolypin to return to Saratov from Moscow by private steamship.[54] In the cities there were strikes, riots, robberies, and terrorist bombings daily. Accounts from Saratov in the Petersburg newspapers reported a steady stream of anarchy and destruction.[55]

As is generally the case, the revolution and obvious strength of radical groups brought about a new self-consciousness and heightened activity on the part of conservative elements. They formed clubs in imitation of revolutionary cells and disseminated propaganda to counteract that of the left. Rightist hoodlums roamed the streets, indiscriminately assaulting students, Jews, and anyone else whom they considered even remotely connected with the revolution. In Saratov, reactionary groups amassed 80,000 rubles for the conflict with the left and divided the city into three sections for intensive work.[56]

In addition to this turmoil, Stolypin had to face insubordination in his own administration. The director of the Peasant Bank, Zeren, convinced the peasants that they should not buy land from the *pomeshchiki* ("landowners"), since soon all land would be given to the peasants. The procurator of the *Sudebnaya palata* (Chamber of Justice), Makarov, an extreme conservative who later held a post under Stolypin and succeeded him as Minister of Internal Affairs, openly displayed hostility to Stolypin.[57]

Stolypin believed that a show of weakness on the part of governors increased disorder,[58] and indeed, the neighboring Governor of Samara province let things get so far out of control that he was forced to appeal to Stolypin for aid.[59] In addition, circulars from the Ministry of Internal Affairs ordered each governor to suppress revolutionary violence and threatened dismissal in cases of laxity or negligence. Some governors actually were dismissed, including the Governor of Kiev *guberniya.*[60]

Stolypin vigorously squelched disorder—whether it was perpetrated by rightists or leftists. He vehemently condemned pogroms, although he asserted that in some instances Jews invited the animosity of reactionary organizations by indulging in revolutionary activity.[61] In

October 1905 Saratov was declared under martial law. Stolypin strengthened the army and the police and announced that in the event that crowds hurled bombs or fired the troops would retaliate.[62] He also used personal appeals. Displaying great bravery, he walked fearlessly into mobs of revolutionaries, oblivious to bombs and gun fire, to exhort mobs to return to peace and order.[63]

Stolypin admitted that he used stringent measures in Saratov, although it appears that the most severe ones were not employed until the appearance of General Sakharov, military general from Petersburg. This individual was detested by the populace and was assassinated by a Socialist Revolutionary on November 27, 1905, while sitting in Stolypin's home.[64]

In any case, unlike many governors who blamed agitation for the upheavals,[65] Stolypin emphasized as he had in Grodno that the real causes of unrest were the hunger, the illiteracy, the poverty of the peasants which were easily exploited by revolutionary agitators.[66] He analyzed the peasant problem in his *Vsepoddanneishii otchet* or "annual report" to the Tsar for 1904, actually, composed some time in 1905. This report repeated some of the ideas Stolypin had expressed at the Grodno committee meetings, but in a much more thorough and finalized form. The poverty of the peasant, Stolypin explained in the report, stemmed from various factors. The peasant seemed unable to accumulate savings because even in a good harvest year much of his income was spent to repay his debts. However, the peasant also wasted a good percentage of his money at the wine shop and on trifles. There seemed to be a spiritlessness, a lack of incentive on the part of the peasant to save or to produce. This apathy, Stolypin stressed, resulted not from any inherent debility, but rather from the peasants communal organization which stifled initiative. The whole tenor of peasant life was at fault—"the Russian peasant has the passion for all to be equal, all to reach one height, and since the mass cannot rise to the height of the most active and intelligent, then the best elements must be leveled to the lower, to the aspiration of the worst, to the inert majority."[67] Although Stolypin claimed that the Russian peasants could not consider any other kind of life, he might have noted that the government had kept them in this bondage by retaining the commune. He did not do so, however, but continued his analysis, maintaining that the one inducement for the peasant to save money was acquisition of land. At this point Stolypin criticized the exploitation of the peasant by the local landowners. Desperate to lease land, despite the bank's curtailment of loans, the peasantry accepted the *pomeshchiki's* disproportionately high rates for leases. The rates were so high, Stolypin revealed, that the peasant could pay them only with difficulty during a good harvest year; after a poor or medium harvest he was forced to indenture himself. Another problem for the peasant was the kulak or more ambitious peasant, who also exploited his neighbors. Stolypin believed that if the kulak were offered a constructive outlet for his energy and initiative he would become a productive member of society.

The remedy for peasant poverty and apathy, the way to channel the abilities of the kulak, in Stolypin's opinion lay in giving each peasant his own individual farmstead. However, a farm alone was not sufficient; other factors were involved. Stolypin conceded, realistically, that the new proprietor must be work-loving, and must be guaranteed water and other agronomic assistance. Then there might appear an "independent, prosperous settler," a type which already existed in the western *gubernii.*[68]

As he had earlier and was to do later, Stolypin emphasized the social and political effects as well as the economic benefits to be derived from a land reform. The *khutor* system would guarantee law and order since small proprietors, having a vested interest in stability and the established order, were innately disposed to disruption[69] and because the peasantry would then be emancipated from their dependence upon the *pomeshchiki,* which Stolypin realized, as surely as did Lenin, "created hatred of one class for another . . . soil on which propaganda is easily implanted and on which revolution springs up."[70] Furthermore, a class of stable, independent yeoman farmers was particularly necessary if the newly created, popularly representative parliament was to be viable.[71]

In his report, Stolypin suggested that the land which was to be turned over to the peasants as separated farmsteads ought to come from the land fund of the Peasant Bank or be carved out of state lands.[72] Privately, however, he confided to his daughter Maria that large estates had outlived their usefulness and gave his own Nizhegorodskii estate to the land bank for distribution, hoping that this might serve as an example for voluntary sale of private estates to the bank.[73]

Stolypin's experiences in Saratov not only confirmed his views on the peasant question, but also shaped his attitude toward so-called liberals. In the early twentieth century, Russian liberals, pressing for civil liberties, a constitution, limited monarchy, a national representative assembly, and parliamentary government, began emerging among

professional people, zemstvo representatives, and the so-called third
element, specialists hired by zemstvos. In 1905 the majority of
professional people and the left wing of the zemstvo liberals and
third element merged to form the Constitutional Democratic or Kadet
party, as it was popularly known. These extremist liberals zealously
pursued their aims, even going so far as to unite in an uneasy
partnership with revolutionary-terrorist groups, for they believed, in
the words of Paul Miliukov, university professor and one of the
founders of the Kadet party, that liberals and leftists could cooperate
"to abolish the autocracy and establish a free, democratic regime on
the foundations of universal suffrage."[74] During the latter months of
1904 and 1905 liberals held banquets, in imitation of the practice in
France in the 1840s, at which discussion, according to one ex-Kadet,
was "determinedly and openly aggressive toward the State authority."[75] Liberals also held mass rallies, particularly in provincial
capitals, at which they debated the plight of the workers and the
agrarian problem.[76] Less radical liberals abhorred this activity and
divorced themselves from the Kadets, forming the more conservative
Octobrist party, which was more accommodating to the government.
A few minor, independent liberal groups also sprang up between
1905 and 1907, but these had limited following and influence.

There is no doubt that the irritation Stolypin displayed toward the
Kadets in 1906 and 1907 was determined to a large extent by their
earlier behavior in Saratov as well as by their actions during that later
period. He acknowledged their "courage, working ability, energy, and
know-how" in his *Vsepoddanneishii otchet* for 1904, but he strongly
criticized both their program and their tactics. He believed that they
ignored historical development and the organic nature of culture
and institutions—as he explained a year or so later, he felt their desire
to transplant British forms of government and laws did not take into
account conditions existing in Russia. Secondly, the liberals' banquets, "at which were exchanged ideas on current issues, the solutions of which were expressed in revolutionary guise," and their public
lectures only incited more radical groups, aroused the masses, and
established an "anti-governmental," "negative," "accusatory" social
atmosphere at a time of military failures and all possible disclosure of
governmental weaknesses. Thus, in Stolypin's opinion, the liberals
were unrealistic (they were "cursed with great theorists") and irresponsible.[77]

Stolypin's mistrust of the radical liberals was confirmed by his
experiences with them in the next years. On the other hand, he was

not opposed to moderate opposition. In the same annual report he sympathized with the liberals' desire to improve the lot of the populace. He vowed that "the local administrative authority does not stand as a barrier to anything in the activity of the 'third element' which appears useful for the population" and acknowledged that the liberals might serve as useful critics of the government if they stayed within bounds.[78] There is at least one newspaper account of cooperative efforts on the part of Stolypin and Saratov zemstvo representatives to restore order in the province,[79] and Stolypin remained friends with moderate liberals such as N. N. Lvov.[80]

In the ordinary course of his administrative duties, Stolypin displayed personal integrity. When the editor of the official Saratov newspaper wrote an expose of police corruption, the police chief tried to prevent publication of the article. Stolypin refused to allow this intimidation—he insisted that the article was accurate and objective and that it would be wrong to suppress it.[81]

Stolypin's cousin, Baron Meyendorff, claimed that Stolypin also attempted to deepen his knowledge of public law while Governor of Saratov. According to Baron Meyendorff, in 1904 or 1905 Stolypin, recognizing his deficiency in legal theory, asked Meyendorff to recommend a comprehensive text. Meyendorff suggested the works of the eminent jurist N. M. Korkunov,[82] and indeed, as we shall see, there appeared to be a great deal of similarity between Stolypin's later ideas on local self-government and the position of Finland in the empire and the theories of Korkunov. Professor A. V. Zenkovsky, active in local affairs in Kiev *guberniya* and a good friend of Stolypin, corroborated Stolypin's interest in public law. He claimed that Stolypin had begun to acquaint himself with Russian and foreign public law while he was still marshal of nobility in Kovno.[83] A newspaper article describing Stolypin in 1907 asserted that he was familiar with the public law of Russia and western European countries,[84] and in fact, evidence we have from that period tends to support this claim.

Whether or not Stolypin sensed that he was preparing himself for bigger things, his administration in Saratov made a favorable impression on the Tsar. On the margin of Stolypin's *Vsepoddanneishii otchet* for 1904, Nicholas wrote: "These thoughts are worthy of consideration."[85] The Petersburg newspaper *Pravitel'stvennyi vestnik* mentioned Stolypin's name frequently in reports from Saratov, portraying him as fearless, decisive, and fair. I. V. Hessen, a Kadet lawyer and journalist, recalled that Stolypin received enormous publicity for quelling a particularly destructive riot in the town of Balashev on November 30, 1905.[86]

In April 1906 Stolypin was appointed Minister of Internal Affairs.[87] There is no doubt that the publicity he had received in Saratov and the sound and constructive thinking he had expressed in his annual reports were responsible, to a great extent, for his being offered this position. However, he was also helped by his personal connections.[88] His brother-in-law, Dmitrii Borisovich Neidhardt, had served in the Preobrazhensky regiment with Nicholas while the latter was doing his term of military service and apparently knew the Tsar well. Another brother-in-law, Aleksei Borisovich Neidhardt, was a member of the State Council. It was rumored that the brothers had proposed Stolypin's name to Nicholas.[89] Stolypin had another supporter in the government, Prince A. V. Obolensky. In October 1905, when Sergei Witte, the newly appointed head of the reorganized government, opened discussions for ministerial posts, Prince Obolensky recommended Stolypin for Minister of Internal Affairs.[90] Stolypin was rejected at that time, but it is conceivable that Obolensky again suggested his name in the months that followed, particularly when Witte was replaced by I. L. Goremykin in the spring of 1906.

In part, chance also played a role in Stolypin's appointment. Nicholas had been considering both Stolypin and the Governor of Smolensk, N. I. Zvegintsev, for the position. The Tsar asked Goremykin, after he was appointed Chairman of the Council of Ministers, to choose between the two candidates. Since Goremykin knew neither, he asked the opinion of V. I. Gurko, Assistant Minister of Internal Affairs. Gurko was only slightly acquainted with Stolypin, but since Zvegintsev had the reputation of being a grafter and an embezzler, Gurko advised Goremykin to choose Stolypin.[91]

Immediately after learning of his appointment, Stolypin hurried to St. Petersburg to ask the Tsar to withdraw it, for he did not feel that he had enough experience. However, Nicholas commanded Stolypin to take the post. He told him that he had been following his activity in Saratov and considered him an exceptionally able administrator.[92]

Thus, Stolypin and his family moved to Petersburg. Less than three months later, Stolypin was named Chairman of the Council of Ministers—the head of the Russian government—while retaining his post in Internal Affairs.

The most obvious thing about Stolypin, as he closed his career in the provinces, was that he was a man of action. While his ideas on education were reminiscent of conservative nationalists of the late nineteenth century, such as Pobedonostsev,[93] there is no evidence that he was influenced by current theories or even that he read widely. Indeed, the only analytical work pertaining to contemporary Russia which we have some documentation of his reading is Korkunov's, and evidence of this author's possible influence appeared only after Stolypin entered the central government. Stolypin's ideas, thus, were empirical. Furthermore, while his ideas were in no way avant-garde and were held by other thoughtful provincial landowners, his thinking was moderately progressive as well as imbued with common sense. While he was not extraordinary, and while his rise was due in part to good luck, he possessed characteristics needed at the helm of Russia in 1906. He was in touch with two widely diverse provincial areas and was interested in socioeconomic improvement. In addition, he apparently was a capable and efficient administrator who could handle dissidents. He even had a certain amount of charisma. But whether he would be a match for the internecine politics of the capital and for the magnitude of Russia's problems remained to be seen.

Notes

1. *Russkii biograficheskii slovar* (St. Petersburg, 1909), pp. 439-40. A. A. Stolypin's correspondence with Speransky may be read in *Russkii Arkhiv,* 1869, nos. 5, 10, 11, pp. 1682-1708, 1966-84; 1870, nos. 4-6, pp. 880-93, 1125-56.

2. "Arendnye khutora" was published in *Russkii vestnik,* 220 (1892), no. 5, pp. 355-64. An earlier brochure, entitled *Zemledelcheskii poryadok do i posle uprazdneniya krepostnogo prava,* appeared in 1874.

3. Baron Alexander Meyendorff, "Memoirs," pp. 1-2, 11-28. This unpublished manuscript, written in 1942, is in the possession of Stolypin's eldest daughter, Maria Petrovna von Bock, who lives in San Francisco. Baron Meyendorff, eight years Stolypin's junior, lived with Stolypin's parents while a student in the legal faculty of St. Petersburg University, ca. 1888. He later became a member of the Third Duma, authored three books, and served as a professor at the London School of Economics.

A basic biography of Arkadii Dmitrievich is contained in Brockhaus and Efron, eds., *Entsiklopedicheskii slovar* (St. Petersburg, 1890-1904), vol. 62, p. 685. On Arkadii Dmitrievich's capacity for dinner party conversation, see the society gossip Count Paul Vassili Radziwill, *Behind the Veil at the Russian Court* (New York: John Lane Company, 1914), p. 353. On Arkadii Dmitrievich see also Maria Petrovna von Bock, *Vospominaniya o moem ottse, P. A. Stolypine* (New York: Chekhov Publishing House, 1953), pp. 43-48.

Arkadii's *Khronika Genrikha Latysha* (Vilna: Tipografiya R. M. Romma, 1867), can be read in the New York Public Library.

4. The correspondence between Tolstoy and both P. A. and A. A. Stolypin, 1907-1908, is contained in "Perepiska Tolstogo s A. A. Stolypinym," in N. Guseva, ed., *Literaturnoe nasledstvo* (Moscow: Izdatelstvo Adademii Nauk, SSSR, 1939), vols. 37-38, pp. 324-29. Tolstoy asked Stolypin to abolish private property.

The Stolypin family also had entree at court, but apparently they enjoyed no real influence. Nicholas Savickij, "P. A. Stolypine," *Le monde slav,* November 1933, p. 227.

5. Bock, *Vospominaniya o moem ottse,* pp. 48-51.

6. *Ibid.,* pp. 43, 103.

7. *Ibid.,* p. 51; Alexandra Stolypine, *L'homme du dernier Tsar* (Paris: Alex Redier, Librairie de la *Revue Française,* 1931), pp. 133-34.

8. Letter of Maria Petrovna von Bock to the author, July 3, 1964. Apparently, Stolypin's mother commonly spoke in French, as was common among Russian upper classes.

9. From an article by Count A. Patem Kin in *Predsedatel' soveta ministrov, Petr Arkad'evich Stolypin,* ed. E. Verpakhovsky (St. Petersburg: Izdanie sostavitelya, 1909) p. 275.

10. Letter of Maria Petrovna von Bock to the author, June 7, 1964; conversation with Mrs. Bock, June 23, 1964. Also, Bock, *Vospominaniya o moem ottse,* pp. 59, 110; Stolypine, *L'homme du dernier Tsar,* p. 8; A. V. Obolensky, *Moi vospominaniya i razmyshleniya* (Stockholm: Izdanie Zhurnala Rodnye Perezvony, 1961), p. 79.

11. Bock, *Vospominaniya o moem ottse,* pp. 57-58, 97-100, 120; also Savickij, "P. A. Stolypine," *Le monde slav,* pp. 227-28.

12. Baron Alexander Meyendorff, "A Brief Appreciation of P. Stolypin's Tenure of Office," p. 5 of chapter on "Agrarian Problems," 1932-1947. MS, Russian Archive, Columbia University. See below, p. 17, for Dmitrii's connection with Nicholas.

13. Meyendorff, "Memoirs," pp. 8-11; Bock, *Vospominaniya o moem ottse,* pp. 22-23.

Apukhtin (1841-1893) is discussed in Prince D. S. Mirsky, *Contemporary Russian Literature, 1881-1925* (New York: Alfred A. Knopf, 1926), pp. 70-71.

14. According to the 1897 census, the percentages of various nationalities in Kovno were as follows: Great Russian, 4.7; Little Russian, 0.1; White Russian, 2.44; Polish, 9.03; Lithuanian, 68.28; Jewish, 13.72. Statistics from which percentages were computed are found in: *Pervaya vseobshchaya perepis naseleniya Rossiiskoi imperii, 1897: Obshchii svod po imperii rezultatov razrabotki,* ed. N. A. Troinitskii (St. Petersburg: Ministerstvo vnutrennikh del, 1905), vol. 2, table 13, pp. 20-22, 28, 30. (Only pertinent nationalities are included above.)

15. A description of Kovno in the 1890s is contained in Brockhaus and Efron, vol. 15, pp. 510-15, and in Savickij, "P. A. Stolypine," *Le monde slav,* pp. 229-30.

16. Bock, *Vospominaniya o moem ottse,* p. 53.

17. A full account of the peasant question is contained in Geroid T. Robinson, *Rural Russia Under the Old Regime* (New York: Macmillan Co., 1961). Of course, technically the peasant was not given land, but had to redeem it over a 49-year period.

18. Brockhaus and Efron, vol. 10, pp. 205-15; vol. 19, pp. 423-25. I have limited discussion to the office of *uezd* marshal of nobility because Stolypin did not become provincial (*guberniya*) marshal until 1899, and because the former position involved more fundamental activity and closer contact with the peasantry. For this reason Stolypin preferred the position of *uezd* marshal to provincial marshal. The provincial marshal dealt with peasants only in the appellate instance, as a member of the Provincial Gathering for Peasant Affairs.

19. Stolypin to the editor of *Volga* (a Saratov newspaper) in 1909. Quoted in *Gosudarstvennaya deyatel'nost' predsedatelya soveta ministrov stats sekretarya Petra Arkad'evicha Stolypina,* ed. E. Verpakhovsky, chast 1 (St. Petersburg: Izdanie sostavitelya, 1911), p. 4.

20. Brockhaus and Efron, vol. 19, pp. 424-25; vol. 15, pp. 513-14.

21. Trudy mestnykh komitetov o nuzhdakh sel'skokhozyaistvennoi promyshlennosti, vol. 11, Grodnenskaya Guberniya (St. Petersburg: Tipografiya Izadora Gol'dberga, 1903), pp. 158-63.

22. Bock, Vospominaniya o moem ottse, p. 43.

23. Ibid., p. 31.

24. Obolensky, Moi vospominaniya i razmyshleniya, p. 78.

25. Bock, Vospominaniya o moem ottse, p. 31; Vladimir Alexandrovich Skripitsyn, Bogatyr mysli, slova i dela (St. Petersburg: Gorodskaya Tipografiya, 1911), p. 13.

26. Bock, Vospominaniya o moem ottse, pp. 32-33, 55, 71, 75, 109-13.

27. Obolensky, Moi vospominaniya i razmyshleniya, p. 78. The State Council in 1902 was a body whose members were appointed by the Tsar. The council examined law proposals developed by the ministers, discussed the budget and all state expenditures, but had no authority to propose modification of the laws.

28. According to the 1897 census, the percentages of the various nationalities in Grodno were as follows: Great Russian, 4.62; Little Russian, 24.47; White Russian, 44.22; Polish, 10.08; Jewish, 17.3. Statistics from which percentages were computed are found in: Pervaya vseobshchaya perepis naseleniya Rossiiskoi imperii, 1897: Obshchii svod po imperii rezultatov razrabotki, vol. 2, pp. 20-22, 28, 30.

29. Bock, Vospominaniya o moem ottse, p. 116.

30. Obolensky, Moi vospominaniya i razmyshleniya, pp. 78-80, 84.

31. Meyendorff, "A Brief Appreciation of P. Stolypin's Tenure of Office," p. 15 of chapter entitled "Stolypin and Finland," and p. 14 of chapter entitled "Stolypin and the First Duma"; Savickij, "P. A. Stolypine," p. 231.

32. Bock, Vospominaniya o moem ottse, pp. 114-117.

33. Skripitsyn, Bogatyr mysli, slova i dela, p. 2.

34. An interesting description of the work preceding the enactment of the agrarian reforms of 1906 is presented by George Yaney, "The Imperial Russian Government and the Administration of the Stolypin Reforms" (Ph.D. dissertation, Dept. of History, Princeton University, 1962).

35. Trudy mestnykh komitetov, vol. 11, pp. 1-5.

36. Ibid., passim.

37. Ibid., p. 76.

38. Ibid., p. 32.

39. Ibid., pp. 158-63, 205.

40. Materialy: Vysochaishe Uchrezhdennoe Osoboe Soveshchenie o nuzhdakh sel'skokhozyaistvennoi promyshlennosti (St. Petersburg, 1904), passim.

41. Trudy mestnykh komitetov, vol. 11, p. 76.

42. Peter Ivanovich Liashchenko, History of the National Economy of Russia to the 1917 Revolution (New York: Macmillan, 1949), pp. 654-58, 651-60.

43. Trudy mestnykh komitetov, vol. 11, p. 32.

44. Ibid., p. 23. Stolypin also advocated more education for women and special women's educational institutions.

45. Ibid., p. 32.

46. Ibid., p. 31.

47. Ibid., p. 3.

48. Ibid., pp. 10, 89, 63, 181.

49. Bock, Vospominaniya o moem ottse, pp. 117-18.

50. Uchenye zapiski: vypusk istoricheskii posvyashchennyi 50 letyu pervoi russkoi

revolyutsii, LV Ministerstvo vysshego obrazovaniya SSSR Saratovskii gosudarstvennyi universitet. (Saratov: Izdatelstvo "Kommunist," 1956), p. 277. Also Savickij, "P. A. Stolypine," pp. 239, 248, 251. A dessiatine is a measure of land equal to 2.7 acres.

51. *Uchenye zapiska,* pp. 27-88, 193, 307.

52. The activity of the Social Democrats is presented in *Uchenye zapiski, passim.* That of the Social Revolutionaries is in *Vserossiiskii Krest'yanskii soyuz: Otchety o zasedaniyakh delegatskogo sezda Vserossiiskogo Krest'yanskogo soyuza,* 6-10 *noyabrya* 1905 g, pp. 41-44, as quoted in Robinson, *Rural Russia Under the Old Regime,* pp. 174-75. The strikers' grievances were economic, not political. They demanded an eight-hour day, higher wages, payment during absence due to illness, etc. *Uchenye zapiski,* pp. 193-94.

53. From the statistics of the Ministry of Internal Affairs, S. N. Prokopovich, *Agrarnyi krisis i meropriyatiya pravitelstva* (Moscow, 1912), .p. 61, as quoted in Robinson, *Rural Russia Under the Old Regime,* p. 175. The ruble was worth about $.50 at the.time.

54. Bock, *Vospominaniya o moem ottse,* pp. 147-50. Revolutionaries made several attempts on Stolypin's life and threatened to kidnap his infant son if their demands were not fulfilled.

55. Reports from Saratov in *Pravitel'stvennyi vestnik,* October 22, 1905-December 30, 1905.

56. Bock, *Vospominaniya o moem ottse,* p. 149.

57. *Ibid.,* p. 137.

58. Stolypin to Durnovo, Minister of Internal Affairs during 1905, quoted in N. I. Karpov, *Agrarnaya politika Stolypina* (Leningrad: Rabochee Izdatelstvo "Priboi," 1925), pp. 173-74.

59. The Governor of Samara, Zasyadko, refused to strengthen the army and restore order. In the end, things got so far out of control that he was forced to appeal to Stolypin for aid. A. N. Naumov, *Iz utselevshikh vospominanii* (New York: Izdanie A. K. Naumovoi i O. A. Kisevitskoi, 1955), vol. 2, pp. 26-27.

60. Great Britain, Public Record Office, Foreign Office (hereafter cited F.O.) 371, vol. 125, no. 1703, November 21, 1905, Spring-Rice.

61. Skripitsyn, *Bogatyr mysli, slova i dela,* pp. 3-4.

62. *Pravitel'stvennyi vestnik,* October 22 and 23, 1905, *passim.*

63. Bock, *Vospominaniya o moem ottse,* pp. 148-49, 154-55. Also, *Pravitel'stvennyi vestnik,* October 22 and November 13, 1905. Corroborated by I. V. Hessen, "Reminiscences"; MS, Hoover Library, Stanford, California. Hessen was a liberal and therefore, although he apparently was on good terms with Stolypin (see below, chapter 2, p. 30), he was not likely to praise Stolypin unduly.

64. Stolypin admitted that the revolution had been crushed with stringent measures in a letter to Durnovo on January 11, 1906, quoted in Karpov, *Agrarnaya politika Stolypina,* p. 172.

65. General Sakharov arrived in Saratov on November 3, 1905; *Pravitel'stvennyi vestnik,* November 4, 1905, p. 2. He was succeeded by General-Adjutant Maximovich on November 29; *Ibid.,* November 29, 1905. A full description of the General's assassination is given by Alexandra Stolypin, Stolypin's youngest daughter, in *L'homme du dernier Tsar,* pp. 24-26. The woman assassin, who screamed, "I did it to save Russia from a tyrant," later was the only woman in the delegation to Brest-Litovsk.

65. *Krest'yanskoe dvizhenie v revolyutsii 1905 goda v dokumentakh,* ed. N. I. Karpov (Leningrad, 1926), pp. 94-97, as cited in Robinson, *Rural Russia Under the Old Regime,* pp. 154-55.

66. Stolypin to Durnovo, in Karpov, *Agrarnaya politika Stolypina*, p. 173.

67. "Vsepoddanneishii otchet saratovskogo gubernatora P. Stolypina za 1904 god," *Krasnyi arkhiv*, 17 (1926), p. 84.

68. *Ibid.*, p. 85.

69. *Ibid.*, pp. 84-85. Also, Stolypin to Durnovo, in Karpov, *Agrarnaya politika Stolypina*, p. 173.

70. "Vsepoddanneishii otchet . . . za 1904 god," *Krasnyi arkhiv*, 17, pp. 84-85.

71. *Ibid.*, p. 85.

72. *Ibid.*

73. Maria Petrovna von Bock, *Vozrozhdenie*, no. 3850, December 18, 1935, p. 6; Bock, *Vospominaniya o moem ottse*, p. 205.

74. P. N. Miliukov, *Vospominaniya* (New York: Chekhov Publishing House, 1955), vol. 1, pp. 242-44, 258-59, 264, 283-84, 293-309, 316-30, 335-50, 411.

75. D. N. Shipov, *Vospominaniya i dumy o perezhitom* (Moscow: Tipografiya "Pechatnya S. P. Yakovleva," 1918), pp. 393-94.

76. *Ibid.*, pp. 394-404. Shipov left the Kadet party on this account. Since in later years he was not sympathetic to Stolypin, his statements can be taken to corroborate Stolypin's.

77. "Vsepoddanneishii otchet . . . za 1904 god," *Krasnyi arkhiv*, 17, pp. 85-87.

78. *Ibid.*

79. *Pravitel'stvennyi vestnikh*, October 27, 1905, p. 4. On October 26, Stolypin met with the municipal duma and the members of the *guberniya* and *uezd* zemstvos in Saratov province. The self-governing officials stated at this meeting that there was no need for severe measures, since there was a city militia and the citizens were capable of self-defense. Stolypin replied that he could permit relaxation, but he hoped the people would be able to use their freedom.

80. See below, chapter 6, p. 156.

81. Skripitsyn, *Bogatyr mysli, slova i dela*, p. 6.

82. Meyendorff, "A Brief Appreciation of P. Stolypin's Tenure of Office," p. 5 of chapter entitled "Agrarian Measures." Although Meyendorff claims he recommended Korkunov's *General Theory of Law* (Boston, 1909), he probably meant Korkunov's *Russkoe gosudarstvennoe pravo* (St. Petersburg: Tipografiya M. M. Stasyulevicha, 1905), for two reasons: first, he wrote these memoirs in English and, therefore, might have used the English title for convenience; second, inferring from the memoirs, Meyendorff made the recommendation while Stolypin was Governor of Saratov. Thus he would have suggested the 1905 edition, not the 1909 edition.

Korkunov was a professor of law at St. Petersburg University. He lived from 1853 to 1904.

The eulogistic Baron Meyendorff was the same member of the Octobrist party in the Third Duma period (1907-1912) who vehemently disagreed with his cousin Stolypin's Finnish policy, the proposal for the southwestern zemstvos, and Stolypin's behavior during the zemstvo crisis of 1911. Geoffrey A. Hosking, *The Russian Constitutional Experiment, Government and Duma, 1907-1914* (New York, London: Cambridge University Press, 1973), pp. 112, 130, 143-44.

83. Zenkovsky, "Moi dopolnitelnye vospominaniya o P. A. Stolypine," p. 2. MS in Russian Archive, Columbia University. According to Zenkovsky, Stolypin said that he "recognized that it was extremely important to be acquainted with public, administrative and civil law. When I was appointed Governor, at first of Grodno and then of Saratov, I . . . began energetically to study our Russian laws . . . and Senate decisions on . . . a range of questions."

84. *Predsedatel' soveta ministrov Petr Arkad'evich Stolypin*, ed. E. Verpakhovsky, p. 275.

85. Stated in the introduction to Stolypin's "Vsepoddanneishii otchet . . . za 1904 god," *Krasnyi arkhiv*, 17, p. 81.

86. I. V. Hessen, "Reminiscences," vol. 2, p. 19.

87. Notice of the appointment appeared in *Novoe vremya*, April 23, 1906.

88. Stolypin had some personal contacts of a social nature with the Tsar. For instance, while Governor of Saratov, Stolypin and his daughter Maria attended an Easter breakfast given by the Tsar and Tsarina at the Kremlin palace. Bock, *Vospominaniya o moem ottse*, pp. 120-22. However, as this contact was quite minimal, it was undoubtedly those of Stolypin's relatives and friends that helped pave his way.

89. Vladimir Nikolaevich Kokovtsov, *Out of My Past*, trans. Laura Matveev (Stanford, California: Stanford University Press, 1935), p. 569, note 8, and p. 576, note 6; Lev Moiseevich Klyachko, *Povesti proshlogo* (Leningrad: Izdatelstvo pisatelei, 1929), p. 25.

90. Shipov, *Vospominaniya i dumy o perezhitom*, p. 343. Stolypin's old friend Prince A. V. Obolensky had served under Stolypin in the chancellery while Stolypin was Governor of Grodno. In 1903, Obolensky had been appointed secretary in the Department of General Affairs in the Ministry of Internal Affairs.

91. Vladimir Iosifovich Gurko, *Features and Figures of the Past*, trans. Laura Matveev (Stanford, California: Stanford University Press, 1939), pp. 460-61.

82. Bock, *Vospominaniya o moem ottse*, p. 159.

93. Edward C. Thaden, *Conservative Nationalism in Nineteenth-Century Russia* (Seattle: University of Washington Press, 1964), pp. 183-203.

Chapter 2:
Stolypin, the Autocracy, and Loci of Power

Stolypin's family by the spring of 1906 included five daughters, Maria, Natalya, Elena, Olga, Alexandra, and a two-year-old son, Arkadii. On August 12, 1906, the summer home on Aptekarsky Island, which the family had been lent by the Tsar, was destroyed by a terrorist's bomb. Natalya was seriously injured and several family servants and others were killed. Upon the Tsar's invitation, the family moved into the Winter Palace, where they stayed until 1910. In that year they moved to the Ministry of Internal Affairs' house on Fontanka Street.[1]

During the summer the family lived in the Elagin palace, which was situated on an island of the same name, north of the central part of St. Petersburg. The palace had been designed by the famous Italian architect C. I. Rossi in the latter part of the reign of Alexander I. It was, and still is, a beautiful white neoclassical structure, surrounded by wooded grounds and a rear garden ornamented with pseudo-classical statuary. In 1907, as a result of the attempt on Stolypin's life the previous summer, the palace was protected, according to the British ambassador, Sir Arthur Nicolson, "by high palisades, triple rows of barbed wire entanglements, and a large force of mounted and foot gendarmes holding watch round the grounds, while water patrols keep guard in the river."[2]

Stolypin was forty-four years old. Photographs of him show a handsome, slightly balding, bearded man, impeccably groomed, with an intent, serious expression. To the well-known Russian scholar Sir

Donald MacKenzie Wallace, who visited Stolypin in August 1906, he
was a "tall thin man" of "sympathetic manner and appearance." He
"speaks remarkably well, especially when he is using . . . his native
language. Unlike many of his countrymen, he never indulges in
vague, philosophical phrases, but speaks simply, earnestly and to the
point. His whole manner and bearing suggest a large reserve supply of
quiet determination, energy and perseverence." It was Wallace's
impression that if Stolypin succeeded it would be due to "those
qualities, combined with a large amount of common sense," rather
than to "any exceptionally brilliant intelligence."[3]

Stolypin held meetings of the Council of Ministers and received
visitors at Elagin palace as well as in town. According to a press
release from that period and the recollections of his colleagues,
Stolypin was an indefatigable worker. He kept a continental schedule
which lasted far into the night—meetings of the Council of Ministers,
which were held nearly every day, often lasted until one o'clock in the
morning. Afterward, Stolypin sometimes continued to work until two
or three. Despite this, he was at his desk again by eight o'clock in the
morning, reading newspapers and greeting officials from the ministries, the Duma, and the State Council. After lunch he worked alone
until four in the afternoon, when he again received visitors. When the
Duma was in session he made it a point to attend the sittings.[4]

As a regular course, Stolypin avoided Petersburg and court society,
preferring to spend his moments of relaxation with his family (in all
accounts he appears to have been a devoted husband and father) or in
solitary half-hour walks. His exclusiveness may have resulted from the
viciousness of the elite. Taking malicious delight in the Tsarina's
errors in French and court etiquette, these gossips also disliked
Stolypin's wife, whom they considered too bourgeois.[5] Nevertheless,
Stolypin gave the dinners and balls which his position required. He
periodically dined with the British ambassador[6] or attended evening
parties and court functions. He was particularly fond of meeting
provincial officials from whom he could obtain information about the
state of the provinces and public or official opinion in a firsthand,
informal way.[7]

As Chairman of the Council of Ministers, Stolypin was in no way
the equivalent of a prime minister of the British type. According to
article 81 of the Fundamental State Laws of 1906, ministers were
appointed by the Tsar and were individually responsible to him.
Furthermore, it was categorically stated in these laws that "to the
Emperor of All Russias belongs supreme autocratic power." Modern

historians have attempted to prove that the term "autocrat" meant sovereign, but from the evidence we have of Nicholas' thinking on the subject, this was not how he construed the term.[8]

After 1906, the Tsar was to share legislative power with a bicameral parliament. The upper chamber consisted of the revised State Council, half the members of which were, as formerly, appointed by the Tsar. Supposedly, both the president of the State Council and the Chairman of the Council of Ministers could make recommendations. The remaining half were, after 1906, elected corporately by the zemstvos, Holy Synod, Academy of Sciences, universities, nobility, and business groups. During Stolypin's term of office the State Council contained some liberals, a large center group, a group of moderately conservative nationalists, and a small but powerful body of reactionaries.[9] The lower chamber, the Duma, was popularly elected. The political complexion of the first three Dumas will be discussed in a later chapter. The powers of the Duma had been diluted by the Fundamental Laws of March-April 1906. The monarch was to determine the length of the Duma's annual session, one-third of the state budget was beyond the Duma's control, the government was allowed to implement important measures in emergency situations which had the force of laws but were not subject to the Duma, and the government could dissolve the Duma. Thus, Geoffrey Hosking rather misses the mark with his criticism that Stolypin was "not adept at handling the weapons which have to constitute a major part of the armoury of a constitutional statesman, those of persuasion, manoeuvre and compromise."[10] As we shall see, Stolypin did not necessarily believe that Russia had a constitution. In any case, he did not derive his power from the Duma, but from the Tsar. In this political situation, Stolypin needed some cooperation from the Duma to implement his policies, but his chief concerns were to muster support from his fellow ministers, to squelch opposition on the part of those in the State Council, at court, or in the country at large who had influence over Nicholas and above all, to get the approval of the Tsar.

S. Frederick Starr has asserted, in his incisive work on Russian local administration and local self-government in the nineteenth century, that "one man rule, if it ever existed, was giving way to bureaucratic rule" as early as the 1830s and 1840s and that "individual bureaucrats at or below the ministerial level had a great deal of influence in formulating autocratic policy."[11] George L. Yaney, in his provocative work on the internal mechanism of the Russian government before 1905, has noted ministerial challenges to the Tsar.[12] As we shall see, Stolypin, in the tradition of strong bureaucrats like

Speransky and Witte, periodically conflicted with Nicholas or stubbornly insisted on a course of action. On the other hand, it is also true that just as frequently he gave in to Nicholas or found his program thwarted because of capricious influences on the Tsar. Furthermore, there was always the possibility that he might be summarily dismissed as his predecessors had been.

Actually, Stolypin's relationship to the Tsar was very much like that of the chief operating officer of a firm to the corporate chief executive. And Nicholas was a difficult boss to work for, not because he was strong, but because he was weak. Having succeeded his father Alexander III in 1894, Nicholas was fairly intelligent, concerned enough about the country to promote agrarian reform after the disturbances of 1902, a kind father, a loving husband, and a man of integrity. He appreciated capable officials, particularly Stolypin. On the other hand, from his diary and correspondence, as well as from recollections of his contemporaries, he also seems to have been shallow, somewhat callous, indecisive, and easily influenced. V. I. Gurko, who served in the Ministry of Internal Affairs before and during Stolypin's administration, caustically claimed that Nicholas hated to dismiss a minister, not because he was kind, "for actually he was indifferent to the feelings of the person he dismissed, but because it disturbed his peace of mind and obliged him to make an effort of will which he always found difficult."[13] Gurko, of course, bore a personal grudge against Nicholas, but the Tsar's treatment of Witte substantiates Gurko's evaluation.

Nicholas also was reluctant to alter the autocracy too greatly and was unhappy about sharing authority with the State Duma. In 1905, shortly after he issued the October Manifesto, he wrote his mother bemoaning the fact that those who wished the autocracy preserved had not publicized their opinions sooner.[14] In 1907, shortly after the Second Duma began, he fumed that it was too early to dissolve it, but he warned that once the Duma stepped too far out of line—"slap!"— like an insect it would be gone.[15] Even after the tractable and hardworking Third Duma had been in session for more than a year, Nicholas admitted that he had created the Duma to advise him, not to order him.[16] He was easily convinced that the Duma's interest in the military and in state defense threatened his prerogatives and, in fact, a governmental crisis arose on this score in 1909.[17]

With this mentality, Nicholas gratefully accepted the support of conservative organizations such as the Union of Russian People.[18] According to its bylaws of 1908, the union dedicated itself to maintenance of the autocracy and preservation of the Orthodox faith, recommended a consultative rather than a legislative Duma, and was in favor of abolishing some rights of non-Russian nationalities.[19] The union was also anti-Semitic.

Unlike the Kadets and the Octobrists—moderate reformers who supported a limited monarchy—Stolypin, with the practicality noted by Wallace, accepted the Tsar on Nicholas' own terms. While constitutional theorists hotly debated the extent to which the autocracy had been diluted by the October Manifesto, the new Fundamental Laws, and the strength of representative government in Russia, Stolypin informed an American newspaper correspondent in 1907 that he was not sure that the term "constitution" could be properly applied to the October Manifesto. The word "constitution," he explained, referred to an agreement between the people themselves, as in America, or a reciprocal contract between the crown and the people, as in Prussia. The October Manifesto and the Fundamental Laws (of 1906), he pointed out, had been given by an "autocratic Sovereign"; the matter of whether or not Russia had a constitution needed further study.[20] Upon occasion, Stolypin paid homage to the autocracy in public speeches, many of which were written by I. Ya. Gurland, a civil servant who was devoted to the autocratic system.[21] One such occasion was the opening of the Third Duma, when Stolypin described the historical development and greatness of the autocracy.[22] On another occasion Stolypin found the autocracy a convenient escape hatch. During the zemstvo crisis of 1911, which will be discussed in a later chapter, he forced the Tsar to prorogue both chambers of the parliament and pass a bill, using exceptional procedure. Later, he justified his action before the Duma and the State Council as an expression of the imperial will; it was the Tsar's prerogative to use exceptional measures at exceptional times; any attempt to contest the action would be a limitation on the rights of the crown.[23] Despite the fact that he pressured Nicholas in this instance, almost always the fact that the Tsar was his superior—however the Tsar viewed himself or whatever the Tsar's legal position—was for Stolypin a constant frame of reference. He had to retain the Tsar's support at whatever cost.

The published correspondence between Stolypin and Nicholas indicates that the two were usually on good terms. Nicholas frequently asked Stolypin's advice, Stolypin often concurred with the Tsar's judgment and praised him for his farsightedness on the land question and other matters.[24]

On the other hand, Stolypin and Nicholas differed on several significant issues and on some occasions Stolypin expressed irritation and frustration with the limitations of his position. In the first year of his administration, Stolypin and Nicholas disagreed on the necessity of ameliorating, even modestly, the conditions of the Jews. Nicholas vetoed a proposal, on which Stolypin and other ministers had labored, for increasing Jewish rights. Despite this, Stolypin had the records of the Council of Ministers' meetings doctored to protect the Tsar's public image.[25] As we shall see, Stolypin was more tolerant of the Duma than was Nicholas, but he found his relationship to the Duma restricted by his need to retain the Tsar's support.

A major issue on which Stolypin and Nicholas disagreed was the Tsar's affiliation with reactionary, anti-Semitic groups. I. V. Hessen, the liberal Jewish lawyer, recalled, for example, that in 1907, while he was visiting Stolypin late one evening, the latter received a telephone call from the Tsar informing him that Nicholas would receive a deputation from the Union of Russian People on the following day. According to Hessen, "Stolypin's expression grew darker as he spoke and his tone plainly betrayed irritation." Hessen felt that Stolypin was "conscious of his impotence."[26] Stolypin vociferously opposed the rabble-rousing, anti-Semitic monk Iliodor[27] and Rasputin,[28] who, of course, was an obscurantist rather than reactionary presence.

A related problem for Stolypin was the clique of his enemies at court, in Petersburg society, and in the State Council. Some of these individuals were ideologically opposed to Stolypin's reform program, others were simply resentful of his power. Sir Bernard Pares reported to the British Foreign Office in 1907 and 1908 that there were three main reactionary groups at court, all of whom had easier access to the Tsar than did Stolypin.[29] Prince A. V. Obolensky, an old friend of Stolypin and an assistant in the Ministry of Internal Affairs, and V. N. Kokovtsov, Minister of Finance during Stolypin's administration, testified to the intrigue against Stolypin at court and in the capital. Kokovtsov cited as particularly hostile Dr. Dubrovin, the founder of the Union of Russian People, and Prince Meshchersky, the editor of a Petersburg scandal sheet *Grazhdanin* (The Citizen).[30] Alexandra Feodorovna, the Tsarina, strongly disliked Stolypin. She also disliked Olga Borisovna and was jealous, fearing an encroachment on her position when Stolypin's family moved into the Winter Palace.[31] On less personal terms, she and Stolypin were opposed on the issue of Rasputin, and she believed her husband belittled his own position by conferring with and relying upon Stolypin.[32] Although the sick woman probably had no effect on Nicholas' attitude toward

Stolypin, she apparently was responsible for the appointment of P. G. Kurlov to the post of commander of gendarmerie, a branch of the police, against Stolypin's wishes, despite the fact that Stolypin, as Minister of Internal Affairs, was nominal head of the police and should have concurred with the Tsar on police appointments. Kurlov intercepted Stolypin's correspondence and opposed his efforts to reform the police department. Stolypin tried to remove him several times, but each time was thwarted by Alexandra, who considered him indispensible to Nicholas' protection.[33] Stolypin may have been referring to Kurlov when he complained to his son-in-law Boris Bock that Russia was the only country in which it was not possible for a chief minister to choose his subordinates.[34] Finally, Stolypin's enemies in the State Council blocked Stolypin's legislative proposals, embarrassed him, and caused major ministerial crises in 1909 and 1911.

Stolypin employed both frontal attacks and guerrilla tactics in dealing with personal adversaries, reactionaries, or others who threatened his programs or the general order in Russia. On the one hand, he admonished Nicholas for receiving members of the Union of Russian People and tried to prevent their access to the Tsar.[35] According to a member of the union, Stolypin forbade mass demonstrations of the organization and tried to destroy it by creating dissention within its branches.[36] In 1909 Stolypin prosecuted Dr. Dubrovin for implication in the murder of a liberal Duma deputy.[37] He periodically fined reactionary editors and confiscated their papers for anti-Semitic, as well as antigovernmental, articles. Furthermore, he threatened local authorities with legal penalties should any anti-Semitic outbreaks occur.[38] He was particularly disgusted with Rasputin, whom the Tsar sent to try to cure the injuries Stolypin's daughter Natalya had suffered in the Aptekarsky explosion.[39] Stolypin warned Nicholas that Rasputin was harming the imperial family's image and twice tried to have him exiled to Siberia, but his efforts were to no avail.[40] In February 1911 Stolypin also warned Nicholas about Iliodor who was spreading anti-Semitic propaganda in Saratov province. He urged the Tsar not to dismiss the Chief Procurator of the Holy Synod, for it might appear that this church authority, whom Iliodor repudiated, had been sacrificed to the renegade monk.[41]

On the other hand, with characteristic pragmatism, Stolypin also tried to buy off obstructionist or hostile individuals and groups. Spicing his remarks with an old Russian proverb, he told Kokovtsov: "I think the same of [Prince] Meshchersky [the editor of *Grazhdanin*] as you do, but if one lives with wolves one has to howl like them. We

can't afford to have him spiteful to us, and surely, Vladimir Nikolaevich, you and I are worth more than 200,000 rubles to Russia."[42]
With this philosophy, according to Kokovtsov and Assistant Minister
of Internal Affairs S. E. Kryzhanovsky, Stolypin gave about 3,000,000
rubles annually to rightist groups, subsidizing about thirty newspapers all over Russia—including two papers of the notorious Markov
II, Dubrovin's *Russkaya znamya,* and the official government newspaper, *Rossiya*—as well as rightist student groups and some local
officials.[43] Stolypin also subsidized the Nationalists, a political party
formed about 1908, whose platform stressed Russia's national
interests but otherwise was moderately progressive. In 1910, for
example, Stolypin gave a large subsidy to the Nationalist Club in St.
Petersburg.[44]

Periodically, Stolypin received assurances of the Tsar's trust and
appreciation. In October 1906 Nicholas had written to his mother that
he thought highly of Stolypin,[45] and on January 2, 1908, the Tsar
made Stolypin secretary of state.[46] On April 13, 1909, on the eve of
the naval general staff crisis, Nicholas bestowed upon Stolypin the
title "Knight of the White Eagle" and proclaimed to the whole nation
his "wholehearted appreciation of Stolypin's talented activity" and his
"hearty gratitude" for Stolypin's "unwearied work, so useful for the
country."[47] Immediately after the crisis, which had been perpetrated
by his enemies, Stolypin secured the privilege of nominating persons
for appointed seats in the State Council.[48] Throughout 1910 Nicholas'
letters to Stolypin expressed warm sentiments: "I wish you a good rest
and goodbye until Riga,"[49] and "Peter Arkad'evich, with satisfaction I
learned about your safe return from the interesting trip to Siberia . . .
Goodbye. I firmly grasp your hand."[50] Nevertheless, the machinations
of his enemies caused Stolypin a great deal of anxiety and exhausted
him. Finally, as we shall see in a later chapter, he precipitated the
so-called zemstvo crisis partly in order to force Nicholas to choose
once and for all between himself and his adversaries, and in so doing
he possibly sealed his own doom.

Because ministers were individually responsible to the Tsar there
was no principle of unanimity in the Russian ministry.[51] However, it
appears that major ministerial changes were discussed and agreed
upon by Nicholas and Stolypin. Such was the case with the dismissal
of Kaufman as Minister of Education in 1907 and the appointment of
A. N. Schwarts in his stead. Believing that Kaufman was weak and
that a firmer hand was needed to manage the country's youth,
Stolypin informed the Tsar that he would speak with both Schwarts

and L. A. Kasso (who succeeded Schwarts) to see which might be better qualified for the post.[52] Kaufman was dismissed because of Stolypin's recommendation and Schwarts inaugurated a more stringent rule in the schools.

Only one ministerial change seems to have been not to Stolypin's liking. This was the appointment of V. A. Sukhomlinov as Minister of War in place of A. F. Roediger. Apparently the Tsar effected this change in part because he could not tolerate Roediger's criticism of the country's defense system. Stolypin had clashed with Roediger, but according to the Assistant Minister of War, A. A. Polivanov, Stolypin and Kokovtsov were almost constantly at odds with Sukhomlinov.[53]

The fact that ministers could and did report matters privately to the Tsar at times posed problems for Stolypin. Such was the case with the Foreign Minister, A. P. Izvolsky, during the Bosnian crisis of 1908-1909. In that crucial time, according to Kokovtsov, Izvolsky informed Stolypin that "he had been explicitly instructed by his Majesty not to discuss matters of foreign policy in the Ministers' Council . . . without first receiving special permission from the Tsar, the one supreme director of our foreign policy." Stolypin, Kokovtsov recalled, "reddened, but said nothing."[54]

In his day-to-day direction of the Council of Ministers, Stolypin as would be expected, felt his way during his first year in office. P. P. Mendeleev, an official in the Ministry of Internal Affairs, remarked that during this year Stolypin spoke little but listened attentively to the views of others and tried to reconcile them.[55] Records of the Council of Ministers' meetings for 1906 and early 1907 show that Stolypin met stiff opposition from the other ministers on proposals such as the prohibition of land leasing for Jews within the Pale and changes in the system of local administration. In these instances the opinion of his fellow ministers superseded Stolypin's.[56]

After 1907, however, it appears that Stolypin was primus inter pares within the Council of Ministers. Mendeleev, who came to dislike Stolypin, claimed that he became a tyrant, totally confident of his own opinion and intolerant of opposition.[57] This is not borne out by the records of the meetings of the council where there is evidence of discussion and opposition to Stolypin's policies after 1907. For example, Izvolsky and Kokovtsov strongly disagreed with some aspects of Stolypin's Finnish policy and Kokovtsov repeatedly opposed Stolypin's and the other ministers' proposals to improve the army by increasing state expenditures.[58] Nevertheless, after 1907 Stolypin's opinion predominated in the ministry's official reports.

In addition to serving as Chairman of the Council of Ministers, Stolypin was Minister of Internal Affairs and, as such, was titular head of the provincial administration and the police. However, it is difficult to estimate how much actual authority he had over the officials in these areas.

Outside of the regular channels of communication between Petersburg and the provinces, Stolypin tried to keep abreast of local conditions by informal meetings, often with zemstvo leaders and marshals of the nobility rather than with administrative personnel.[59] He was particularly well informed on developments in Finland, judging from his voluminous correspondence with the Governor General of Finland and the Minister State Secretary for Finnish Affairs.

Nevertheless, local officials sometimes acted independently of Stolypin's orders. For example in 1906, shortly after Stolypin assumed office, a pogrom broke out in Bielostok. The governor of the province notified the Duma instead of Stolypin, causing him great embarrassment. Furthermore, his subsequent demands to the governor went unheeded.[60] Apparently, local authorities, even on the gubernatorial level, aided and abetted reactionary organizations, sent telegrams to the Tsar asking for the Duma's dissolution, and did not cooperate with committees arranging the agrarian reform or prosecute those who impeded it.[61] All these actions were counter to Stolypin's policy and expressed commands.

As we shall see, in 1907 Stolypin tried to improve the local administrative apparatus. However, his proposal met opposition from his fellow ministers and from one influential governor. The latter apparently turned the Tsar against the reform and it was never implemented.[62]

The police must have been more difficult to manage, for some of their work was of a conspiratorial nature, and judging from their memoirs, policemen themselves were not always aware of what their close colleagues were doing.[63]

The Department of Police within the Ministry of Internal Affairs included the Okhrana, or intelligence division; the *Glavnoe upravlenie otdelnago korpusa zhandarmov* (the main administration of the separate corps of the gendarmes); port, railway, and fortress police; and a unique mounted command stationed in Odessa. The headquarters of the Okhrana and the gendarmerie were in St. Petersburg; in addition the Okhrana had branches in Moscow, Warsaw, Finland, and in the provincial capitals, districts, and major cities in Russia.

There was also a branch of the Okhrana in Paris which kept surveillance on revolutionaries abroad.[64]

The branches of the police in all provincial capitals and one hundred districts were subject to both civil and military officials on the provincial level, to the directors of the police, and ultimately to Stolypin and the Tsar. The police employed a staff of several thousand double agents—in fact each local police chief was free to recruit his own.[65] Often these former revolutionaries who were paid to inform for the police were not thoroughly converted. Such was the case with Azef, whom the Okhrana permitted to become a member of the Socialist Revolutionary party's combat union. He directed the assassination of Minister of Internal Affairs, V. K. von Plehve, in 1904 and the uncle of Nicholas and Governor of Moscow, Grand Duke Sergei Aleksandrovich, in 1905 before he was exposed, censured by his party, and fled Russia in 1908.[66]

The Okhrana had access to official secrets, as well as to revolutionary information, through its so-called black cabinets established under the auspices of the post and telegraph offices in every major city of the empire. Larger cities sometimes had two or three black cabinets and temporary ones were set up in other cities when the Okhrana felt conditions warranted them. Letters of magistrates, Duma members, governors, court dignitaries, and ministers—including Stolypin—filtered through the black cabinets. Though for obvious reasons statistics are difficult to come by, it has been estimated that three to four thousand letters per day were opened at the Petersburg office alone. The information acquired by the double agents and black cabinets was fed to the Secret Section of the Okhrana. There it was translated into a pattern of varicolored circles, somewhat inappropriately known as dactylographs, which enabled the Okhrana to trace the movements of both revolutionaries and governmental figures.[67]

The Secret Section sent all information, along with strategic plans, to provincial chiefs and to the Tsar through trimonthly conferences and a biweekly newspaper the Okhrana *Gazette*.[68] The Tsar marked certain passages and returned the paper to the Okhrana, supposedly via the Minister of Internal Affairs.[69]

Some high-ranking police officials were members of the Union of Russian People or were engaged in anti-Semitic activity, although most of these cases occurred before Stolypin became Minister of Internal Affairs or in the first year of his administration. One Ratchkovsky, director of the police department until 1906, directed

activities of the union and was implicated in a pogrom.[70] General
A. V. Guerassimov, head of the Petersburg Okhrana, had helped to
found the union in the winter of 1905-1906 but later dissociated
himself from it.[71] V. F. von Launits, Governor of St. Petersburg
until his assassination in 1907 and one of the prefects of the Okhrana,
also was a cofounder of the union, and remained in it. He formed a
combat section of the union, which he provided with arms, using its
members to conduct searches. It was said that the Tsar protected
him.[72] M. I. Trussevich, director of the police department from 1906
to 1909, reputedly created his own intelligence agency, which was a
center of anti-Semitic provocation.[73] At least one secret press used to
print literature inciting pogroms was discovered in the Okhrana headquarters at 16 Fontanka Street in June 1906.[74]

Apparently, Stolypin tried to keep informed of Okhrana activity
and to keep some sort of rein on at least its chief officials. General
Guerassimov claimed that in 1906 he made a report to Stolypin
almost every night, after midnight.[75] Kurlov, commander of the
gendarmerie, maintained that Stolypin was vitally interested in the
work of his department.[76] On the other hand, Polivanov asserted that
Stolypin was too credulous of police reports.[77] And A. T. Vasiliev, a
police chief, believed that Stolypin knew very little about the Azef
affair.

Stolypin's assertion of authority over lower level policemen was
limited mainly to the issuance of policy pronouncements. In 1906 he
sent a circular to local officials warning of the danger of double
agents, urging that policemen be adequately armed, and suggesting
methods of increasing police efficiency. On this last subject he
stressed that police be freed from activities not connected with their
primary duty.[78]

At the end of 1906, during the period of his great reforming
activity, Stolypin appointed an interdepartmental commission under
the chairmanship of Assistant Minister of Internal Affairs Makarov,
to draw up a thorough plan of reorganization and general upgrading
of the police. The survey of the police department as it then existed
and plans for improvement were published in eleven volumes in 1911,
affording valuable insight into the flaws of the police department. The
proposals for improvement included coordinating some of the
branches of the police, raising pay and qualifications for policemen,
and removing extraneous duties.[79] Unfortunately, the reform never
was implemented, and given the actions of police officials in high

places and the independence of local chiefs, it seems safe to conclude that Stolypin's authority over the police was limited.

Other departments within the Ministry of Internal Affairs included the Land Section, which was concerned in conjunction with the Ministry of Agriculture, with agriculture and the peasantry; the Chief Administration for the Affairs of the Local Economy, which supervised the national food supply, public charities, and the institutions of local self-government, the zemstvos and municipal dumas; the Department of General Affairs of the Ministry, which attended to ministerial personnel, the elections of marshals of nobility, and Jewish and other nationality affairs; the Chief Administration for the Affairs of the Press; the Chief Administration of Posts and Telegraphs; and the Department of Foreign Religions. The effect of Stolypin's management of these departments will be considered in later chapters.

How then can we assess the degree of Stolypin's power? Due to the vast expanses of Russia and the time lag in communications, he probably had tenuous control over most governors, not to mention lesser officials. However, as we shall see, in sensitive areas of the empire such as Finland and the Caucasus, he enjoyed a considerable amount of authority. Although he set repressive policies, his control over police officials, even the highest, appears to have been slight. Nevertheless, since Stolypin's repressive policies coincided with the mentality of lower police officers, these policies probably in effect were enforced by the police.

At the central level, Stolypin was by no means as powerful as he has been depicted. Within the ministry he had to coerce as well as to persuade in his attempt to get his programs accepted and he was not always successful. Then there were the Tsar and those who exerted influence over him to contend with. Thus, although Stolypin largely set Finnish policy, many of his proposals were rejected by Nicholas or stymied by pressure groups or strong individuals. As the years went by his position because increasingly precarious. While Nicholas realized Stolypin's abilities and probably was relieved to have such a capable manager of the country, hostile forces embarrassed Stolypin and gradually wore him out. Finally, many of his programs suffered from the dilatoriness of the legislative procedure—but that is part of a later chapter.

Notes

1. Alexandra Stolypine, *L'homme du dernier Tsar* (Paris: Redier, Librairie de la *Revue Française,* 1931), p. 129; also, Maria Petrovna von Bock, letter to the author of June 19, 1973. Alexandra Stolypin claimed the family moved because the Ministry of Internal Affairs house was "more habitable and suitable for receptions and balls." There will be further discussion on the Aptekarsky Island incident and its affect on Stolypin's policy in chapter 4, below.

The fact that Stolypin was living at the Winter Palace did not result in any closer relations between him and the Tsar. According to memoirs of family intimates such as Anna Vyrubova (Viroubova), *Memories of the Russian Court* (New York: The Macmillan Co., 1923), *passim,* the Tsar either spent after-duty hours with his family in their private apartments, traveling to other palaces, or relaxing on board the imperial yacht, or at the messes of the different regiments with his aides-de-camp; see also Count Paul Vassili Radziwill, *Behind the Veil at the Russian Court* (New York: John Lane Co., 1914), p. 363.

2. Great Britain, Public Record Office, Foreign Office (hereafter cited F.O.) 371, vol. 326, no. 29515, p. 2.

3. F. O. 371, vol. 127, no. 27544, August 4 (July 22), 1906, p. 4.

4. Count A. Patem Kin, *Predsedatel' soveta ministrov, Petr Arkad'evich Stolypin,* ed. E. Verpakhovsky (St. Petersburg: Izdanie sostavitelya, 1909), pp. 275-76. Aleksei Andreevich Polivanov, Assistant Minister of War, described the nocturnal meetings of the Council of Ministers; A. A. Polivanov, *Iz dnevnikov i vospominanii voennogo ministra i ego pomoshchika, 1907-1916* (Moscow: Vyshii voennyi redaktsionnyi sovet, 1924), *passim.*

5. Count A. Patem Kin, *Predsedatel' soveta ministrov Petr Arkad'evich Stolypin,* p. 275.

For society's repudiation of both Alexandra Feodorovna and Olga Borisovna see Count Paul Vassili Radziwill, *Behind the Veil at the Russian Court,* pp. 228-34, 360.

6. F. O. 371, *passim.*

7. "Dnevnik A. A. Bobrinskogo (1910-1911 gg.)," *Krasnyi arkhiv,* 26 (1928), pp. 138, 139, 141, 143 (19 noyabrya, 25 noyabrya, 15 dekabrya, 1910, yanvarya 13 dyna, 1911). Bobrinsky, who disliked Stolypin, criticized him for wearing in these years swallow tails instead of the more egalitarian frock coats he had formerly worn.

Stolypin's relationship with provincial leaders is described by A. V. Zenkovsky, *Pravda o Stolypine* (New York: Vseslovyanskoe Izdatel'stvo, 1956), *passim,* and is discussed in chapter 3 of this work, p. 62.

8. In *Polnoe sobranie zakonov Rossiiskoi imperii. Sobranie tretie, March 1, 1881-December 31, 1913,* 33 vols. (St. Petersburg, 1885-1916), see "The Fundamental Laws," no. 27805, glava pervaya, articles 78, 81, 4. Also see chapter 6, pp. 169-70 below, for the ministry's comments on the term "autocrat."

9. Sir Bernard Pares, in F. O. 371, vol. 1217, no. 29095, July 4, 1911, p. 4.

The State Council had approximately 196 members. The Council sat for a nine-year term; one-third of the members were elected every three years. Howard D. Mehlinger and John M. Thompson, *Count Witte and the Tsarist Government in the 1905 Revolution* (Bloomington: Indiana University Press, 1972), pp. 291-92.

10. *The Russian Constitutional Experiment, Government and Duma, 1907-1914* (New York, London: Cambridge University Press, 1973), p. 25.

11. *Decentralization and Self-Government in Russia, 1830-1870* (Princeton, New Jersey: Princeton University Press, 1972), p. 185.

12. *The Systematization of Russian Government: Social Evolution in the Domestic Administration of Imperial Russia, 1711-1905* (Urbana: University of Illinois Press, 1973), p. 300.

13. Vladimir Iosifovich Gurko, *Features and Figures of the Past,* trans. Laura Matveev (Stanford, California: Stanford University Press, 1939), p. 485. One of the intimates of the imperial family, Anna Vyrubova, similarly testifies to the Tsar's indecisiveness. Anna Viroubova, *Memories of the Russian Court,* p. 82 and *passim.*

14. *The Secret Letters of the Last Tsar,* ed. Edward J. Bing (New York: Longmans, Green and Co., 1938), p. 188.

15. *Ibid.,* p. 228.

16. Polivanov, *Iz dnevnikov i vospominanii voennogo ministra i ego pomoshchika, 1907-1916,* p. 69.

17. See below, chapter 6, pp. 162-68.

18. F. O. 371, vol. 513, no. 8956; *ibid.,* vol. 512, no. 30901, September 4, 1908.

19. Charles Bentinck, in F. O. 371, vol. 513, no. 7145.

20. Quoted in P. A. Tverskoi, "K istoricheski materialam o pokoinom P. A. Stolypine," *Vestnik evropy,* no. 4 (April 1912), p. 188.

21. Pavel Pavlovich Mendeleev, "Svety i teni v moei zhizni. Obryvki vospominanii," book 2, pp. 154-155; MS, Russian Archive, Columbia University. Mendeleev served in the chancellery of the Council of Ministers from 1906 to 1909.

22. *Gosudarstvennaya Duma: Stenograficheskie otchety,* Tretii sozyv, sessiya I, Zasedanie 7, November 16, 1907, cols. 311-12, 349-54.

23. See chapter 6, pp. 174-78, for discussion of the zemstvo crisis of 1911.

24. "Iz perepiski P. A. Stolypina s Nikolaem Romanovym," *Krasnyi arkhiv,* 30 (1928), on the land question: pp. 82-83, letter of Stolypin to Nicholas, September 26, 1910; on changes in the Ministry of Education: pp. 81-82, letters of Stolypin to Nicholas, December 22 and 30, 1907. "Perepiska N. A. Romanova i P. A. Stolypina," *Krasnyi arkhiv,* 5 (1924), Stolypin suggests that Nicholas deal severely with attempted assassination: p. 105, letter of December 3, 1906; on an appointment to the State Council: p. 113, letter of Stolypin to Nicholas, May 13, 1907; Stolypin suggests postponing elections in the Caucasus: p. 113, letter of May 30, 1907.

Stolypin helped eliminate popular criticism of Nicholas for his veto of the Jewish civil rights bill, *ibid.,* p. 107, letter of Stolypin to Nicholas, December 10, 1906, and of Nicholas to Stolypin, December 11, 1906; Stolypin prevented a possible conflict between the Tsar and the Third Duma, *Krasnyi arkhiv,* 30, p. 80, letter of Stolypin to Nicholas, November 9, 1907. The above are just some examples of the cooperation between Stolypin and the Tsar.

25. "Perepiska N. A. Romanova i P. A. Stolypina," *Krasnyi arkhiv,* 5, pp. 105-07, letters of Nicholas to Stolypin, December 10 and 11, 1906, and letter of Stolypin to Nicholas, December 10, 1906.

26. I. V. Hessen, "Reminiscences," pp. 20-21; MS, Hoover Library, Stanford, California.

27. Iliodor, who accepted the patronage of Rasputin, was a problem of a different sort. He preached a mixture of anti-Semitism and socialism and particularly hated Stolypin, whom he publicly castigated. Iliodor (Sergei Michailovich Trufanoff), *The Mad Monk of Russia, Iliodor* (New York: Century, 1918), pp. 48-71.

28. On Stolypin's behavior toward Rasputin, see below, p. 31.

29. F. O. 371, vol. 326, no. 32625, pp. 11-16, July 9, 1907; also Sir Arthur Nicolson, F. O. 371, vol. 729, no. 17374; and Bernard Pares, *ibid.,* vol. 512, no. 31810, September 4, 1908.

30. Vladimir Nikolaevich Kokovtsov, *Out of My Past*, trans. Laura Matveev (Stanford, California: Stanford University Press, 1935), pp. 435-36; A. V. Obolensky, *Moi vospominaniya i razmyshleniya* (Stockholm: Izdanie zhurnala "Rodnye Perevony," 1961), p. 81. Prince Obolensky also commented about the intrigue which swirled around Stolypin and against which Stolypin had to contend, during two interviews which the author had with the Prince in Stockholm, July 1963.

31. Letter of Boris von Bock to Professor A. V. Zenkovsky, June 24, 1953, pp. 1-2 (Russian Archive, Columbia University); letter of Maria Petrovna von Bock to Zenkovsky, July 11, 1953, pp. 1-2 (Russian Archive, Columbia University).

32. "Dnevnik A. A. Bobrinskogo (1910-1911 gg.)," *Krasnyi arkhiv*, 26, p. 144, January 15, 1911. Bobrinsky claimed that an anecdote circulating through Petersburg in 1911 had Alexandra saying to Nicholas: "Il faut consulter Stolypine . . . N'est tu pas souverain? Quel besoin de demander d'autres avis?"

33. Mendeleev, "Sveti i teni v moei zhizni," p. 149. Mendeleev described Kurlov as "without scruples and clever. His cunning was well known in Petersburg society and bureaucratic life."

34. Letter of Boris Bock to Zenkovsky, June 10, 1953 (Russian Archive, Columbia University).

35. General Alexandre Vasilevich Guerassimov, *Tsarisme et terrorisme* (Paris: Librairie Plon-Plon et Nourrit, 1934), p. 239; F. O. 371, vol. 512, no. 30901; *ibid.*, vol. 318, no. 26798, August 15, 1907; *ibid.*, vol. 732, no. 28888, July 23, 1909.

36. Testimony of Markov II in *Padenie Tsarskogo rezhima*, ed. P. S. Shchegolev (Moscow-Leningrad: Gosudarstvennaya tipografiya, 1926), vol. 6, pp. 194-95; corroborated by General Pavel Grigorevich Kurlov, *Gibel' imperatorskoi Rossii* (Berlin: Otto Kirchner and Co., 1923), p. 95.

37. F. O. 371, vol. 732, no. 28888, July 23, 1909.

38. F. O. 371, vol. 318, no. 30841, September 14, 1907; *ibid.*, vol. 513, no. 16037, May 6, 1908; *ibid.*, vol. 732, no. 28888.

39. Alexandra Stolypin recalls the first and only visit Rasputin made to the Stolypin household. One of Stolypin's daughters, Natalya, had severely injured legs, the result of the Aptekarsky explosion of 1906. The Tsar told Stolypin that Rasputin was a "grand, magnetic, beneficent force" and suggested that Stolypin allow Rasputin to see Natalya, and perhaps cure her. Rasputin came and "mumbled" prayers over Natalya, but he never returned. Alexandra corroborates Guerassimov's story. She stated that Stolypin spoke several times to the Tsar regarding Rasputin, but the Tsar insisted that it was a personal and private matter, regarding only the imperial family. Stolypine, *L'homme du dernier Tsar*, pp. 117-18.

40. Guerassimov, *Tsarisme et terrorisme*, pp. 261-63; Prince A. D. Golitsyn, "Vospominaniya," p. 297; MS, Russian Archive, Columbia University.

41. "Iz perepiski P. A. Stolypina s Nikolaem Romanovym," *Krasyni arkiv*, 30, pp. 84-85. Letter of Stolypin to Nicholas, February 26, 1911; A. I. Guchkov, "Iz vospominanii A. I. Guchkova" *Posledniya novosti*, no. 5633 and 6537 (August 26 and 30, 1936) as quoted in Gurko, *Features and Figures of the Past*, p. 723.

42. Kokovtsov, *Out of My Past*, p. 435. Two hundred-thousand rubles equalled about 100,000 U.S. dollars at that time.

43. *Ibid.*, p. 285; Sergei Efimovich Kryzhanovsky, *Vospominaniya* (Berlin: Speer and Schmidt, n.d.), pp. 103-104. The money came from the so-called ten million or reptile fund. This fund was a special part of the budget and was used to cover unforeseen

expenses in all ministries. Withdrawal of funds required authorization of the Tsar, after a report by the Minister of Finance and examination by the State Controller. By the budget laws of March 6, 1906, this part of the budget was free from debate by the legislature.

Accounts of those who had received funds are given by Plehve in *Padenie tsarskogo rezhima*, vol. 6, p. 56, and Markov II, *ibid.*, p. 181.

44. Bobrinsky, "Dnevnik A. A. Bobrinskogo," *Krasnyi arkhiv*, 26, p. 143, December 22, 1910.

45. Letter of Nicholas to Maria Feodorovna, October 11, 1906, in *Archives secretes de L'Empereur Nicolas II*, trans. from the Russian by Vladimir Lazarevski (Paris: Payot, 1928), p. 84.

46. F. O. 371, vol. 513, no. 457, January 2, 1908. Secretaries of state were heads of departments in the State Council and State Chancellery; the title was also conferred as an honor on high-ranking officials.

47. *Pravitel'stvennyi vestnik*, April 11, 1909, recorded in F. O. 371, vol. 729, no. 14217, April 13, 1909. The Order of the White Eagle was a first-degree award in the Russian Table of Honors.

48. F. O. 371, vol. 729, no. 19347, May 10, 1909.

49. "Perepiska N. A. Romanova i P. A. Stolypina," *Krasnyi arkhiv*, 5, p. 121, letter of Nicholas to Stolypin, May 30, 1910.

50. *Ibid.*, pp. 121-22, letter of Nicholas, September 22, 1910.

51. Besides Internal Affairs, ministries of the Russian government included Finance, Education, Ways of Communication, Trade and Industry, Agriculture and the Organization of Land Exploitation, State Bank, State Control, War, Navy, Justice, and Foreign Affairs, as well as some special departments for administration of state and crown properties.

52. "Perepiska N. A. Romanova i P. A. Stolypina," *Krasnyi arkhiv*, 5, p. 117, letter of Nicholas to Stolypin, December 22, 1907; "Iz perepiski P. A. Stolypina s Nikolaem Romanovam," *Krasnyi arkhiv*, 30 p., p. 81, Stolypin to Nicholas, December 22, 1907.

53. Polivanov, *Iz dnevnikov i vospominanii*, pp. 62, 68, 71, 72, 75-77. According to A. V. Zenkovsky, Stolypin complained to him of Minister of Finance Kokovtsov's fiscal conservatism, which lead the minister to oppose grants to zemstvos and spending in general; Zenkovsky, "Moi dopolnitelnye vospominaniya o P. A. Stolypine," pp. 72-75, 86; MS, Russian Archive, Columbia University.

54. Kokovtsov, *Out of My Past*, p. 271.

55. Mendeleev, "Sveti i teni moei zhizni," pp. 148-50.

56. See below, chapter 3.

57. Mendeleev, "Sveti i teni moei zhizni," p. 151.

58. Maria Petrovna von Bock substantiates this view of Kokovstov on the part of her father in a letter to Zenkovsky, July 11, 1953 (Russian Archive, Columbia University). Also see chapters 5 and 6 below.

59. "Tsirkulyar predsedatelya soveta ministrov P. A. Stolypina ot 15 sentyabrya 1906 g. general-gubernatoram, gubernatoram i gradonachalnikam," *Krasnyi arkiv*, 32 (1929), pp. 163-81; "Pismo P. A. Stolypina na imya kn. Nikolaya Nikolaevicha ot 27 yanvarya, 10 fevralya, 1908 g.," *Krasnyi arkhiv*, 19 (1926), pp. 215-21; Circular, Spring 1910, quoted in *Gosudarstvennaya deyatel'nost predsedatelya soveta ministrov, stats sekretarya, Petra Arkad'evicha Stolypina*, ed. E. Verpakhovsky (St. Petersburg: Izdanie sostavitelya, 1911), pp. 52-54.

On Stolypin's informal relationship with local leaders see Zenkovsky, *Pravda o Stolypine*, pp. 201, 204, 208-209; Bobrinsky, "Dnevnik A. A. Bobrinskogo," *Krasnyi*

60. Kokovstov, *Out of My Past*, p. 138.

61. *Gosudarstvennaya Duma: Stenograficheskie otchety*, May 29, 1906, col. 1834; Hessen, "Reminiscences," p. 19; F. O. 371, vol. 321, February 22, 1907; *ibid.*, vol. 318, no. 6673, February 28, 1907; *ibid.*, vol. 318, no. 8615, March 14, 1907; *ibid.*, vol. 321, no. 15469, April 30, 1907; *ibid.*, vol. 326, no. 23525, July 9, 1907; *ibid.*, vol. 318, no. 30841, September 14, 1907; *ibid.*, vol. 513, no. 457, January 2, 1908; Obolensky, *Moi vospominaniya i razmyshleniya*, p. 93.

62. See chapter 3, below.

63. Guerassimov, *Tsarisme et terrorisme*. Maurice Laporte, *Histoire de l'Okhrana* (Paris: Payot, 1935); Laporte had access to the Okhrana files. Aleksei Tikhonovich Vasiliev, *The Ochrana, The Russian Secret Police* (London: George C. Harrap and Co., 1930); Vasiliev was a police officer in the latter years of the empire. Pavel Pavlovich Zavarzin, *Rabota tainoi politsii* (Paris: Izdanie avtora—tipografiya "Franco-Russkaya pechat," 1924); Zavarzin also was a police officer. P. G. Kurlov, *Gibel' imperatorskoi Rossii* (Berlin: Otto Kirchner and Co., 1923); Boris Ivanovich Nikolaevsky, *Istoriya odnogo predatelya* (Berlin: Petropolis-Verlag, 1932).

64. Ministerstvo vnutrennikh del, *Zhurnal': mezhduvedomstvennoi komissii po preobzovaniyu politsii v Imperii*, 11 vols. (St. Petersburg: Gosudarstvennaya tipografiya, 1911), *passim*. See also, Edward Ellis Smith *"The Okhrana," The Russian Department of Police* (Stanford University: The Hoover Institution, Bibliographical Series: 33, 1967), p. 16. The files of the Paris branch of the Okhrana are in the Hoover Library, Stanford University.

65. Vasiliev, *The Ochrana, the Russian Secret Police*, p. 57; Zavarzin, *Rabota tainoi politsii*, pp. 16-32; Laporte, *Histoire de l'Okhrana*, pp. 23, 61.

66. Kurlov, *Gibel' imperatorskoi Rossii*, p. 111; Guerassimov, *Tsarisme et terrorisme*, p. 135; Nikolaevsky, *Istoriya odnogo predatelya*, *passim*.

67. Vasiliev, *The Ochrana, the Russian Secret Police*, pp. 90-91; Zavarzin, *Rabota tainoi politsii*, pp. 42-46; Laporte, *Histoire de l'Okhrana*, pp. 32, 39-41.

68. Vasiliev, *The Ochrana, the Russian Secret Police*, pp. 89-90.

69. Laporte, *Histoire de l'Okhrana*, p. 29.

70. Guerassimov, *Tsarisme et terrorisme*, p. 119.

71. Nikolaevsky, *Istoriya odnogo predatelya*, p. 252.

72. Guerassimov, *Tsarisme et terrorisme*, pp. 239-40.

73. *Ibid.*, pp. 183-86; Guerassimov, *Tsarisme et terrorisme*, p. 142.

75. F. O. 371, vol. 126, no. 23098, June 26, 1906. The policeman indicted was Kommissarov. One of the directors of the police resigned as a consequence, but Kommissarov remained unpunished.

75. Guerassimov, *Tsarisme et terrorisme*, pp. 117, 269.

76. Kurlov, *Gibel' imperatorskoi Rossii*, p. 81.

77. Polivanov, *Iz dnevnikov i vospominanii*, p. 34.

78. "Tsirkulyar predsedatelya soveta ministrov P. A. Stolypina ot 15 sentyabriya 1906 g. general-gubernatoram, gubernatoram i gradonachalnikam," *Krasnyi arkhiv*, 42, pp. 163-81.

79. *Zhurnal': mezhduvedomstvennoi komissii po preobrazovaniyu politsii v imperii*, vol. 6, pp. 26, 82. An example of an extraneous function of the Okhrana was its enlistment, in 1909, to prevent a marriage between Grand Duke Michael Alexandrovich and one Mme Wolfert. Guerassimov, *Tsarisme et terrorisme*, pp. 287-91.

Chapter 3:
Plans for Improvement

The summer of 1906 to the spring of 1907 was a period of feverish activity for Stolypin and the government. From July 1, 1906, to February 20, 1907, while the Duma was not in session, some fifty-eight matters were decided under the terms of article 87 of the Fundamental State Laws.[1] Fifty-three of these temporary laws were introduced to the Second Duma for confirmation, including the agrarian, Old Believer-sectarian reforms.

In September 1906 a wide list of reforms which the government was planning was published in an official manifesto.[2] Stolypin told the British ambassador, Sir Arthur Nicolson, that he hoped these proposals would be freely discussed at public meetings and in the press.[3] The Council of Ministers discussed the reform program in January 1907, and it was unveiled for the Second Duma in March. The program was comprehensive and contained several innovative measures.

The Ministry of Justice submitted proposals on reform of the local courts, involving abolition of the position of *zemskii nachal'nik* and concentration of local judicial matters in the hands of elected justices of the peace. There also were proposals on civil and criminal responsibility of officials, improvements in criminal law procedure which dealt with preliminary hearings, admittance of controversial evidence during trial, and the establishment of conditional censure and possible reduction of sentences.

The Department of Land Administration pledged to make credit easier, facilitate consolidation of land held in scattered strips, speed up land reclamation and internal migration, and increase land at the disposal of the Peasant Bank. There also were proposals for workers: improvement of health care, workingmen's insurance, and additions to the statutes limiting hours and types of labor for women and children. The government committed itself to less interference in management-labor disputes and more freedom for the formation of bonafide professional organizations by workers. It also promised to abolish penalties for strikes based on economic grievances.

The Ministry of Communications introduced proposals for extension of the railway network (special attention was focused on the Amur railway), the growth and improvement of internal waterways and necessary laws about navigation and the navy, and the alienation of immovable property for state and public needs.

Two important proposals submitted to the Second Duma concerned compulsory, universal primary education and an increase of teachers. Middle schools were to emphasize technical education. The Ministry of Finance submitted an equally important proposal for the institution of an income tax which was to "free the wide masses of the poor from additional tax burdens." While acknowledging the depleted state of the treasury due to the Russo-Japanese War, the ministry proposed reforms on inheritance taxes and planned to divert some state funds to zemstvos and municipal dumas in order to allow these institutions to perform the responsibilities entrusted to them.[4]

Of the manifold proposals embodied in the governmental program of 1906-1907, we have record of Stolypin's view on those projects emanating from the Ministry of Internal Affairs, namely, the agrarian measures, reorganization of the local administrative apparatus, changes in local self-government, modification of the position of the Jews, sectarians, and non-Orthodox Christians in Russia, and the development of far-eastern Siberia; and on the proposal of the Ministry of Education regarding the advancement of elementary education.

Some of these projects were not implemented due to opposition within and outside the government, the dilatoriness of representative government, and the magnitude of the problems confronted. Nevertheless, examination of them is profitable for it affords us a view of the ideas and attitudes of key governmental officials and of the governmental mechanism in operation.

Most of the proposals specifically sponsored by Stolypin had originated with his predecessors, but in several cases they concerned matters with which Stolypin was intimately familiar and he considerably or entirely modified them. The agrarian reforms and the reform of *volost'* self-government, if realized, might have been the first steps toward Russia's rejuvenation. The proposal on education, which Stolypin heartily endorsed, ought to have resulted in wide-scale improvement. The proposals on the sectarians contained enlightened provisions. The rest of the proposals which Stolypin personally sponsored, were more prosaic. Although the project on local administration included clauses promising real improvement, it did not, as S. Frederick Starr said of an earlier project,[5] fundamentally alter the structure of local government. Nor did the various proposals on the Jews, examined in the Ministry of Internal Affairs during Stolypin's administration, fundamentally change their status. The proposals on local self-government, while appearing to be liberal, ensured supervision and control over these institutions on the part of state officials. Furthermore, for practical reasons, wealthy, better-educated, and Orthodox Russians were favored in several of Stolypin's proposals. Some problems, too, were left unattended to. Nevertheless, as we shall see, Stolypin was at least committed to change and in a manner more in tune with Russian reality than were more radical contemporary reformers.

Agrarian Reform

The agrarian reforms were among the few improvements con-templated just before and during the early stages of Stolypin's administration which actually saw the light of day. Undoubtedly they were key measures, for the principles they embodied might have revolutionized peasant agriculture and they implied also great social and political transformation—which, to be sure, would be realized, only gradually.

Ukases in August and September 1906 released appanage and state lands for peasant purchase and opened the Altai lands of Siberia for peasant settlement.

An ukase of October 5 gave all Russian citizens, regardless of class or former taxpaying status, the same right to enter government service as that of the nobility, stipulated that minor crimes of peasants were to be handled by justices of the peace as were those of other Russians, permitted peasants to vote in the landowners' curia of the zemstvo if they possessed a certain amount of land, restored the peasants' right to elect representatives to the zemstvo, and permitted them legally to leave the commune.[6]

Ukases in October and November reduced interest rates on peasant loans made by the Peasant Land Bank and provided for expansion of its credit activities. The crucial statute was that of November 9, 1906, which provided for hereditary and consolidated tenure of allotment land and stipulated that the head of the household was the sole owner of the family property, thus obliterating the practice of splintering farmland among children and relatives.[7] The Third Duma made easier the process of achieving hereditary and consolidated tenure through laws of June 14, 1910, and May 29, 1911.[8]

The texts of the agrarian statutes had been composed mainly by Sergei Witte, former Minister of Finance; V. I. Gurko, Assistant Minister of Internal Affairs; the assassinated Minister of Internal Affairs, V. K. von Plehve; and A. V. Krivoshein, Minister of Agriculture, on the basis of information gathered by the local committees of 1902-1903, in which Stolypin had participated as Governor of Grodno. A decree of November 3, 1905, paved the way for the reform by abolishing the peasants' redemption payments, which had been one of the government's major reasons for preserving the commune. A decree of March 4, 1906, instituted the machinery necessary for the reform, the land commissions. These were actually responsible for consolidating strips of land through land surveys, establishing equitable property rights, and so forth.[9]

Stolypin had the good fortune to be in office at the time the agrarian reforms were due to go into effect. Nevertheless, he had become convinced of the necessity of such reforms while in provincial government and worked zealously for their success, fighting opposition and obstructionism.[10] As in Grodno and Saratov, he emphasized the political and social implications of the reforms,[11] particularly the establishment of hereditary, separate farmsteads, as well as their economic importance. In August 1908 he told Sir Arthur Nicolson that he had recently read a pamphlet "written by a prominent Socialist, who lamented that the ground was being cut out from under the feet of his party, owing to the impending formation of the Russian peasant into an independent owner. The writer acknowledged that as soon as the peasant acquired property over which he had absolute rights there would be no hope of winning him over to Socialistic or Communistic views."[12] In 1909, in a statement reminiscent of his 1904 annual report to Nicholas from Saratov, he claimed that "it is necessary first to create the citizen, the peasant proprietor, the small landowner, and when this problem is solved the civil state and the

qualities of citizen will of themselves come into existence in Russia
. . . . The great task will be creation of a strong individual proprietor,
the most hopeful support of the state and of enlightenment and
this will be unswervingly carried out by the Government."[13] In a
variation on the same theme, Stolypin informed Nicholas in 1910,
after a trip to Siberia, that although the reform had just begun and
much work still remained to be done, "popular psychology has
changed among the peasants . . . members of the First Duma who
were peasant revolutionaries are now fervent *khutoryan* and people of
order."[14]

Stolypin countered opposition to the formation of separated farmsteads from right and left with equal vigor. While he desired voluntary
sale of landlord estates, he opposed compulsory expropriation of
landlord property as a solution to the peasant problem because he
considered this method "unjust and economically ruinous."[15] Several
times, in fact, he requested treasury subsidies for landowners who had
suffered losses during peasant uprisings.[16] On the other hand,
acknowledging to Nicolson that conservative or reactionary groups
wanted to retain the commune because it kept the peasants in their
place,[17] Stolypin ordered local officials to carry on the reform,
reminded the Tsar that the reform had been Nicholas' idea[18] and that
the government was committed to the establishment of small private
farms,[19] and advised him not to appoint Dmitrii Khomyakov to the
State Council because he was a Slavophile and supporter of the commune.[20]

While throwing his weight behind the key issue of separated farmsteads, Stolypin regarded with greater skepticism the easing of the
peasant land shortage, real or technical, by peasant migration to
Siberia. He insisted that it was "essential to develop the unbounded
resources of Siberia, and also to relieve the congestion of some
provinces in [European] Russia," but he was painfully aware of the
difficulties involved. In a conversation with Sir Arthur Nicolson in
August 1908 he criticized the defects in distribution and reception of
settlers in Siberia, the lack of funds, and the poor railway connections. He stated that he had looked into internal migration in
Canada and the United States and that two important factors were
adequate capital and well-organized private associations to assist
settlers.[21] In the spring of 1909 he ruefully admitted that the conditions of Siberian migration had not greatly improved.[22]

Indeed, despite the bravado he publicly displayed, for instance in
his famous speech to the Second Duma, Stolypin's realism made him

view the future of the agrarian reforms, or any major improvement in Russia, with some pessimism. In the summer of 1908 he confided to Nicolson that "when he contemplated the great problems with which the government had to deal, he felt occasionally appalled by the magnitude of the task, and the want of funds, the dearth of competent men, and the prevailing ignorance of the bulk of the population were great obstacles. If the money could be found to undertake several measures, in a few years such undertakings would be productive and reimburse the outlay. The next four or five years were the difficult period; once they were tided over, the prospect would brighten and the path be easier."[23]

Improvement in the Conditions of the Jews

In December 1906, close on the heels of the agrarian laws, came Stolypin's proposal for increasing Jewish rights. His precedessor in the Ministry of Internal Affairs, Prince P. D. Sviatopolk-Mirsky, had wanted to abolish some of the restrictive statutes pertaining to the Jews, but had not succeeded.[24]

The majority of Jews, amounting to about 6 million or about 5 percent of the population in the early twentieth century, lived in the western border regions of the empire. This area, commonly called the Pale of settlement, had been brought into the empire in the late eighteenth century through Catherine the Great's partitions of Poland-Lithuania.

Jews in early twentieth century Russia were subject to various limitations. A decree of 1882 had forbidden them to live outside towns or larger villages and cancelled the right of Jewish soldiers to remain outside the Pale after their military service was finished, as they had done from 1867. In 1891 large numbers of Jewish merchants and artisans were expelled from Moscow. Jewish merchants of the First Guild—the organization of wealthiest merchants—were allowed to settle outside the Pale, but a law of 1899 required them to obtain individual consent from the Minister of Internal Affairs. In 1891 Jews also were barred from participating in municipal self-government.

Jews were further restricted in their choice of occupation. A decree of 1882 limited the number of Jewish doctors or orderlies in the medical corps to 5 percent and a decree of 1899 required all Jews wishing admittance to the Bar to receive permission from the Minister of Justice; permission was not always given. Civilian Jewish physicians had difficulty practicing and Jewish attendance at secondary schools and universities was limited. A decree of 1897 established a quota for Jews of 3 percent for schools in St. Petersburg and Moscow, 5 percent for schools in other cities outside the Pale, and 10 percent for schools within the Pale. Perhaps more reprehensible than these quotas, which at least were commensurate with the proportion of Jews in Russian society, were the periodical pogroms, often supported by local officials or ignored by them.[25]

Stolypin's views on the Jewish question essentially were conservative. He claimed that the restrictions on the Jews were unwise because they bred revolutionary spirit among the Jews and gave a poor image of Russia abroad.[26] Nevertheless, he candidly admitted to Nicholas that although the Jews were entitled to full civil rights following the manifesto of October 17, 1905, if their rights were partially enlarged, the Duma might postpone granting them equal rights.[27]

The reform bill of 1906, the only comprehensive proposal on Jewish rights issued by the ministry during Stolypin's administration, reflected this cautious thinking. As far as residence was concerned, Jews still were to be confined largely to the Pale; only Jewish heads of household who had plied a trade for ten years outside the Pale were permitted to live in cities outside the Pale. Jews were, however, to be on a nearly equal footing with other Russians when engaged in trade or industry where they were allowed to live.[28] In the matter of land-holding, Stolypin came out firmly against Jews not only purchasing, but even leasing land in rural areas of the Pale. He maintained that Jews competed for land with Christian peasants, in an area where land was at a premium, that they could best the peasants because they were usually richer, and that they then exploited the peasants to whom they subleased the land for high payments.[29] The other ministers rejected the prohibition on leases in the final version of the proposal, on the grounds that it would deprive Jews of a livelihood and also because fraudulent leases had already been contracted. However, the ministry retained the prohibition on Jews buying land within the Pale.[30] The Tsar, as we have mentioned, vetoed this proposal.

There were three other instances in which the Council of Ministers sanctioned meager increase of Jewish rights. Stolypin's opinion was specifically registered in two of the three cases. There were two other instances in which the Council of Ministers did not approve relaxation of restrictions on Jews. It is not clear in these latter cases whether Stolypin shared the majority opinion, although probably, and in one case, most probably, he did. On the whole, even when Stolypin and the Council of Ministers reacted favorably to the Jews, it is clear that he—and the council as a whole—regarded Jews as second-class citizens.

The three occasions on which Stolypin and the ministry appeared somewhat liberal toward the Jews involved Jewish participation in municipal government, norms for Jewish entrance into secondary schools, and rights of Jewish merchants to live in Moscow. Regarding the first issue, the ministry approved a clause in its proposal on local government, discussed in 1907, which permitted Jews once more to participate in city government in the Pale. They had been barred from such participation in 1892. In the new proposal, however, the ministry lowered the number of city duma members which Jews were permitted to elect from the one-third permitted them in 1870 to one-fifth.[31]

In 1909 Stolypin and his fellow ministers argued against the Minister of the Navy and the Minister of Public Education in favor of increasing the percentage of Jews admitted to secondary schools in comparison to the percentage allotted to Jews in higher schools. The naval and education ministers proposed that general percentage norms for Jewish admittance to secondary schools should equal those for universities, namely, 3 percent for schools in the capital, 5 percent for schools in other cities outside the Pale, and 10 percent for schools within the Pale. Stolypin and his camp maintained that the percentage norms for middle schools should be higher than those for universities because many of those attending middle schools never went on to higher. Accordingly, they proposed percentage norms of 5, 10, and 15 percent respectively for state-supported secondary schools in the capital, in cities outside the Pale, and in cities within the Pale. These included agricultural schools, surgical schools, and midwife schools. They also advised that percentage norms for pharmacy schools be higher: 6, 10, and 20 percent for the categories mentioned. Schools not permitting students to go on to higher educational institutions were to have unlimited entry quotas for Jews.[32]

In 1910 the Council of Ministers proposed that Jewish merchants be allowed to live in Moscow and cities of Moscow province if they had resided there since 1897. As bases for their reasoning, the council bluntly admitted that if Jewish merchants were expelled business would suffer and a poor impression would be given abroad. All members of the Jewish merchant's family, however, were not to be granted these privileges. In addition to wives, only unmarried daughters, minor sons, sons necessary to their father's business, or sons not yet finished with university courses were to be permitted to remain.[33]

In contrast to these guarded examples of generosity, in 1910 the Assistant Minister of Internal Affairs, probably representing Stolypin, stated in a meeting of the Council of Ministers that a proposal of 166 members of the Duma asking for abolition of laws restricting Jewish choices of residence was unacceptable.[34] A further instance of negative or unsympathetic attitude toward the Jews on the part of the Council of Ministers was expressed in the same year. Stolypin was probably included in the opinion of the council, although there is no specific mention of his views. Discussion in the council centered on the application, in trade and industrial schools, of the secondary school quotas ordained by the ministry in 1909. The Minister of Trade and Industry urged that application of these quotas in commercial schools within the Pale be postponed for three years in order to prevent financial disaster and possible collapse of these schools, with attendant loss to all Russian youths. According to the minister, Jews often supported the schools and even paid the tuition of individual Christian students in the hope that one or both these measures would enable them to have their sons admitted, despite quota restrictions. The Council of Ministers, in opposition to this suggestion, insisted that the quotas be applied and made the further policy statement that leniency had resulted in Jews filling the schools and that such overcrowding must be stopped.[35]

Reorganization of the *Guberniya* and *Uezd* Administration

Stolypin's plans to reform the local administration were another of the projects, developed by his ministry under his personal supervision, which never came to fruition. Nevertheless, they deserve attention for several reaons. First they illustrate how much the local administrative apparatus needed overhauling. Second, they add a chapter to the story of the rivalry in the provinces between the Ministry of Internal Affairs and the Ministry of Finance, which has been described for the period preceding 1905 by S. Frederick Starr and George Yaney.[36] Third, they are representative of Stolypin's moderate solutions to Russia's major internal problems. Fourth, they emphasize the difficulty he had in implementing even modest proposals. Before the Duma could delay or reject a proposal, it might be curtailed by Stolypin's fellow ministers, fearful of increase in the power of the Minister of Internal Affairs, or shelved because of opposition from more conservative figures in the country at large who could persuade the Tsar of the danger of enacting the project.

The revolution of 1905 had disrupted communications between the central government and the provincial administration and seriously weakened the government of some provinces. But both before and after this period, Russian political theorists were concerned about intrinsic flaws in the provincial administration, resulting in inefficient and arbitrary government.

To begin, the governor was overwhelmed with duties. He was chairman of eleven boards and vice-chairman of one and a member of another.[37] In some respects the governor had too little authority; in other respects he had too much—at least vis-à-vis the central government. The law stated that the governor was a supraministerial figure—the representative of the central government in the provinces. Actually, however, the governor had either partial or no control over important provincial agencies and officials belonging to ministries other than Internal Affairs. In the case of some provincial agencies of the Ministry of Finance, namely the fiscal board (*kazennaya palata*) and the Board of Exise Tax Collection, and the provincial Department of State Domains, the governor received annual business reports and could make investigations. If any irregularities appeared he could order the agency to correct them and inform the responsible minister. If the disorders continued, however, the governor's only recourse was to inform the minister a second time. The governor could not issue immediate orders to other local branches of the Ministry of Finance, namely the mining, forest and salt, and monetary departments, or to local offices of the Ministry of Agriculture and Land Development, but could notify the agency and proximate superior of irregularities. Governors had no control whatsoever over the provincial Board of State Control, provincial offices of the state bank, tariff boards, and the gendarmerie.[38] Although the law stated that the governor had the right to call all provincial officials to him and that they must obey "immediately" and fulfill his "lawful commands," the stipulation was so vaguely worded that it was virtually a dead letter.[39] Furthermore, a contradictory law stated that the governor should confine his dealings with officials of departments outside the Ministry of Internal Affairs to explaining the functions of these officials. He was to enter into "formal" (i.e., disciplinary) relations with them only in cases of "extreme necessity."[40]

In contrast to these limitations on their authority, governors had acquired wide discretionary powers not subject to the control of the central government. The governor had the right to veto, within a two-week period, appointments, transfers, and promotions of provincial officials belonging to all ministries. He also had the authority to approve officials of noble organizations and the members of the *uprava* of zemstvos and municipal dumas, as well as city mayors. The only reason the governor needed to submit, in case of rejection of an appointee, was that the candidate was "unreliable." This decision could not be appealed.[41]

In addition to controlling the regular police, governors were allowed to issue "obligatory regulations" in "emergency situations." Neither of these terms, in the opinion of contemporary jurists, had been adequately defined, and as Minister of Internal Affairs Stolypin had reproved governors for abusing this authority.[42] Obligatory regulations could be appealed to the Senate and changed or abolished by the Ministry of Internal Affairs, but while they existed they had the force of law.[43]

Finally, since there were no requirements for the position of governor, most governors had no judicial training. What is worse, most were chosen from the Petersburg bureaucracy and they were, therefore, unfamiliar with the needs of the provinces to which they had been appointed.[44]

A second provincial institution, the Provincial Administrative Board (*gubernskoe pravlenie*), might have been an aid to the governor, as well as a check on him, and a possible unifying force in the province. According to law, the Provincial Administrative Board was the highest governmental institution in the province, equal to the governor and subordinate to the Senate. In reality, the board had lost its pan-ministerial character and had become an agency of the Ministry of Internal Affairs. Furthermore, it was completely dependent upon the governor.

The Provincial Administrative Board consisted of a general assembly and a chancery. All the members of the general board—the vice-governor, councillors, medical inspector, engineer, architect, surveyor, assessor, and prison inspector—were appointed by the Minister of Internal Affairs.[45] Most important business in the provinces was handled by the agencies of other ministries and outside the jurisdiction of the Provincial Administrative Board. Officials of these agencies were practically immune from control by the board. Although the law gave the judicial instance of the board the right to bring all officials of all departments and ministries to trial for misdemeanors, the board needed the sanction of the accused's superior and this usually was not forthcoming. In addition, another law contradicted the first, as in the case of the governor, and stated that agencies of one ministry were forbidden to interfere in the affairs of another.[46]

In defining the relationship of the board and the governor, the law stipulated that they were to cooperate in judicial and administrative matters of the "second instance," that is, matters not urgent or requiring secrecy. These latter issues were termed matters of the "first instance" and were to be decided by the governor alone. Actually, however, the journals of the general assembly of the board indicate that it usually unanimously echoed the governor's opinion,[47] and governors further diminished the boards' power by extending the meaning of the term "urgent and secret business" so that they could decide many matters without interference from the boards.[48] The Provincial Administrative Board, thus, was left with only two real functions. It had the right to notify the governor, and if he agreed, the Senate, about discrepancies or lack of clarity in a law; and it controlled the police, in conjunction with the governor.[49]

Stolypin's predecessors in the central government had attempted to reform the local administration, but had not succeeded. Stolypin, of course, had experienced firsthand the weaknesses in the local administration while governor as Governor of Grodno during 1902-1903 and as Governor of Saratov from 1903 to 1906. In Saratov, which was one of the provinces hardest hit by destruction during the revolution, Stolypin had emphasized the necessity of preserving and strengthening the provincial administrative apparatus.[50] As Minister of Internal Affairs, he often deplored the fact that it was so difficult to find suitable candidates for provincial positions.[51]

According to S. E. Kryzhanovsky, Assistant Minister of Internal Affairs during Stolypin's administration, Stolypin was fascinated with a truly innovative plan for decentralization in which the empire was to be divided into eleven oblasts, each with a zemstvo assembly and administrative institutions. The plan proposed federal-type separation between oblast and central legislation. However, according to Kryzhanovsky, Stolypin shelved the project when he realized that the Tsar opposed it on grounds that it might be construed as a step toward weakening the unity of the empire.[52]

This account may or may not have been true. In any case, the projects for reform of the local administration which Stolypin presented to the Council of Ministers in the winter of 1906-1907 did not propose drastic change but rather remodeling and reorganization of existing institutions.[53]

The proposal on reform of the provincial administration listed six deficiencies at this level of government: absence in the law of a fixed and exact view of the governor's function, lack of unity in the activity of provincial institutions of various ministries, isolation of the administrative sector from the administrative-economic sector which was managed by publicly elected institutions, the splintering of administrative business among provincial institutions, a lack of assistants for the governor, and the insignificant salaries of officials in provincial administration making it difficult to find suitable candidates for provincial positions. The main aim of the project was to unify provincial government.[54]

In order to give the governor a pan-ministerial cast, his method of appointment, first of all, was to be modified—but only slightly. The Minister of Internal Affairs was to suggest a candidate to the Tsar only after the candidate had been approved by the Council of Ministers. In order to make the governor more truly the representative of the central government in the provinces all orders from the central government which "affected the whole tenor of local life or had general significance for all departments" were to pass through the governor's hands. He was to give corresponding orders to the provincial heads of various departments and to receive information on how these orders had been executed, informing the responsible minister if they had not been carried out. The governor was to supervise the business and behavior of all departments in the province, except judicial institutions, offices of state control, and higher educational institutions, through inspections and periodic reports. He retained the right to veto appointments to positions in administrative bodies and public institutions, "within limits ordained by law." He was explicitly declared chief director of land development and lower and middle schools and was to be responsible for punctual collection of taxes, with the power of imposing penalties for arrears. He was to be chief of all police in the province: regular, military, and special forces.[55] (A thorough reform of the police simultaneously was being worked out under Stolypin's aegis.)[56] As formerly, the governor was to be allowed to issue obligatory regulations for preservation of law and order which carried penalties if they were not heeded.[57]

In line with the state theory of local self-government, the governor continued to enjoy extensive power over local self-governing institutions. He could attend meetings of zemstvos and municipal dumas and make speeches. If self-governing institutions did not fulfill their responsibilities, the governor could do so with the aid of a special fund. He was to submit to the Minister of Internal Affairs an annual recommendation on the amount of treasury funds which ought to be allocated to self-governing institutions.[58]

To make the provincial administration more cohesive and to strengthen its relationship with local self-government, a Provincial Council (*gubernskii sovet*) was to be instituted. The council was to replace the Provincial Administrative Board and all special committees and boards in the province, and its membership was to include representatives from class and publicly elected institutions. The council was to consist of the governor, who served as its chairman, two proposed assistant governors, the highest officials of the various ministries in the provinces, the provincial marshal of nobility, the chairman of the provincial zemstvo *uprava,* the mayor of the provincial capital, and two especially elected individuals, one from the provincial zemstvo, the other from the municipal duma of the capital city of the province. The Provincial Council was divided into three sections: a general assembly which was to assist the governor in an advisory capacity, nine special assemblies, corresponding to the separate ministries and departments in the province, and a disciplinary assembly.[59]

The division of the council into nine special assemblies appeared a bit unwieldy and brought forth the justified criticism of the ministry that instead of streamlining the provincial administration Stolypin had merely reshuffled committees. On the other hand, the proposed disciplinary assembly might have made a real contribution toward increased legality as well as increased unity in the province. Including the chairman of the provincial zemstvo *uprava,* the head of the capital city duma, the procurator of the circuit court (*okruzhnoi sud*), and the highest official of the department to which the person being called to account belonged, the jurisdiction of the disciplinary assembly was to extend to the provincial personnel of all ministries and departments, as well as to publicly elected officials.[60]

In order to relieve the governor of some of his responsibilities he was to be assisted by two vice-governors, one for general administration and one for police affairs.[61] Finally, to raise the caliber of provincial officials, the project proposed salary increases, stipulated that all officials of *nachal'nik* ("managerial") status have a higher education, and required officials aspiring to careers in the central administration to spend at least three years in the provinces.[62] On the matter of higher salaries, Stolypin was forced to fight Minister of Finance V. N. Kokovtsov whose main concern was paring the state budget. In this case, however, Stolypin was supported by the other ministers.[63]

The proposal on the local administration left some important problems untouched, notably the chance for arbitrary action on the part of the governor and his relationship to the Minister of Internal Affairs insofar as supervision and control were concerned. Nevertheless, the proposal appeared to have succeeded in its main aim of establishing cohesion in local government, in restoring the status of the Provincial Board and widening its membership and jurisdiction, in providing a check on the activity of local officials, and in perhaps raising the quality of local officials. While still in its early stages, however, Stolypin's project on provincial administation was emasculated by his fellow ministers who continued to regard the governor and the Provincial Council as creatures of the Ministry of Internal Affairs. They feared that strengthening the authority of the governor and the council would enhance the power of the Minister of Internal Affairs and consequently weaken their own power in the provinces.

Kokovtsov pointed out that according to Stolypin's proposal the governor still was to be appointed by recommendation of the Minister of Internal Affairs and that with the authority given the governor by Stolypin's proposal he would come between the central ministries and their agencies and departments on the local level. He also noted that practically speaking it would be difficult to find a person versed in the business of all the ministries as the governor would now be required to be.[64] The other ministers agreed with him and as a result amended the project significantly. They stipulated that the governor could give orders to personnel of their ministries only regarding matters of "general significance" (matters which had been discussed in the Council of Ministers). He was not to give orders to their personnel on specialized departmental business. If the governor's orders were not executed he was to inform the responsible minister—and the Chairman of the Council of Ministers.[65] The governor was to receive information only regarding matters of "general significance" or in cases where he suspected abuse and was not to receive reports of all business carried on in the various provincial departments. In each case he had to specifically request information, that is, he did not automatically receive it. He was denied even this general supervision over the provincial institutions of state credit.[66] Furthermore, he could not order department heads belonging to ministries other than

Internal Affairs to make inspections of persons subordinate to them, but could only notify the responsible minister and the Chairman of the Council of Ministers. The latter were to decide on the necessity of such an inspection.[67]

The Minister of Internal Affairs was not to be allowed to abolish obligatory regulations issued by the governor and the Provincial Council. Rather, persons who had complaints about these regulations could appeal to the ministry with which they were affiliated and this ministry, after consultation with Internal Affairs, was to petition the Senate to abolish the obligatory regulation.[68]

In the event of absence or sickness of the governor, his place was to be taken by the director of the *kazennaya palata* ("fiscal board") or by the head of the Board of Land Development and State Properties, rather than by the governor's assistant for administrative affairs.[69]

The ministers deprived the disciplinary assembly of the Provincial Council of authority over persons appointed by the government. The assembly was to have jurisdiction only over publicly elected officials, not over administrative personnel. Simultaneously, the Minister of Justice, I. G. Shcheglovitov, proposed that the courts and the pro-curator, an agent of *his* ministry, have the right to bring to trial administrative officials hitherto granted immunity for crimes com-mitted in office.[70]

The ministers' opposition effectively neutralized Stolypin's reform of the local administration, but according to Kryzhanovsky, the project was dealt its death blow by the campaign of two individuals, Governor of Nizhnii-Novgorod A. N. Khvostov and representative of the Saratov provincial zemstvo S. A. Panchulidzev. These two contended that the project would diminish the Tsar's power and their criticism apparently upset Nicholas.[71] Whether or not this actually occurred,[72] Stolypin's proposal for the provincial administration never was put into effect.

Stolypin's Plans for Improving Uezd-Volost' Administration

The deficiencies in the *uezd* administration were as serious as those on the provincial level. First, *uezd* government was essentially class government. The *uezd* marshal of nobility and the *uezd* assembly of nobility played a dominant role in *uezd* affairs.[73] In addition, the *uezd* marshal of nobility was not subject to the governor's control. Furthermore, statistics assembled by Stolypin showed that *uezd* marshals were negligent. During 1908, for example, only two *uezd* marshals had attended every meeting of which they were chairmen. Less than half the marshals fulfilled half their responsibilities; about one-third did not fulfill them at all. About one-half the *uezd* marshals did not live in their *uezdy*.[74]

As on the provincial level, the central government' had no supra-ministerial representative in the *uezd* other than the district police chief (*uezdnyi ispravnik*), and the *uezd* administration suffered from the same confusion and duplication of ministerial agencies as the provincial.[75]

In the *volost', zemskie nachal'niki* or "land captains," usually chosen from the local nobility, exercised administrative and judicial authority over *volost'* and settlement self-government and individual peasants. Before Stolypin's administration, V. I. Gurko, Assistant Minister of Internal Affairs, had tried to enlist more qualified men in the posts of *zemskie nachal'niki* by establishing a training course and examination for candidates. He also formulated a special manual of regulations for these officials. Finally, in 1904, the government undertook a special investigation of *zemskie nachal'niki*.[76]

The major aims of Stolypin's proposal for the *uezd-volost'* admin-istration, which he presented to the Council of Ministers in 1906, were to abolish the class character of *uezd-volost'* government and to give it more unity by establishing a representative of the central govern-ment and a pan-ministerial council on the *uezd* level. To head the *uezd* administration, Stolypin created an *uezd* governor, the *uezdnyi nachal'nik*. Like the provincial governor in Stolypin's project for provincial administration, the *uezdnyi nachal'nik* was to supervise and coordinate administrative officials and agencies of all ministries which were located in the *uezd* and to preside over another new institution, the *uezd* council.[77]

This council or *uezdnyi sovet* was to be composed of all ministerial representatives in the *uezd,* representatives from the *uezd* zemstvo and municipal duma in the *uezd,* and the *uezd* marshal of nobility. The council was to replace all collegiate committees on army affairs, *volosti,* land administration, and police administration.[78] Thus, it simplified the *uezd* administration and linked it more closely with popularly elected bodies.

With the advent of the *uezdnye nachal'niki,* the *uezd* marshals of nobility were to have significance only as representatives of the noble class. Their function was to be reduced to supervising public schools and to presiding over meetings of the *uezd* zemstvo and *uezd* Land Exploitation Commission.[79]

Stolypin's proposal completely abolished the *zemskie nachal'niki.* In their place were to be established *uchastkovye nachal'niki.* These latter were to supervise the activity of the proposed all-class *volost'* and settlement zemstvos (institutions which Stolypin proposed to the Council of Ministers in 1907)[80] as to the legality of their actions and also were to examine complaints arising from their decisions.[81] Unfortunately, Stolypin did not stipulate qualifications for the future *uchastkovye nachal'niki* or provide for much supervision over them.

As in the case of Stolypin's plans for the provincial administration, his proposals for the *uezd-volost'* administration never were put to the test. First, his fellow ministers strongly opposed his plans. They feared, as they had in the case of the governor, that the *uezdnye nachal'niki* would come between them and their subordinates in the *uezdy.* Therefore, they limited the unifying function of the *uezdnye nachal'niki* to presiding over the *uezd* council and to supervising and inspecting all civil departments in the *uezd.* The *uezdnyi nachal'nik* was to enter into "immediate relationship" with personnel of ministries other than Internal Affairs only in regard to matters of "great significance."[82]

The Council of Ministers took greater objection to demoting marshals of nobility. Ministers delivered long dissertations on the service rendered by marshals of nobility, service which the ministers claimed was above class interest and which had been praised in testimonials from several tsars. In the light of this contribution of the marshals of nobility the ministers urged that marshals be appointed to the post of *uezdnyi nachal'nik* whenever possible.[83]

According to Kryzhanovsky, it was because of the opposition of the united nobility that Stolypin's project was never implemented. Resenting a limited role in *uezd* and *volost'* administration, they agitated against the project, and Stolypin did not defend it as well as he might have. He did not, for example, present the statistics which documented his claims about the poor performance of marshals of nobility because, according to Kryzhanovsky, he feared they presented too bleak a picture of the *uezd* administration.[84] He steadfastly maintained that the government did not intend to diminish the position of the nobility. For instance, in an interview with the editor of *Volga* in 1909[85] and in meetings of the Council of Ministers he stated that the government depended upon the nobility in local administration and in local self-government because of their education, expertise, and economic resources.[86]

To summarize, then, Stolypin's plans for improving the local administration were not as far-reaching as they might have been. The proposals on the provincial administration did not deal with some major problems. The class character of the lowest level of administration was retained. Nevertheless, Stolypin's plans promised greater legality and unity in the local administration and a closer relationship between the local administration and local self-government. But these promises, indeed any improvement in local government, were forestalled by the ministers' desire to preserve their vested interests and by a similar outlook on the part of rightist pressure groups in the country at large.

Changes in Local Self-Government

Progressives in Russia had been demanding improvement in local self-government almost from its inception. During the 1880s many zemstvo leaders called for the replacement of peasant *volost'* government by a so-called all-class *volost'* institution, the function and representation of which were to be modelled on the *uezd* and *guberniya* zemstvos, and which was to be subordinate to the *uezd* zemstvo.[87] Agitation for wider representation and power for the *guberniya* and *uezd* zemstvos increased after the central government placed restraints upon these bodies in the late 1880s and 1890s.[88] Zemstvo leaders found the local administration's right to veto decisions on the basis of their subject matter especially frustrating. Zemstvo finances were in bad shape. In some areas schools and hospitals were closed and roads and veterinary work suspended due to lack of funds.[89] During the hectic years of 1904 and 1905 progressive zemstvo circles called for modernization of local self-government, along with the creation of a national parliament.

By 1902 even the government had decided to increase zemstvo power and was debating the possibility of creating an all-class *volost'*. V. K. von Plehve, Minister of Internal Affairs at the time, devised a plan for decentralization and closer cooperation between zemstvo and administrative activity.[90] An imperial ukase of 1903 and another of 1904 promised to restore the representation and power the zemstvo had enjoyed before the last decades of the nineteenth century.[91] V. I. Gurko and others in the Ministry of Internal Affairs discussed the establishment of an all-class *volost'* government, although, strangely enough, in the project as actually formulated the *volost'* remained purely peasant-based.[92] Plehve also planned to create an advisory body in the Ministry of Internal Affairs which was to include representatives, appointed by the central government, from the zemstvos and the local administration. It was to be called the *Sovet po delam mestnago khozyaistva.*[93]

How did Stolypin's attitude toward local self-government fit into this picture? As Governor of Grodno in 1902-1903 he emphasized that local persons and zemstvos ought to play a more significant part in land reclamation. (He also opposed at this time public discussion on the question of the introduction of zemstvos into the western provinces.) At an evening reception for zemstvo leaders in 1906, he announced that one of his policies was decentralization in economic and social matters. He stated that the government must allocate many of its responsibilities to local institutions of self-government. Within the administration, he asked ministers and department heads to draw up lists of their affairs which could be transferred to the zemstvos.[94] Throughout his tenure of office as Chairman of the Council of Ministers, he requested treasury grants-in-aid for the zemstvos and municipal dumas in the face of Kokovtsov, who was more concerned about a balanced budget.[95] Stolypin had good friends among zemstvo and provincial figures and periodically held informal interviews with them on the state of affairs in their localities. These local leaders included A. V. Zenkovsky from Kiev *guberniya,*[96] Feodor Vladimirovich Shlipie, member of the Moscow provincial zemstvo and head of the Land Development Commission of the *guberniya,*[97] and Prince A. D. Golitsyn, member of an *uezd* zemstvo in Kharkov *guberniya* and Octobrist deputy to the Third Duma.[98] According to Zenkovsky, Stolypin personally participated in the organization of an all-Russian congress of specialists in zemstvo economy.[99]

Stolypin's specific program for local self-government was fourfold. First, he attempted to rescind some of the restrictions which had been placed upon the representation and taxing power of the zemstvos and municipal dumas. Second, he attempted to create all-class zemstvos on the *volost'* and settlement levels. Third, he attempted to integrate local self-governing institutions with local administrative agencies, principally by instituting the *gubernskii* and *uezdnyi* soviets, described in the preceding section of this chapter, in which administrative personnel mingled with representatives from the zemstvos and municipal dumas. Fourth, he activated the *Sovet po delam mestnago khozyaistva* and included in it persons elected by the zemstvos in addition to local persons appointed by the government. (It will be noted that although three of these projects had originated with Stolypin's predecessors, he had considerably modifed two—on the *volost'* zemstvo and on the *Sovet po delam mestnago khozyaistva*—and one, on the *gubernskii* and *uezdnyi* soviets, was entirely his own.)

However, none of these changes in local self-government (and herein lay the crux of Stolypin's thinking with regard to popular government) implied diffusion of political power. Rather, they were built on what N. M. Korkunov, the eminent nineteenth century Russian jurist, described as the state theory of local self-government. This theory, propounded by two political theorists, Rudolph Gneist and Lorenz Stein, was advocated, according to Korkunov, by the majority of political theorists of the time.[100]

The state theory held that zemstvos and municipal dumas were qualitatively different from the local branches of the central administration in that they were not directly subordinate to the central administration. However, because they performed vital public services the government could not regard them in the same way as it regarded private societies and corporations. According to the state theory, wrote Korkunov,

the essence of self-government lies in the fact that the government has made local society responsible for fulfilling certain tasks of the state administration. . . . In this theory . . . the legislation of all states views the activity of local self-governing societies not as additional only, but as a partial substitute for state activity.[101]

Because of this the central administration not only had to guard against illegal actions of zemstvos and municipal dumas, but had to ensure that these institutions fulfilled the vital tasks entrusted to them. If the public institutions neglected their duties, administrative authorities were to perform them in their stead:

Since the organs of self-government are carrying out the tasks of the state administration, the state cannot regard their activity indifferently, cannot limit, as in regard to a free society, supervision merely to the fact that they do not violate any laws. . . . The state watches not only that the local organs of self-government do not violate the rights of others . . . but also that they actually fulfill the functions of state administration placed upon them.[102]

Whether Stolypin read Korkunov, as he had been urged to do by his cousin Baron Alexander Meyendorff in 1904 or 1905,[103] is unknown. Nevertheless, the echo in Stolypin's projects on self-government of the ideas expressed in Korkunov indicates that he was conversant with the principles of the state theory.

The fullest expression of the state theory was contained in his bill on the establishment of settlement zemstvos:

The correct application of supervision over the activity of self-government is one of the most important conditions in the growth of these institutions. However, the degree of supervisory authority over the organs of self-government which will guarantee both the interests of the local unit and of the whole administration is very difficult to establish, and in practice depends upon varying conditions.

The general principle by which we are directed . . . in the decision of the question is . . . that governmental supervision over the activity of public agencies must be confined predominantly to observation over the legality of these agencies' activity. However . . . there is not one state in the world in which governmental power has limited its influence over self-governing units only to questions of legality. . . . Self-governing institutions not only have the right, but the responsibility before the state to fulfill a whole range of tasks, whence arises the right of the state to observe that these tasks are executed, and in the ordained sense.[104]

Other of his bills affirmed that in other countries increased competence in local self-governing institutions was accompanied by an increase in supervision on the part of the administration.[105]

In accordance with this outlook, Stolypin, in his several projects on local self-governing institutions, augmented their jurisdiction, widened their representation, and made provision for their influence on administrative agencies. At the same time, he established controls which curtailed policy making on the part of these institutions and prevented them from becoming a counterweight to the administration.

Guberniya and Uezd Zemstvos and Municipal Dumas

Stolypin presented the project on "The Transformation of the *Guberniya* and *Uezd* Zemstvos and Municipal Dumas" to the Council of Ministers early in 1907.[106] The first concern of the project was with zemstvos' and municipal dumas' revenue-raising and decision-making power. The project abolished the restriction placed upon zemstvo taxation by the law of June 3, 1900, which had stipulated that zemstvo tax revenues were not to increase by more than 3 percent each year and allowed the Minister of Internal Affairs to veto budgets in excess of this amount. Stolypin's project also repealed laws of 1885, 1887, and 1898, which had increased the amount of trade and industrial taxes destined for the treasury at the expense of zemstvo revenue from these enterprises.

Stolypin's bill once more allowed zemstvo revenue to rise more than 3 percent annually and gave the zemstvos a greater share in treasury taxes. It removed from the cities the duty to quarter troops, gave the zemstvo control over roads and ports with no strategic importance,[107] and put additional police forces at the zemstvos' disposal. To pay the policemen's salaries the government permitted the zemstvos to collect a special police tax.

The bill also redressed laws of August 19, 1879, and June 12, 1890, which had severely limited the zemstvos' decision-making power. The former law had required that every technician whom the zemstvo *uprava* ("managing board") hired be approved by the governor. It also had allowed governors to remove zemstvo employees whom they considered "politically undesirable," a term obviously capable of wide extension. The law of June 12, 1890, had removed the immediate supervision of the Minister of Internal Affairs over zemstvo activity and gave governors the power to reject candidates for zemstvo offices and to appoint their own candidates if a zemstvo had twice refused to appoint those proposed. Governors also had been permitted by this law to prohibit implementation of zemstvo resolutions, not only if they did not conform to the laws of the land, but also if they "did not harmonize with the general interests and needs of the state or clearly violated the general interests of the local populace."[108]

Stolypin's project shortened the list of matters demanding confirmation by administrative officials, allowed these officials to approve only the chairman of the *uprava* of the zemstvos and municipal dumas, and revoked the right of the officials to suppress zemstvo decisions if they deemed them unsuitable. Henceforth, administrative authorities could annul zemstvo resolutions only if they contradicted the law.[109]

The second item attended to in the bill was the democratization of the suffrage. In the case of municipal dumas, Stolypin proposed that property qualifications be lowered by one-half, that tax qualifications for trade and industry be lowered by 1 percent, and that the "highest class" of persons leasing apartments be allowed to vote. The project also asked that the right of Jews to participate in municipal duma elections, sit on the *uprava,* and hold other administrative posts be restored.[110]

As far as the zemstvos were concerned, representation was to be hybrid. The peasants' right to elect representatives (limited in 1890) was restored. The project stated that the zemstvos were to be class-less, yet class distinctions were in evidence. Furthermore, although voting qualifications were to be based on tax payments, rather then on the amount of property owned, these taxes were assessed on land or other immovable property, which had to be owned, according to the project, for at least one year. Electors for *uezd* representatives were to be divided into three categories: *volost'* deputies, landowners, and owners of other immovable property and commercial and in-dustrial enterprises. The right of suffrage for the second and third categories was conferred by an annual tax payment of twenty-five rubles. (It was estimated that the amount of property on which such a tax would be levied would be between fifty and one hundred des-siatines.) Voters entitled only to elect representatives to the *volost'* zemstvo assembly or *sobranie* (the *volost'* zemstvo was to be instituted according to another project of Stolypin, already introduced into the Duma) and owners of immovable property who paid less than twenty-five rubles were to annually chose their delegates to the *uezd* zemstvo indirectly. Deputies to the *guberniya* zemstvo, therefore, were to be elected indirectly on this semi-class basis in two or three stages. The old bias in favor of the large landowners was discarded. Representa-tion was to be apportioned according to the amount of taxes paid by each group.[111]

At first glance it appeared that the zemstvo stood to gain con-siderably. Certainly the financial measures offered in the project would have fulfilled very real needs of the zemstvo. Abolition of the local administration's right to veto a zemstvo resolution on the basis of substance unquestionably would have benefited the zemstvo. Nevertheless, these grants were offset by further restrictions on zemstvo competence.

Although the bill diminished the authority of local administrative officials over the zemstvos, it made supervision over these institutions on the part of the Minister of Internal Affairs more immediate. The bill gave the Minister of Internal Affairs the right, formerly accorded only to governors, to inspect zemstvos and municipal dumas, to demand information concerning their business, and to introduce proposals into zemstvo meetings. It permitted the Minister of Internal

Affairs (with the Tsar's sanction) to prorogue a zemstvo for a period not exceeding three years if he felt that "the activity of a zemstvo did not answer the needs of society." The Council of Ministers, with the Tsar's approval, was given the right to dissolve a zemstvo or municipal duma and to replace it with appointed officials for a period not exceeding three years if the zemstvo or municipal duma were unable to cope with a national calamity such as famine or flood, if its activity in dispensing public services were inadequate, or if its finances were in prolonged disorder.[112]

In the matter of representation, the tax qualification was eliminated from the final version of the bill because of opposition from an all-zemstvo congress, which reviewed the project in July-August 1907, and because of opposition on the part of the Council of Ministers.[113] More important, Stolypin ensured the presence in the zemstvo of a sufficient number of large landowners. According to the original proposal, individual landowners worth more than 150,000 rubles on the basis of the zemstvo tax rate could sit in the *uezd* zemstvo without being elected. The maximum number of these persons was fixed, however, so they could never form a majority.[114] In addition, a minimum was set for representatives from both the landowning class and from the peasantry, while a maximum was established for representatives from the commercial-industrial classes.[115]

Stolypin included these stipulations in his proposal because he feared there would not be enough educated (*kul'turnyi*) persons in the zemstvos. He stressed that the major problem with regard to zemstvo representation was to establish a suffrage qualification low enough to allow sufficiently wide participation, but high enough to ensure persons of suitable educational level. Such persons, he felt, were predominantly large landowners.[116]

In the case of the maximum set for the commercial-industrial classes in the zemstvo, Stolypin stated that since the new suffrage qualification was based on zemstvo tax payments, and since industrial revenue and hence industrial taxes had risen spectacularly during the past years, commercial-industrial classes might receive a greater percentage of representation in the zemstvo than their numbers warranted.[117]

Volost' and Settlement Self-government

The mixture of stimulation and control which characterized Stolypin's plans for the zemstvos and municipal dumas also was applied to the zemstvos he created on the *volost'* and settlement level. The project on "Settlement and *Volost'* Administration" which he presented to the Council of Ministers in February 1907 proposed the establishment of an all-class *volost'* zemstvo and, in addition, a special self-governing unit, the settlement gathering (*skhod*). The *volost'* zemstvo was to be the second-smallest administrative-social unit. It was to include all land, property, and persons found within the boundary of several villages and a certain rural area. Voting qualifications were to be the same as those for the *uezd* zemstvo. Responsibilities of the *volost'* zemstvo were to include policing, matters of military conscription, keeping of family records, some tax activity, and so forth.[118] For larger villages and those with foreign (*postoronnyi*) peasants, special settlement administrations were to be set up.[119] The settlement gathering was to care for the immediate economic and social needs of the populace.[120] The right to vote at this level was given to anyone who had owned land in the area for three years or who had paid two rubles in taxes on a trade or industrial establishment.[121]

Unfortunately, the all-class principle in *volost'* self-government was offset, as in the case of the *uezd* zemstvo, by the inclusion of the right of "personal representation," although again, the number of persons thus admitted was to be limited. Stolypin justified the measure by the same reasons as that given in the *uezd* zemstvo bill.[122]

In addition, the powers given the settlement and the *volost'* gathering were curtailed by higher authority. As in the case of the *guberniya* and *uezd* zemstvos, supervision was to be confined primarily to determining the legality of the settlement and *volost'* gatherings' activity. However, administrative officials could interfere in case of lack of activity, and certain matters were removed from the jurisdiction of the *volost'* and settlement gatherings.

Who was to be responsible for overseeing the smallest units of self-government? The project rejected the idea of entrusting supervision to the zemstvos, as liberal zemstvo leaders had demanded in the 1880s, on the grounds that the zemstvos were "not sufficiently disinterested."[123] The ultimate guardian of the smallest zemstvos was to be the Minister of Internal Affairs. In practice, he was to delegate this authority to his deputies, the newly created *uezdnyi nachal'nik*[124] and the *uezdnyi sovet*. The *uezdnyi nachal'nik* and his council were required to approve alienation of real estate, expenditures of public capital, and loans which exceeded the annual budget of the *volost'* or settlement gathering. The *uezdnyi nachal'nik* was to supervise and investigate the legality of the actions of the *volost'* and settlement gatherings and their individual members. He also was allowed to impose fines for unlawful activity and to suspend resolutions which contradicted the law.[125]

Ironically, despite all the energy expended on the projects for the transformation of *guberniya, uezd,* municipal, *volost',* and settlement self-government, they came to nothing. Although Stolypin presented the proposals to the Second Duma, only those on *volost'* and settlement self-government were considered, but by the Third, not the Second Duma. The settlement bill was introduced to the Third Duma in September 1908. On November 5, 1910, the Dumas's Finance Committee referred to the bill, but it was not mentioned again. On February 14, 1911, the Committee on Local Self-Government reported to the Duma on the *volost'* bill and in May of that year the entire *volost'* bill was read in the Duma.[126] It was greatly changed by the Duma, which gave the *volost'* zemstvo more power and more democratic representation. The bill was not passed until the Fourth Duma, however, after Stolypin's death, and was rejected by the State Council in 1914, owing to the efforts of the reactionary bloc who deemed it too democratic.[127]

Sovet po Delam Mestnago Khozyaistva

Since Stolypin's projects on local self-government were never implemented, we can only surmise how they might have fared. But in the matter of his plan to provide for the influence of public opinion on both the local and central administration, we have actual case studies in which to observe his theory of local self-government at work.

On the local level, in the mixed administrative-public bodies, the *gubernskie* and *uezdnye sovety,* administrative personnel were given preponderance over representatives from the municipal dumas and zemstvos.[128]

At the central level, in the *Sovet po delam mestnago khozyaistva,* public opinion also was effectively neutralized. When Stolypin activated the *Sovet,* more commonly called the *Preddumy,* in 1907 (though conceived by Plehve, it had never met), he introduced, as we have said, elected representatives from the provinces. He was very enthusiastic about the *Preddumy,* which was to serve him as a sounding-board, discussing legislation destined for the provinces prior to its introduction into the Duma and informing him of the further needs and desires of the provincial population. He announced to the Duma in the fall of 1907[129] and informed the Tsar in 1910[130] that the *Preddumy*'s existence would prevent legislation for the provinces from having a bureaucratic tenor and would ensure that this legislation was feasible and met genuine needs.

In reality, the meetings of the *Preddumy* had the character of a puppet show in which the puppets were getting out of hand. Some of the most interesting meetings were those held from March 4 to 16, 1909, on the subject of Stolypin's proposed reforms of the local administration. The specific topic of conversation was the power of the governor and the *gubernskii sovet* or provincial council. The chief fears of the provincials in the *Preddumy* were that zemstvo and municipal duma representatives (or "public men," as they were called) would not have sufficient influence in the *gubernskii sovet* and that the *sovet* would usurp some of the powers belonging to self-governing institutions. To prevent this they passed a resolution, changing from 15:5 to 7:7 the ratio of representatives from the provincial administration and corporations of nobility to representatives from the provincial zemstvo and municipal duma of the capital city.[131] In the same vein, they were greatly disturbed that Stolypin's project gave the *gubernskii sovet* the right to request treasury aid for self-governing institutions. The provincial members of the *Preddumy* believed that the right to request treasury aid was a prerogative of the self-governing institutions and a guarantee of their independence from control of local administrators.[132]

The public men of the *Preddumy* also questioned the right of the disciplinary board of the *gubernskii sovet* to investigate zemstvo employees or members.[133] Clearly opposing the state theory of self-government, they stressed that the governor had the right to supervise zemstvos and municipal dumas only concerning the lawfulness of their activity.[134] They also agitated for the right of self-governing institutions to stop obligatory regulations, issued by the governor, with which they disagreed.[135]

The suggestions and complaints of the public men were doomed to be ineffectual. Although the *Preddumy* was merely an advisory body, the *dokladchik,* an emissary from the Ministry of Internal Affairs, quashed the provincial delegates at every turn. One example was his reaction to their contention that the zemstvo's power would be lessened by allowing the *gubernskii sovet* to request treasury aid on its own initiative. "This would be true," the *dokladchik* piously intoned, "only if public and administrative institutions were two separate worlds."[136] More undemocratically, when a majority of the

Preddumy declined an amendment, offered by the chairman, that the *sovet* be granted the right to request treasury aid only after prior consultation with the self-governing institutions, the *dokladchik* attempted to force a second vote on the issue.[137] The hapless *Preddumy* was finally forced to accept the resolution that the *gubernskii sovet* be given the power only if it appeared "really necessary, within the limits of local needs."[138]

Although Stolypin's policies concerning local self-government would not have altered the prevailing situation along the lines desired by progressives, they were a step forward compared to the views expressed by reactionary groups.

The Kadets and Social Democrats, in addition to agitating for an all-class zemstvo unit smaller than the *uezd* zemstvo to replace the separate peasant administration, wanted both property and tax qualifications abolished and advocated giving the vote to persons who had reached their majority. The Kadets included a residence requirement of six months (during the two years preceding the election) and established the age limit at twenty-one. The Social Democrats would have given the vote to anyone over twenty years of age. Both parties gave the vote to women; both stood for the principle of "one man, one vote" and for secret suffrage.

In addition, the Social Democrats desired elections at all levels of self-government (they wanted to replace the *guberniya* zemstvo with an *oblast'* zemstvo). The Kadets were in favor of direct elections to the settlement and *volost'* (in their project termed *uchastkovoe*) zemstvos, but advocated direct election of only part of the *uezd* deputies—large cities were to send representatives to the *uezd* zemstvo through their dumas; some of the deputies to the *uezd* zemstvo from rural areas were to be elected by the *uchastkovye* zemstvos. Furthermore, the Kadets stipulated that deputies from the cities to the *uezd* zemstvo could not amount to more than one-third of the *uezd* zemstvo *sobranie* and deputies from the *uchastkovye* zemstvos could not amount to more than one-half. As deputies to the *guberniya* zemstvo were to be chosen in the *uezd* zemstvo *sobranie,* elections to the *guberniya* zemstvo were in two or three stages. In the matter of jurisdiction, the Kadets were not so progressive as Stolypin. They left the competence of the zemstvo as it was, except for giving the *uezd* zemstvo ultimate authority over the regular *uezd* police.[139]

Stolypin's policy was not so avant-garde as those proposed by the Kadets and the Social Democrats, but it was probably more realistic.

Although it frankly discriminated against bourgeois elements, it took into account the very real problem of peasant illiteracy. For better or for worse, the large landowners were educated and had political experience. To allow often illiterate and politically inexperienced peasants to dominate the zemstvos might have damaged local self-government.

It is significant that middle-of-the-road groups supported Stolypin's policy. Not only was his paternalistic concept of self-government held by most political theorists of his day, but his concrete proposals for local self-government were, for the most part, accepted by the Octobrist party. The Octobrist project for the election of *uezd* and *guberniya* deputies, presented to the Third Duma on January 25, 1908, proposed a tax, rather than a property, qualification for voting and did not, of course, include any provision for "personal representation." It did, however, place voters in categories, preserving the separate status of the communal peasant.[140]

The issue of tax versus property qualification brought Stolypin under pressure from commercial-industrial circles that wanted the tax qualification, not because of its democratic nature, but because of their own vested interest. Although, as we have noted, the tax qualification would have lowered the voting requirement and would have increased the electorate as the national income rose (which was the justification Stolypin used for the proposal), this was not the main reason the commercial-industrial circles lobbied for it. They did so because they would have benefited if suffrage and representation were based upon taxes.[41]

In comparison with conservative-reactionary views on local self-government, Stolypin's proposals, even with their undemocratic clauses and provisions for extensive supervision on the part of the Minister of Internal Affairs, would have improved local self-government. The Minister of Roads and Communications (who was generally more conservative than Stolypin) was opposed to the increased competence given the zemstvo, in Stolypin's bill, over certain roads and waterways, until it was pointed out to him that in most cases these arteries were not vital to the nation.[142] Other ministers wanted the parish, rather than the settlement or *volost'*, to be the lowest unit of self-government.[143] Kokovtsov's disapproval of the idea that zemstvos should be granted funds or given a share in national taxes has already been cited.

Reactionary landowners wished to preserve the class character of local self-government and to emphasize the role of the nobility in it.

They raised a great outcry about the establishment of a tax rather than a property requirement for electors to the *uezd* zemstvo, even sending a deputation to the Tsar. They issued proclamations reviewing the role of the nobility as a support for the crown throughout history, intimating that it would be disastrous for the autocracy if the position of the nobility were reduced. The nobility demanded that they and an all-zemstvo congress (the zemstvos were at that time dominated by reactionary landowning elements, although the all-zemstvo congress was not) be allowed to review Stolypin's proposal for *guberniya, uezd,* and municipal self-government.[144]

Stolypin's policies, in comparison with the ideas of the reactionary landowners, would have widened zemstvo representation and would have made possible, at least on the *volost'* level, the integration of the peasant into the rest of society. In addition, greater supervision over the zemstvo on the part of the Minsiter of Internal Affairs might have checked the influence of the reactionary elements on the local level.[145]

Improvements in the Central Administration

Professor A. V. Zenkovsky, a financial expert from Kiev who had become good friends with Stolypin, claimed that in May 1911 Stolypin dictated to him a lengthy proposal for improving the central administration. He has included this proposal in his monograph *Pravda o Stolypine* (The Truth About Stolypin).[146] It is intriguing to think of such a proposal, but unfortunately we have only Zenkovsky's word that it existed. The project was never found and no other of Stolypin's contemporaries, even those closely associated with him in the government, mentioned a comprehensive plan for the central government. Among Stolypin's relatives, Boris Bock, the husband of Stolypin's eldest daughter Maria, claimed that he had once seen such a project. However, he recalled of it only a plan for introducing zemstvos into the western provinces, a plan for establishing autonomy in Tsarist Poland, and a preface in which Stolypin described the chaotic state of affairs in the administration when he assumed office. Maria Bock stated that she had never seen any such proposal.[147]

Furthermore, while some elements of the supposed project square with Stolypin's documented views, other features contradict policies recorded in Stolypin's extant proposals. According to Zenkovsky, Stolypin wanted to create seven new ministries, namely, Labor, Local Self-Government, Nationalities, Social Security, Beliefs, Investigation and Exploitation of the Mineral Wealth of Russia, and Health. The ministries of Local Self-Government, Nationalities, and Beliefs were to be offshoots of the Ministry of Internal Affairs,[148] and it seems questionable that Stolypin would have wanted to prune this much authority from his ministry. Then, Stolypin supposedly told Zenkovsky that the Ministry of Local Self-Government ought to develop projects for the introduction of zemstvos into the western provinces and for *volost'* zemstvos—projects which had already been drafted by Stolypin's own ministry. Moreover, the qualifications for voting in the *volost'* suggested in the alleged proposal seem more like those proposed by the Kadets and parties to their left: suffrage was to be granted to all over twenty-one years of age, independent of belief or nationality, who owned even a small amount of immovable property and paid zemstvo taxes and lived in the area for two years.[149] There are several references in Zenkovsky's account to Stolypin's plans to grant full rights to Jews,[150] which does not coincide with the policy he had always subscribed to—unless he had had a change of heart. In addition, in Zenkovsky's account Stolypin referred to national minorities—all of whom were to be fully equal citizens with no limitations—in modern terminology, that is as Little Russians, Latvians, Lithuanians, Tatar, Kirghiz, etc.,[151] whereas he did not refer to the nationalities in these terms in his proposals for Kholm province, for the western zemstvos, and so on. The zemstvos, in Stolypin's plans as described by Zenkovsky, were to be given a great deal of authority, especially over education and even higher educational institutions,[152] whereas in Stolypin's officially recorded statements on education ultimate policy was to remain in the hands of the central government, although zemstvos were to be encouraged to assume responsibility.[153]

Zenkovsky's description of Stolypin's plans for improvements in existing ministries and proposals for new ministries,[154] other than those mentioned above, seem in line with Stolypin's thinking. According to Zenkovsky, Stolypin was desirous of exploiting Russia's mineral wealth, building railways, providing social security for workers and others, providing better health care, granting higher salaries to priests and *chinovniki* ("governmental clerks"), and increasing educational institutions at all levels. In order to accomplish this, according to Zenkovsky, Stolypin proposed foreign loans and higher internal taxes on vodka, as well as a progressive income tax. This latter project had already been proposed to the Second Duma by Kokovtsov. Stolypin's suggestion for certain educational requirements for governmental personnel, as recalled by Zenkovsky, also was in line with his thinking.

The most astounding improvements in the proposal allegedly dictated to Zenkovsky were to be implemented in the position of the Chairman of the Council of Ministers. He was to become more a prime minister, with the right of proposing ministers for the Tsar's confirmation. No report was to be submitted to the Tsar without his approval.[155]

Freedom of Belief

In order to implement the promise of freedom of conscience contained in the manifesto of October 17, 1905, Stolypin submitted two proposals for discussion by the Council of Ministers during the fall of 1906 and the winter of 1907, one regarding Old Believers and sectarians, and the other, Catholics, foreign Christians, and non-Christian religions.

The Old Believers, imbued with the fifteenth-sixteenth century conception of Russia as the repository of the one, true faith, separated from the Orthodox church in the mid-seventeenth century on the question of alteration of ritual. They soon divided among themselves, however, into the Priestists, who retained basic Orthodox doctrine, and the Priestless. The latter, influenced by older Russian heresies and German evangelical and pietistic Protestantism, splintered in the eighteenth and nineteenth centuries into various sects which were greatly divorced from Orthodox belief. Some of these, like the Stundists and Molokanes, were harmless; others, like the Khlysts, indulged in orgies, or like the Skoptsy, practiced self-castration, or like the Dukhobors, repudiated governmental authority, taxes, recruitment, and oaths of allegience. Paradoxically, among the moderate Priestless and the Skoptsy were wealthy merchants and entrepreneurs with commercial and manufacturing contacts all over the country, whose enterprise contributed to Russia's industrial development. Other sectarians were sober and hard-working assets to a developing country. In any case, the Old Believers and sectarians amounted to a sizable portion of the population, perhaps as much as 16 to 20 percent in 1907—three to four times as many as the more vociferous Jewish minority. Unlike the bulk of the Jews, they were not confined to a particular locality but were scattered throughout European Russia and the borderlands.

The government alternately persecuted and tolerated the Old Believers and sectarians. Classified in 1842 as "moderate," "pernicious," or "most pernicious," they were periodically restricted in building prayer houses and conducting worship services. Their marriages were not recognized, their children were considered illegitimate until 1883, they were to be raised as Orthodox, and so forth. In 1903 the Old Believers, who formed a minority of the schismatics, were allowed to register their children as Old Believers; in 1905 they were awarded the same status as Catholics and Lutherans regarding the right to have their own primary schools, military exemption for their priests, and the opening of civil service and military positions to their laymen. The sectarians, however, were not granted these rights.

Paul Miliukov, the historian and Kadet leader in the Third Duma, claimed that the government ignored the practical application of these rights during the First Duma and only presented an unsatisfactory bill to the Third Duma.[156] However, Stolypin's proposal of 1906 was designed to carry out the government's promises. It stipulated that Old Believers and sectarians not belonging to "wild sects, or those whose activity is forbidden by law" had the right to profess their beliefs, openly practice religious ceremonies, and form religious communities which had the judicial status of persons, and it recognized their religious leaders as clergy, with attendant privileges. The proposal also recognized the validity of marriages conducted in the rites of the sect and the legality of births resulting therefrom. Marriages and births were to be henceforth recorded in the registration books (*metricheskie knigi*) of the sect. In conjunction with this proposal, Stolypin petitioned for the abolition of existing laws which prohibited the spreading of heresy and dissemination of dissenting (from the Orthodox Church) beliefs, and which applied discriminatory regulations for Baptists and other non-Orthodox Christians.[157]

The second proposal, concerning Catholics, foreign Christian sects, and non-Christian religions, was composed of several sections, the chief of which concerned the permitting of individuals to transfer from one faith to another; the freedom of all religious groups to worship, build prayer houses, and form societies; and the right to enter into mixed marriages in which spouses had the right to decide upon the religious upbringing of their children. The proposal also called for abolition of civil and political disabilities on the non-Orthodox.[158]

These proposals on freedom of belief, which were quite liberal, were not entirely well received by the Council of Ministers. In regard to the proposals on the Old Believers, the council objected to abolishing existing discriminatory statutes and decided that the term "dangerous sects" would be too difficult to apply. The council also considered the term "open meetings" too inexact to be included in the proposals since in the ministers' opinion public meetings of Old Believers might be prohibited by criminal law. The Council of Ministers stipulated that if the activity of the religious community appeared to be violating the law or hurting public morals the governor or municipal authority could suppress it.[159] The ministry also decided that no decision could be taken on the question of registration of marriages and suggested that police registration of marriages of dissenters should be continued until the civil laws were thoroughly examined.[160] The Council of Ministers further opposed abolishing the civil and political disabilities on non-Christians because the ministry felt that these referred primarily to Jews and could not be considered apart from the general Jewish question.[161]

In 1908 a proposal was introduced on the migration of Old Believers to Siberia. It was stated that since conditions in the Far East had not been favorable for Russia since the Russo-Japanese War, increasing the number of Russians in the area would benefit the Empire. Old Believers were deemed suitable candidates because they were hard-working, and their emigration from the internal provinces would relieve some land shortage there. Relocation of the Old Believers, thus, was to have a triple result. The details of the project were to be worked out by the Chief Director of Land Exploitation and Agriculture and by the Minister of Internal Affairs.[162]

Although Stolypin defended the freedom to transfer from one belief to another and the freedom of worship, he also opposed Duma amendments which appeared to lower the status of the Orthodox church. In a speech to the Duma on May 22, 1909, he affirmed that education must conform to the tenets of the Orthodox church, that the Orthodox church must be considered a state church, and that Russia was ruled by an Orthodox Tsar. He likened the situation which must prevail in Russia to that in other European countries in which there were state churches.[163] In the opinion of historian Edward Chmielewski, Stolypin was attempting by this speech to gain the support of the Nationalist faction in the Duma and to publicly affirm his support for the Tsar and the status quo after the attacks on him perpetrated by the Right and the ministerial crisis of April 1909.[164] This may well have been the case. On the other hand, with no documentation to support this theory, it is equally probable that Stolypin genuinely supported the position of the Orthodox church as a state church and considered the Duma amendments a violation of his principle of moderate reform.

Development of Far Eastern Siberia

Stolypin's promotion of the migration of Old Believers to Siberia was closely connected with his interest in general development of the region from Lake Baikal to the Pacific. He considered especially important the left and right banks of the Amur River, known as the Amur and Ussuri regions. Russia had acquired these territories from China in the treaties of 1858 and 1860.

Settlement of the area had begun before Stolypin's administration —he estimated that Molokanes had already settled 800,000 dessiatines in the Amur region—but he was convinced that Russia should accelerate exploitation of Siberia for several reasons: there were mineral wealth and forests there which the state economy needed, there was land for cultivation, and settlement of the area was necessary for security reasons.[165]

In addition to the proposal for migration of Old Believers to Siberia, sponsored by Stolypin in 1908, the government approved the building of an Amur railway. This railway was to be built along the left bank of the Amur River, connecting the Ussuri region with the rest of Siberia and European Russia. It was to facilitate colonization, removal of lumber and mineral wealth, and defense, in the event of another far eastern war.

Stolypin defended the importance of the railway before the Duma in April 1908. There had been objections to the allocation of 238 million rubles for construction of the railroad, but the Duma voted the appropriations.[166]

Education

As long ago as the Grodno committee meetings, Stolypin had stressed the importance of increasing educational opportunities in Russia. He reiterated this theme in a speech to the Second Duma in which he introduced the government program. In August 1908 he confided to Ambassador Nicolson that the education problem was "very urgent" and "very difficult." Stolypin stated that it was "essential" to increase the number of primary schools and also agricultural and teacher training schools. He criticized as "ridiculous" the fact that the "government spent only 8 million pounds annually on education out of a total revenue of some 250 million pounds."[167]

In August 1906 and January 1907 the Council of Ministers discussed a project presented by the Minister of Education. It proposed one teacher for not more than fifty pupils and a school in each three-verst radius. It fixed minimum requirements for teachers' salaries and for curricula. The ministry admitted that the shortage of teachers would make attainment of the projected goals very difficult. They also noted the depleted state of the treasury. But despite this, they hoped to raise teachers' salaries and thereby attract more people into the teaching profession.[168]

The chief controversy in the area of primary education was raised by the question of who was going to control it—the state, the church, or institutions of self-government. The proposals approved by the Council of Ministers in 1906 and 1907 emphasized that the central government must be responsible for establishing and managing universal primary education. The ministry arrived at this conclusion for two reasons. First, it was felt that the zemstvos and municipal dumas did not have funds to implement compulsory primary education. Second, the ministry believed that "schools must be the cement of the state, as in the west . . . the direction of education must agree with the state outlook."[169] In practice this meant that the opening of new schools, the establishment of a network of normal schools, and school inspection and supervision was to be in the hands of the Ministry of Education.[170]

However, the Council of Ministers acknowledged that the Minister of Education's proposal ought to be coordinated with the proposal Stolypin was simultaneously working out for the widening of zemstvo and municipal duma jurisdiction. Therefore, they determined that the zemstvos would be given state subsidies for education and that they could show "concern" for education, while ultimate authority rested in the hands of the central government. In addition, an interdepartmental committee was planned to harmonize the proposals of Stolypin and the Minister of Education.[171]

In March 1909 the Council of Ministers repudiated an education project sponsored by seventy-six members of the Duma. The ministry contended that the project completely contradicted the government's policy and the already completed project of the Minister of Education.[172] The proposal undoubtedly was the one passed by the Duma in 1911, but essentially rejected by the State Council. It entrusted the organization and immediate supervision of primary schools to local self-governing institutions, while reserving guidance and general control for the Ministry of Education.[173]

The 1906-1907 proposal of the Minister of Education was not examined by the Second Duma, but was passed by the Third Duma in May 1908. It provided free, compulsory, four-year instruction for all children from ages eight to eleven. The plan was to be completely in operation by 1922. In 1915, 122,000 primary schools were in existence with an enrollment of 8.1 million as compared with 65,000 primary schools with an enrollment of 3.5 million in 1896.[174]

Would Russia have been different if Stolypin had remained in office after 1911? While Stolypin propelled the government on a course of reform, the reforms he specifically promoted were not radical, and it is obvious that massive illiteracy, large-scale poverty, shortage of funds and expertise, disorder and violence, and opposition to reform on the part of influential individuals and pressure groups made real improvement difficult, if not impossible, in the short term.

Notes

1. "Perechen del razreshennykh v poryadke stati 87 svoda osnovnykh gosudarstvennykh zakonov, izdaniya 1906 g. (s 1 Iyulya 1906 g. po 20 Fevralya 1907 goda)," in *Osobyi zhurnal soveta ministrov* (hereafter cited *Osobyi zhurnal;* there were three volumes annually after 1906), 1907, vol. 1, April 17, following entry no. 128.

2. Great Britain, Public Record Office, Foreign Office (hereafter cited F. O.) 371, vol. 128, no. 31317, p. 4; and F. O. 371, vol. 128, no. 30374 (no. 206), September 7, 1906.

3. F. O. 371, vol. 128, no. 30374, (no. 206). The discussion of the government program in the Council of Ministers is contained in "Po voprosu o zakonoproektakh, podlezhashchikh vneseniyu v Gosudarstvennuyu Dumu," *Osobyi zhurnal,* 1907, vol. 1, no. 28, January 12.

4. Presentation of the government program in the Second Duma is contained in *Gosudarstvennaya Duma: Stenograficheskie otchety* sessiya II, zasedanie 5, March 6, 1907, cols. 106-120.

5. *Decentralization and Self-Government in Russia, 1830-1870* (Princeton, New Jersey: Princeton University Press, 1972), p. 28.

6. Discussion of the Law of October 5 is contained in "Ob otmen nekotorykh ogranichenii v pravakh sel'skikh obyvatelei i lits drugikh byvshikh podatnykh sostoyanii," *Osobyi zhurnal,* 1906, no. 68, September 2 and 12; the actual law of October 5 follows no. 68.

The former taxpaying classes were all peasants, Russian and foreign artisans, Jews, colonists who had settled in Russia after the time of Catherine II, and national minorities. Merchants were exempt from the soul tax after 1775, but were obliged to pay a one percent capital tax. The nontaxable classes included hereditary and honorary nobility, clergy, and persons holding advanced academic degrees.

7. The terms of the law of November 9 are given in "O dopolnenii nekotorykh postanovlenii deistvuyushchago zakona, kasayushchiksya krest'yanskago zemlevladeniya i zemlepol'zovaniya," *Osobyi zhurnal,* 1906, no. 98, October 10, pp. 4-5, 17-19.

8. The terms of these laws are contained in Geroid Tanquary Robinson, *Rural Russia Under the Old Regime,* 3rd ed., (New York: Macmillan, 1961), pp. 212-25.

9. An interesting account of the preparation of the agrarian legislation of 1906 is given by George Yaney, "The Imperial Russian Government and the Stolypin Land Reform," (Ph.D. dissertation, Dept. of History, Princeton University, 1962), pp. 82-88, 90, 97, 100-11, and *passim.*

10. In 1906. Stolypin again emphasized that the chief cause of low peasant productivity and hence peasant poverty was the commune, and he had to fight for immediate abolition of the commune by the government, without waiting for the approval of the Second Duma (through the use of article 87), against other members of the Council of Ministers including Kokovtsov and Obolensky who believed the reform could be achieved more gradually. "O dopolnenii nekotorykh postanovlenii deistvuyushchago zakona, kasayushchikhsya krest'yanskago zemlevladeniya i zemlepol'zovaniya," *Osobyi zhurnal,* 1906, no. 98, October 10, pp. 4-19.

11. For the agrarian reforms themselves, see S. M. Dubrovskii, *Stolypinskaya zemel'naya reforma* (Moscow: Akademiya nauk SSSR, Institut Istorii, 1963), and W. E. Mosse, "Stolypin's Villages," *The Slavonic and East European Review,* 43 (June 1965), pp. 257-74. Also, of course, Geroid T. Robinson, *Rural Russia Under the Old Regime* (New York: Macmillan, 1961).

12. F. O. 371, vol. 519, no. 30064 (no. 383), August 27, 1908.

13. F. O. 371, vol. 733, no. 39159 (no. 558), October 16, 1909, pp. 1-2. Also recorded in *Gosudarstvennaya deyatel'nost predsedatelya soveta ministrov, stats sekretarya, Petra Arkad'evicha Stolypina,* ed. E. Verpakhovsky (St. Petersburg: Izdanie sostavitelya, 1911), part 1, pp. 3-4.

14. "Iz perepiski P. A. Stolypina s Nikolaem Romanovym," *Krasnyi arkhiv,* 30 (1928), p. 83, December 26, 1910.

15. Stolypin to Nicolson, F. O. 371, vol. 126, no. 23110 (no. 412), July 2, 1906. The Kadets demanded compulsory expropriation in the First and Second Dumas.

16. There are several examples in the *Osobyi zhurnal* of Stolypin's requests for remuneration for landowners who had suffered losses from peasant uprisings. One such instance relating to landowners in Kursk and Smolensk was recorded in 1908, vol. 3. no. 263.

17. F. O. 371, vol. 519, no. 30064 (no. 383).

18. "Iz perepiski P. A. Stolypina s Nikolaem Romanovym," *Krasnyi arkhiv,* 30, p. 83, December 26, 1910.

19. "Perepiska N. A. Romanova i P. A. Stolypina," *Krasnyi arkhiv,* 5 (1924), p. 111, April 16, 1907.

20. *Ibid.*

21. To Nicolson, F. O. 371, vol. 519, no. 30064 (no. 383), August 27, 1908, p. 2.

22. F. O. 371, vol. 729, no. 18277 (no. 202), May 7, 1909.

23. F. O. 371, vol. 519, no. 30064 (no. 383), p. 2.

24. Vladimir Iosifovich Gurko, *Features and Figures of the Past,* trans. Laura Matveev (Stanford, California: Stanford University Press, 1939), p. 297.

25. Hugh Seton-Watson, *The Decline of Imperial Russia* (New York: Frederick Praeger, 1960), pp. 158-60.

26. Stolypin to Nicholas, "Perepiska N. A. Romanova i P. A. Stolypina," *Krasnyi arkhiv,* 5, p. 106, December 10, 1906; Stolypin to Kokovtsov, in Vladimir Nikolaevich Kokovtsov, *Iz moego proshlago* (Paris, The Hague: Mouton, 1969), vol. 1, p. 236. Original edition, 1933.

Baron Alexander Meyendorff recounted Stolypin's concern about the restrictions on the Jews prior to his entrance into the central government; see his "Memoirs," p. 45; MS in possession of Stolypin's daughter Maria Petrovna von Bock, San Francisco.

27. "Perepiska N. A. Romanova i P. A. Stolypina," *Krasnyi arkhiv,* 5, p. 106, December 10.

28. *Osobyi zhurnal,* 1906, no. 157, October 27 and 31 and December 1.

29. *Ibid.,* pp. 33-35.

30. *Ibid.,* pp. 36-37.

31. Ministerstvo vnutrennikh del: Glavnoe upravlenie po delam mestnago khozyaistva kantselyariya (hereafter cited MVD), "Ob ustanovlenii glavnykh osnovanii preobrazo-vaniya zemskikh i gorodskikh uchrezhdenii," February 7, 1907, pp. 107-108; *Osobyi zhurnal,* 1907, vol. 3, no. 356, pp. 42-43.

32. *Osobyi zhurnal,* 1908, vol. 2, no. 140; "Ob usloviyakh priema evreev v sredniya uchebnyya zavedeniya," *Osobyi zhurnal,* 1909, vol. 1, no. 89, June 23; Stolypin's proposal, *ibid.,* pp. 10-11, 15-16.

In August 1906, the Minister of Education, von Kaufman, had drawn up a proposal which allowed Jews to open private schools bound only by the regulations on curriculum and teacher licensing pertaining to private schools in general. The proposal applied to Jews in all areas of the empire; see "Po delu predostavlenii evreyam prava otkrytam povsemestno chastnyya uchebnyya zavedeniya vsekh tipov na osnovanii zakona 19 Fevralya 1868," *Osobyi zhurnal,* 1906, no. 43, August 11.

33. "O poryadke vypolneniya Vysochaishe utverzhdennago 22 Avgusta 1909 polozheniya Soveta Min. ob ostavlenii na zhitel'stvo v gor. Moskve i prochikh gorodakh Moskovskoi gubernii evreev-kuptsov pervoi gil'dii," *Osobyi zhurnal,* 1910, vol. 2, no. 164, August 24.

34. *Osobyi zhurnal,* 1910, vol. 3, no. 212, February 2.

35. "Po voprosu o primenenii k kommercheskim uchilishcham pravil 22 Avgusta 1909 goda ob usloviyakh priema evreev v sredniya uchebnyya zavedeniya [po predstavl. Min. Torg. i Prom (Otd. Ucheb.) 24 Maya 1910 g., no. 2654]," *Osobyi zhurnal,* 1910, vol. 3, no. 120, June 11.

36. Starr, *Decentralization and Self-Government in Russia, 1830-1870, passim;* Yaney, *The Systematization of Russian Government* (Urbana: University of Illinois Press, 1973), pp. 319-76.

37. The eleven boards of which the governor was chairman dealt with military affairs, factories, alcoholic beverages, zemstvo and urban affairs, statistics, forest conservation, administration, public charity, public food, and postal affairs. The governor was vice-chairman and member of the prison inspection committee, special provincial board for the protection of the Orthodox clergy, and special board for the appellate court. He also was honorary trustee of women's gymnasia, head of the police in the province, and judge in certain criminal and civil cases. N. M. Korkunov, *Russkoe gosudarstvennoe pravo* (St. Petersburg: Tipografiya M. M. Stasyulevicha, 1905), vol. 2, pp. 311-12, V. M. Gribovskii, *Gosudarstvennoi ustroistvo i upravlenie Rossiiskoi imperii* (Odessa: Tipografiya "Teknik," 1912), p. 134.

These boards were composed of administrative officials from several departments, the provincial marshal of nobility, procurator of the circuit court (*okruzhnoi sud*), and in certain cases, representatives from the provincial zemstvo or the duma of the capital city of the province. The boards mainly handled complaints about official activity in matters within the boards' jurisdiction. Legally, decisions were made on a collegiate basis, but apparently the governor controlled boards whose chanceries were under his control, for the policies of the boards actually were formulated by their chanceries. N. I. Lazarevskii, *Lektsii po Russkomu gosudarstvennomu pravu* (St. Petersburg: Tipografiya "Slovo," 1910), vol. 2 (Administrativnoe pravo), pp. 233-34.

38. Lazarevskii, *Lektsii po Russkomu gosudarstvennomu pravu*, p. 228. Of course, it was only sensible that State Control be independent of the governor if it were to fulfill its function.

39. I. Blinov, *Gubernatory* (St. Petersburg: Tipografiya K. L. Tsenkovskago, 1905), pp. 268-69; Lazarevskii, *Lektsii po Russkomu gosudarstvennomu pravu*, pp. 226-29.

40. Lazarevskii, *ibid.*, pp. 229-30.

41. *Ibid.*, pp. 231-32. The term which I have translated as "unreliable" was *blagonadezhnyi*. In addition, all requests for awards were sent via the governors.

42. Stolypin stressed that obligatory regulations, which governors were permitted to issue under states of exceptional law, were intended only to protect state order and public security. He warned local officials not to issue obligatory regulations, as had been their practice, for such matters as traffic regulations, theater ticket "scalping," billiard parlor usage, the playing of harmonicas, the sale of kosher meat, untinned samovars, and books on sexual questions, prostitution, peasants leaving their children without supervision, swimming too close to steamships, shaking carpets from balconies, and so on. "Tsirkulyarnoe obrashchenie P. A. Stolypina k gubernatoram i grado-nachal'nikam—o stremleniyakh tsentral'noi vlasti v otnoshenii vnutrennei politiki," in *Gosuarstvennaya deyatel'nost' predsedatelya soveta ministrov, stats sekretarya, Petra Arkad'evicha Stolypina*, ed. E. Verpakhovsky (St. Petersburg: Izdanie sostavitelya, 1911), part 1, pp. 52-54.

43. Korkunov, *Russkoe gosudarstvennoe pravo*, pp. 313-14.

44. Blinov, *Gubernatory*, pp. 264-65; Lazarevskii, *Lektsii po Russkomu gosudarstvennomu pravu*, p. 225.

45. Only the vice-governor, councillors, and assessor always were present; outsiders could be invited to meetings of the general assembly if it were necessary. Each member of the general assembly, except the assessor, headed a section of the Provincial Administrative Board chancery which dealt with his speciality. Councillors headed the administrative section, the vice-governor supervised all activity of the chancery. Korkunov, *Russkoe gosudarstvennoe pravo*, vol. 2, pp. 317-20.

46. Lazarevskii, *Lektsii po Russkomu gosudarstvennomu pravu*, pp. 236-37. The judicial instance of the provincial board also settled altercations arising from the jurisdiction of municipal and *uezd* institutions. Altercations concerning the jurisdiction of agencies of different ministries were settled by the First Department of the Senate.

47. Lazarevskii believed that the governor's opinion was printed before the board's discussion and simply signed by the members; *Lektsii po Russkomu gosudarstvennomu pravu*, pp. 235, 239-40. Blinov thought similarly, *Gubernatory*, p. 280.

48. Blinov, *ibid.*, p. 271.

49. Lazarevskii, *Lektsii po Russkomu gosudarstvennomu pravu*, pp. 237-38.

50. Maria Petrovna von Bock, *Vozrozhdenie*, no. 3850 (December 18, 1935).

51. A. V. Zenkovsky (member of the Kiev quasi-zemstvo institution and friend of Stolypin), "Moi dopolnitel'nye vospominaniya o P. A. Stolypine," 1953, pp. 52-53;

MS, Russian Archive, Columbia University. Also, Zenkovsky, "Petr Arkad'evich Stolypin," 1952, p. 67; MS, Russian Archive, Columbia University

52. Sergei Efimovich Kryzhanovsky, *Vospominaniya* (Berlin: Speer and Schmidt, n.d.), pp. 130, 132.

53. Kryzhanovsky claimed that the projects on the reform of the local administration received their final form under Stolypin, *ibid.,* p. 137.

54. "Ob ustanovlenii glavnykh nachal' ustroistva gubernskikh uchrezhdenii," *Osobyi zhurnal,* 1907, vol. 1, no. 43, January 20 and 27, pp. 1-2. This project seems very similar to that of the Governor General of Kiev, which was proposed in the 1850s, and to other projects of the same era discussed by S. Frederick Starr, *Decentralization and Self-Government in Russia, 1830-1870,* pp. 163-70. However there is no evidence that Stolypin referred to these projects when formulating the one which he sponsored in 1906-1907.

55. *Osobyi zhurnal,* 1907, vol. 1, no. 43, 2-5.

56. Ministerstvo vnutrennikh del, *Zhurnal': mezhduvedomstvennoi komissii po preobrazovaniyu politsii v imperii,* 11 vols. (St. Petersburg: Gosudarstvennaya tipografiya, 1911).

57. The governor was to issue obligatory regulations only after discussion of them by the *gubernskii sovet* (provincial council), described below. Self-governing institutions possessed a similar power.

58. "Ob ustanovlenii glavnykh nachal' ustroistva gubernskikh uchrezhdenii," *Osobyi zhurnal,* 1907, vol. 1, no. 43, p. 5.

59. *Ibid.*

60. "Ob ustanovlenii glavnykh nachal' ustroistva gubernskikh uchrezhdenii," *Osobyi zhurnal,* 1907, vol. 1, no. 43, p. 6.

61. *Ibid.,* p. 5.

62. *Ibid.,* pp. 6-7.

63. In 1908, Kokovtsov suggested a "rank" system, rather than indiscriminate raises for all officials. He proposed that salaries of provincial officials be tabulated according to the complexity of the job and the living costs in the province to which the official was assigned.

The rest of the ministers sided with Stolypin rather than Kokovtsov. They stated that a "rank" system was too complicated and ignored the fact that posts in areas where living was cheap might be hardship posts. Thus, they approved the scale of raises proposed by Stolypin. On the whole, these were from 500 to 1,000 rubles higher than those approved by Kokovtsov. "Po schtatu gubernskago upravleniya," *Osobyi zhurnal,* 1908, vol. 1, no. 51, March 4.

64. "Ob ustanovlenii glavnykh nachal' ustroistva gubernskikh uchrezhdenii," *Osobyi zhurnal,* 1907, vol. 1, no. 43, pp. 7-10.

65. *Ibid.,* p. 10.

66. *Ibid.,* pp. 11-12.

67. If the minister and Chairman of the Council of Ministers decided an inspection was necessary, the governor was to be allowed a representative on the scene. *Ibid.,* pp. 12-13.

68. *Ibid.,* p. 14.

69. *Ibid.,* p. 21.

70. *Ibid.,* pp. 22-31.

71. *Vospominaniya,* pp. 145-51.

72. In the records of the *Sovet po delam mestnago khozyaistva,* an advisory committee in the Ministry of Internal Affairs in which this discussion allegedly took

place, there is no mention of this accusation on the part of the two local officials. Khvostov opposed the project on the grounds that it was premature and did not suit the needs of the provinces. Panchulidzev, who was frequently absent, merely noted that the members of the governor's chancery ought to be fewer and better paid. Unnamed representatives from the Ministry of Finance and Ministry of Ways and Communications spoke in favor of retaining the assorted provincial committees, claiming that their work was too specialized to consolidate them in the provincial council which Stolypin proposed. *Ministerstvo vnutrennikh del. Sovet po delam mestnago khozyaistva. Zhurnal* komissii po proektu preobrazovaniya uchrezhdenii gubernskago upravleniya, zasedanie 3, March 9, 1909, p. 6; zasedanie 9, March 15, 1909, pp. 1, 3; zasedanie 4, March 10, 1909, pp. 1-2. But perhaps Khvostov had great influence—in 1911 he was being considered as Stolypin's replacement. See below p. 193, note 8.

73. Blinov, *Gubernatory,* p. 275. In addition to representing the nobility in the *uezd* and presiding over the *uezd* zemstvo assembly, the *uezd* marshal of nobility helped draw up lists of persons eligible for the office of justice of the peace and was responsible for calling up peasant recruits.

74. Kryzhanovsky, *Vospominaniya,* p. 139.

75. A description of *uezd* government is given in Korkunov, *Russkoe gosudarstvennoe pravo,* vol. 2, pp. 331-33, and in Lazarevskii, *Lektsii po Russkomu gosudarstvennomu pravu,* pp. 254-57. Administrative agencies operating in the *uezd* included the tax inspector, forest and agricultural departments, and postal and telegraph agencies.

76. Gurko, *Features and Figures of the Past,* pp. 144-47.

77. "Ob ustanovlenii glavnykh nachal' ustroistva mestnago upravleniya," *Osobyi zhurnal,* 1907, vol. 1, no. 7, December 19 and 22, 1906, and January 3 and 6, 1907, pp. 6-7.

78. *Ibid.*

79. "Ob ustanovlenii glavnykh nachal' ustroistva mestnago upravleniya," *Osobyi zhurnal,* 1907, vol. 1, no. 7, p. 7.

80. The *volost'* and settlement zemstvos are discussed in Mary S. Conroy, "Stolypin's Attitude toward Local Self-Government," *The Slavonic and East European Review,* 46, no. 107 (July 1968), pp. 454-56, and below, pp. 67-69.

81. "Ob ustanovlenii glavnykh nachal' ustroistva mestnago upravleniya," *Osobyi zhurnal,* 1907, vol. 1, no. 7, pp. 7-8.

82. *Ibid.,* pp. 18-20.

83. *Ibid.,* pp. 20-22.

84. Kryzhanovsky, *Vospominaniya,* pp. 138-40.

85. Quoted in *Gosudarstvennaya deyatel'nost'predsedatelya soveta ministrov, statssekretarya, Petra Arkad'evicha Stolypina,* part 1, pp. 5-6.

86. For example, MVD, "Ob ustanovlenii glavnykh osnovanii preobrazovaniya zemskikh i gorodskikh uchrezhdenii," February 7, 1907, pp. 90-93.

87. V. Yu. Skalon, *Po zemskim voprosam* (St. Petersburg, 1905), pp. 242-75.

88. A. Kornilov, *Iz istorii voprosa ob izbiratel'nom prave v zemstve* (St. Petersburg, 1906).

89. M. Prokof'yev, *O sovremennom polozhenii zemstve* (*Vestnik Novgorodskago Zemstva,* no. 16) (Novgorod, 1906).

90. Gurko, *Features and Figures of the Past,* p. 123.

91. "Ob ustanovlenii glavnykh nachal' ustroistva mestnago upravleniya," *Osobyi zhurnal,* 1907, vol. 1, no. 7, pp. 8-9.

92. Gurko, *Features and Figures of the Past,* pp. 133-34, 137-41, 160-63, 170, 176.
93. *Ibid.,* pp. 123-27.
94. Konstantin Konstantinovich Troitsky, "Iz vospominanii chinovnika osobykh poruchenii v V kl. pri ministerstve vnutrennikh del," book 2, pp. 1-11; MS, Russian Archive, Columbia University. Troitsky served in the land section of the Ministry of Internal Affairs.
95. *Osobyi zhurnal,* 1907, vol. 1, no. 25, April 10; *ibid.,* 1908, vol. 1, no. 16, January 22; *ibid.,* 1908, vol. 3, no. 357, December 2; *ibid.,* 1910, vol. 3, no. 209, December 9; Prince A. D. Golitsyn, "Vospominaniya," book 10, pp. 240-41, MS, Russian Archive, Columbia University. Golitsyn was a member of the Budget and Local Self-Government committees of the Duma.

During a meeting of the Council of Ministers, November 25, 1910, Stolypin stated that the central government had to subsidize local self-governing institutions because they were fulfilling certain state duties and therefore they should not be indebted to private institutions and companies. As he frequently did, Stolypin cited examples from western European countries which were to serve as models for the organization of zemstvo credit. *Osobyi zhurnal,* 1909, vol. 3, no. 249.

96. A. V. Zenkovsky, *Pravda o Stolypine* (New York: Vseslovyanskoe Izdatel'stvo, 1957), pp. 199, 201. Between 1906 and August 1911, Zenkovsky met Stolypin nineteen times, on which occasions they discussed affairs, including finances, in Kiev *guberniya.* See also Zenkovsky, "Petr Arkad'evich Stolypin," pp. 1-28.
97. Schlipie describes his relationship with Stolypin in his *Vospominaniya,* pp. 106-07.
98. Golitsyn discussed the all-class *volost'* zemstvo and subsidies for zemstvos with Stolypin in August 1906 and during the period 1908-1910. "Vospominaniya," book 8, pp. 202-03, and book 10, pp. 242-45.
99. *Pravda o Stolypine,* p. 204.
100. *Russkoe gosudarstvennoe pravo,* 1905 ed., vol. 2, pp. 353-54.
101. *Ibid.,* pp. 354-57.
102. *Ibid.,* pp. 360, 364.
103. Baron Alexander Meyendorff, "A Brief Appreciation of Stolypin's Tenure of Office," p. 5 of section entitled "Agrarian Policy"; MS, Russian Archive, Columbia University. See also above, chapter 1, p. 16.
104. Ministerstvo vnutrennikh del: Zemskii otdel, "Polozhenie o poselkovom upravlenii," no. 34012, December 18, 1908, pp. 64-65.
105. "Po proektu preobrazovaniya zemskikh i gorodskikh uchrezhdenii," *Osobyi zhurnal,* 1907, vol. 3, no. 356, December 7 and 18, p. 5.
106. The project actually was a composite of three projects: "Ob ustanovlenii glavnykh nachal' ustroistva mestnago upravleniya," *Osobyi zhurnal,* 1907, vol. 1, no. 7, December 19 and 22, 1906, and January 3 and 6, 1907; MVD, "Ob ustanovlenii glavnykh osnovanii preobrazovaniya zemskikh i gorodskikh uchrezhdenii," February 7, 1907; "Po proektu preobrazovaniya zemskikh i gorodskikh uchrezhdenii," *Osobyi zhurnal,* 1907, vol. 3, no. 356, pp. 11-36, 37-39, 44-45.

I have discussed the three versions as one for reasons of convenience.
107. MVD, "Ob ustanovlenii glavnykh osnovanii preobrazovaniya zemskikh i gorodskikh uchrezhdenii," February 7, 1907, pp. 117-19; "Po proektu preobrazovaniya zemskikh i gorodskikh uchrezhdenii," *Osobyi zhurnal,* 1907, vol. 3, no. 356, pp. 11-36, 37-39, 44-45.
108. MVD, "Ob ustanovlenii glavnykh osnovanii preobrazovaniya zemskikh i gorodskikh uchrezhdenii, February 7, 1907, p. 18.

109. *Ibid.*

110. *Ibid.*, pp. 95-99. Kokovtsov refused to allow the vote to apartment dwellers who paid high rents because this would have involved turning over to the cities part of the state apartment tax.

111. *Ibid.*, pp. 90, 137-39. The third category was subdivided into persons who paid the full tax rate and persons who paid less than, though not one-tenth of, the full tax rate. In *uezdy* where the average tax rate was below norm, the norm could be lowered but not by more than 5 percent. How would the tax rate have affected the electorate? It was estimated by Boris Veselovsky, a contemporary political theorist and authority on the zemstvo, that a tax rather than a property qualification would have lowered the electoral qualification on the average by 35 percent. Veselovsky, *Istoriya zemstva,* 4 vols. (St. Petersburg, 1911), vol. 4, p. 167.

112. MVD, "Ob ustanovlenii glavnykh osnovanii preobrazovaniya zemskikh i gorodskikh uchrezhdenii," February 7, 1907, pp. 19-21. The bill stipulated that this measure was to be taken only in exceptional cases. Even so, some ministers protested that withholding elections for three years was too long. Those who supported Stolypin maintained that the six months which the opposition suggested was too short a time in which to rectify the causes which had necessitated prorogation.

Stolypin took examples from western European countries (England, Austria, France, Italy, and Germany) to show that the central government had the right to control local self-governing bodies in this fashion. "Po proektu preobrazovaniya zemskikh i gorodskikh uchrezhdenii," *Osobyi zhurnal,* 1907, vol. 3, no. 356, pp. 4-10.

113. Veselovsky, *Istoriya zemstva,* vol. 4, pp. 167-68; Neville Henderson in F. O. 371, vol. 318, no. 22429, July 4, 1907. According to Mr. Henderson, the congress consisted of 150 delegates—80 Octobrists, 40 "Right," and 30 Kadets. Rodzyanko was president, Guchkov vice-president. The congress also rejected a proposal for universal suffrage, but passed a resolution in favor of lowering existing property requirements. Discussion of the tax qualification in the ministry is recorded in "Po proektu preobrazovaniya zemskikh i gorodskikh uchrezhdenii," *Osobyi zhurnal,* 1907, vol. 3, no. 356, pp. 1-2.

114. "Ob ustanovlenii glavnykh nachal' ustroistva mestnago upravleniya," *Osobyi zhurnal,* 1907, vol. 1, no. 7, p. 4.

115. MVD, "Ob ustanovlenii glavnykh osnovanii preobrazovaniya zemskikh i gorodskikh uchrezhdenii," pp. 93-95. Members from the landowning class could not constitute less than one-fourth of the total number of representatives; members from the *volost'* could not constitute less than one-third of the total number of representatives; members from the commercial-industrial classes could not amount to more than five-twelfths of the total. Although this scale weighted representation in favor of the large landowners, the project also stipulated that the number of large landowners was to be lowered in areas where there were too many. (It did not specify how many were "too many.")

116. *Ibid.*, pp. 90, 93. Stolypin frankly acknowledged this policy of the government to the Duma in March 1907: "The project on zemstvo representation which has been introduced to the Duma stands on the principle of tax qualification, widening by this means the circle of people participating in zemstvo life, but simultaneously guaranteeing participation in it [zemstvo life] of the cultured class of landowners." *Gosudarstvennaya Duma: Stenograficheskie otchety,* sessiya II, zasedanie 5, March 6, 1907, col. 112.

He continued to maintain that the government would have to ensure a certain number of landowners in the zemstvos because of the landowners' educational caliber.

In an interview with the editor of *Volga*, in 1909, he declared: "The new zemstvo . . . must be classless, but the landowners must preserve their influence in it. The landowners . . . great culture is a strength in the important business of building a state. There is no need to fear that in case the project [on the transformation of the zemstvos] is implemented the old, experienced workers, created during the course of the past forty years, will be replaced by new people in the present zemstvo. They will not be replaced but confirmed." *Gosudarstvennaya deyatel'nost predsedatelya soveta ministrov, stats sekretarya, Petra Arkad'evicha Stolypina*, part 1, p. 6. The other ministers rejected this proposal for "personal representation" as being contrary to the spirit of the zemstvos. "Ob ustanovlenii glavnykh nachal' ustroistva mestnago upravleniya," *Osobyi zhurnal*, 1907, vol. 1, no. 7, pp. 27-28.

117. MVD, "Ob ustanovlenii glavnykh osnovanii preobrazovaniya zemskikh i gorodskikh uchrezhdenii," February 7, 1907, p. 94. This proposal was included in the final ministerial project.

118. The *volost'* bill was read in the Duma on May 13, 1911. *Gosudarstvennaya Duma: Stenograficheskie otchety*. Tretii sozyv, sessiya IV, zasedanie 113.

119. *Gosudarstvennaya Duma: Stenograficheskie otchety*. Sessiya II, zasedanie 5, March 6, 1907, col. 111.

The settlement project is contained in Ministerstvo vnutrennikh del: Zemskii otdel, "Polozhenie o poselkovom upravlenii," no. 29489, October 1908 (hereafter cited as Bill No. 29489), and in Ministerstvo vnutrennikh del: Zemskii otdel, "Polozhenie o poselkovom upravlenii," no. 34012, December 18, 1908 (hereafter cited as Bill No. 34012), If the *skhod* exceeded 150 people it was to be replaced with a settlement assembly (*sobranie*), elected by the settlement gathering through a three-curia system. Bill no. 29489, p. 6.

120. Bill no. 29489, pp. 8-9, articles 35-40. The gathering or assembly also elected an executive agent, the *starosta*.

The settlement gathering had a limited right of self-taxation. Bill no. 34012, pp. 73-81.

121. Bill no. 29489, pp. 3-6. Policemen and monks, even if they owned land in the area, were barred from the settlement gathering. In the case of policemen, the measure was to ensure their disinterestedness.

122. Bill no. 29489, pp. 6-7, articles 26-27; Bill no. 34012, pp. 47-50. The amount of property allowing one to sit in the settlement assembly without being elected was fixed at 7,500 rubles.

123. Bill no. 34012, pp. 34-35.

124. See above, p. 59.

125. Bill no. 34012, pp. 67-72. Stolypin cited examples from western European countries—France and Prussia—to justify supervision and control of local self-government by the central government, as he did in the project on the zemstvos.

126. *Gosudarstvennaya Duma: Stenograficheskie otchety*. Tretii sozyv, sessiya IV, zasedanie 58, zasedanie 113.

127. *Za vseslovnoe volostnoe zemstvo. Rechi, proiznesenniya v Gosudarstvennom sovete* (St. Petersburg, 1914), pp. iii-v.

128. Ministerstvo vnutrennikh del. Sovet po delam mestnago khozyaistva, *Zhurnal' komissii po proektu preobrazovaniya uchrezhdenii gubernskago upravleniya*, zasedanie no. 8, March 13, 1909, p. 3.

129. *Gosudarstvennaya Duma: Stenograficheskie otchety*, Tretii sozyv, sessiya I, zasedanie 7, November 16, 1907, col. 310.

130. Stolypin to Nicholas, "Iz perepiski P. A. Stolypina s Nikolaem Romanovym," *Krasnyi arkhiv,* 30, p. 84, November 20, 1910.

131. Ministerstvo vnutrennikh del. Sovet po delam mestnago khozyaistva, *Zhurnal komissii po proektu preobrazovaniya uchrezhdenii gubernskago upravleniya, zasedanie 8,* March 13, 1909, p. 4.

132. *Ibid.,* zasedanie 7, March 12, pp. 1-2, 5; zasedanie 10, March 15, p. 2.

133. *Ibid.,* zasedanie 6, March 11, p. 5.

134. *Ibid.,* p. 3.

135. *Zhurnal* komissii, zasedanie 7, March 12, p. 6.

136. *Ibid.,* p. 4.

137. *Ibid.,* pp. 5-6.

138. *Ibid.,* p. 6. The *dokladchik* also rejected the demand that self-governing institutions be allowed to stop obligatory regulations. In addition, he suppressed the opinion that the governor and the *gubernskii sovet* had no right to investigate persons not immediately subordinate to them, that is members or employees of zemstvos and municipal dumas. *Zhurnal* komissii, zasedanie 6, March 11, p. 5.

139. The Kadet project on the establishment of settlement and *uchastkovye* zemstvos and on *uezd* and *guberniya* zemstvo electoral reform is described by Veselovsky, *Istoriya zemstva,* vol. 4, pp. 162-64. It was presented to the Second Duma.
The Social Democrats' project for local self-government, described by Veselovsky, *ibid.,* p. 175, was presented to the Third Duma on November 19, 1908.

140. *Ibid.,* p. 175. See Geoffrey Hosking, *The Russian Constitutional Experiment* (New York, London: Cambridge University Press, 1973), pp. 150-77, for a review of the Octobrist's plans for local self-governmental reform.

141. The agitation from commercial-industrial circles for a tax requirement is described by Veselovsky, *Istoriya zemstva,* vol. 4, pp. 170-72.

142. "Po proektu preobrazovaniya zemskikh i gorodskikh uzhrezhdenii," *Osobyi zhurnal,* 1907, vol. 3, no. 356, pp. 11-13.

143. "Ob ustanovlenii glavnykh nachal' ustroistva mestnago upravleniya," *Osobyi zhurnal,* 1907, vol. 1, no. 7, pp. 15-17.

144. Veselovsky, *Istoriya zemstva,* vol. 4, pp. 166-67. Veselovsky claimed that the all-zemstvo congress, as well as the zemstvos, were dominated by reactionaries (p. 168). From the statistics quoted in footnote 125 above, this was not true of the all-zemstvo congress. That the zemstvos, however, were dominated by reactionary elements was verified by C. H. Bentinck, F. O. 371, vol. 318, no. 38729, November 21, 1907, and by Richard Seymour, F. O. 371, vol. 513, March 25, 1908.

145. The measure, of course, would have allowed Stolypin to prevent any interest group from gaining control of the zemstvo. However, at the time in question, it thwarted reactionary elements.

146. "Proekt P. A. Stolypina o preobrazovanii gosudarstvennogo upravleniya Rossii," *Pravda o Stolypine,* pp. 73-113.

147. Letters of Boris von Bock to Zenkovsky, San Francisco, April 24, 1953, and May 23, 1953 (Russian Archive, Columbia University). Letter of Maria Petrovna von Bock to Zenkovsky, July 11, 1953 (Russian Archive, Columbia University).

148. Zenkovsky, *Pravda o Stolypine,* pp. 73-87.

149. *Ibid.,* p. 76.

150. *Ibid.,* pp. 85, 99.

151. *Ibid.,* p. 79

152. *Ibid.,* pp. 74-79.

153. See below, p. 79.

154. Zenkovsky, *Pravda o Stolypine,* pp. 73-87 *passim.*

155. *Ibid.,* pp. 111-113.

156. *Outlines of Russian Culture,* part 1: *Religion and the Church,* ed. Michael Karpovich, trans. Valentine Ughet and Eleanor Davis (New York: A. S. Barnes and Company, 1960), p. 117.

157. "Po proektam 1.) polozheniya o staroobryadtsakh i otdelivshikhsya ot pravoslaviya sektantakh 2.) pravil otnositelno vedeniya dlya oznachennykh lits knig grazhdanskago sostoyaniya," *Osobyi zhurnal,* 1906, no. 100, September 5 and October 13, pp. 1-7. The core of the proposal seems to have been the same as one presented to the First Duma and thus worked out by Stolypin's predecessors in the Ministry of Internal Affairs.

158. "Po zakonoproektam, kasayushchimsya osushchestvleniya svobodny sovesti," *Osobyi zhurnal,* 1907, vol. 1, no. 69, pp. 1-11.

159. "Po proektam 1.) polozheniya o staroobryadtsakh i otdelivshikhsya ot pravoslaviya sektantakh 2.) pravil otnositelno vedeniya dlya oznachennykh lits knig grazhdanskago sostoyaniya," *Osobyi zhurnal,* 1906, no. 100, pp. 7-31.

160. "Po zakonoproektam, kasayushchimsya osushchestvleniya svobodny sovesti," *Osobyi zhurnal,* 1907, vol. 1, no. 69, pp. 14-15.

161. *Ibid.,* pp. 13-14.

162. *Osobyi zhurnal,* 1908, vol. 1, no. 36.

163. *Gosudarstvennaya Duma: Stenograficheskie otchety,* Tretii sozyv, sessiya II, zasedanie 116, May 22, 1909, cols. 1753-1764.

164. "Stolypin and the Russian Ministerial Crisis," *California Slavic Studies,* 4 (1967), pp. 29-32.

165. Stolypin to Nicolson, F. O. 371, vol. 327, no. 35457 (no. 523), October 18, 1907; *ibid.,* vol. 515, no. 8047 (no. 122), March 3, 1908, p. 2; *ibid.,* vol. 519, no. 30064 (no. 383), August 27, 1908, p. 2; *ibid.,* vol. 733, no. 35751 (no. 495), September 12, 1909, p. 2. In the interview of September 12, 1909, Stolypin told Nicolson that he "was anxious to develop migration to the Amur districts so as to check the influx of the Chinese; but there did not seem to be much tendency on the part of the Russian peasantry to move to those regions."

166. Kokovtsov, *Out of My Past,* pp. 209-12; Zenkovsky, *Pravda o Stolypine,* pp. 34-36.

167. F. O. 371, vol. 519, no. 30064 (no. 383), August 27, 1908, p. 2.

168. "Po voprosu o vvedenii v Rossiiskoi Imperii vseobshchago nachalnago obucheniya," *Osobyi zhurnal,* 1906, no. 42, August 8, especially pp. 1-3, 23, 32. A verst equals .66 of one mile.

169. *Ibid.,* p. 28. Also, "Po voprosu o vvedenii v Rossiiskoi Imperii vseobshchago nachalnago obucheniya," *Osobyi zhurnal,* 1907, vol. 1, no. 47, January 26 and 30, pp. 21-23.

170. "Po voprosu o vvedenii v Rossiiskoi Imperii vseobshchago nachalnago obucheniya," *Osobyi zhurnal,* 1906, no. 42, p. 20.

171. *Ibid.,* pp. 15, 19-20, 27-33; "Po voprosu o vvedenii v Rossiiskoi Imperii vseobshchago obucheniya," *Osobyi zhurnal,* 1907, vol. 1, no. 47, p. 19.

172. *Osobyi zhurnal,* 1909, vol. 3, no. 59, March 11.

173. Michael T. Florinsky, *Russia, A History and An Interpretation* (New York: Macmillan, 1963), vol. 2, pp. 1235-36, Florinsky presents other details on the project.

174. *Ibid.,* pp. 1236-37.

Chapter 4:
Law and Order

Although 1905 has been termed a revolutionary year, violence continued to erupt during 1906 and 1907 and sporadically in the years thereafter. According to police statistics, although they may have been exaggerated, 1,126 government officials were killed and 1,506 wounded by terrorists during 1906 and 3,000 were killed and 3,046 wounded during 1907.[1] The Socialist Revolutionary party in particular embarked upon a campaign of assassination directed against high officials. Among those killed were the Governor of Akmolinsk, the prefect of police of St. Petersburg, the chiefs of police of Dagestan and Warsaw, and the Governor of Penza.[2]

It will be recalled that Stolypin's own life was threatened by a bomb attack at his home on Aptekarsky Island on August 12; in that incident thirty-two persons were killed and twenty-two wounded.[3] The threat to the government appeared so serious to Stolypin that he confided in September 1906 to the British Ambassador, Sir Arthur Nicolson, that he had suggested to the Tsar that there be "ministres de reserve" who would be prepared to take charge should ministers and department heads be assassinated.[4]

British observers in Russia notified the Foreign Office that many provincial centers were still cut off from St. Petersburg, governors were fearful, confused, or apathetic, and the administrative apparatus was crumbling—lower-ranking policemen, mindful of everyday assaults and assassination attempts, as well as lower-ranking administrative officials were quitting their posts.[5]

During that first year of Stolypin's administration, mutinies broke out within the elite Preobrazhensky regiment, whose senior non-commissioned officer held the keys to the imperial apartments in the Winter Palace, among the naval forces at Sveaborg and Kronstadt and in the Black Sea squadron, and among the troops stationed along the Trans-Siberian railway and other garrisons of southern Russia.[6]

Peasant disorders declined during the winter of 1905-1906, but from May to August 1906, agrarian disturbances were said to be as numerous and destructive as those which had occurred during the last four months of 1905. In industrial areas the number of strikers in 1906 equalled two-thirds of the total number of factory workers; in 1907, two-fifths of the workers were still on strike.[7]

The Social Democrats and the maximalist section of the Socialist Revolutionary party carried out so-called expropriations or robberies of banks and savings and loan institutions in Moscow and Tiflis.[8] Disorders were especially severe in Poland and in the Baltic provinces where strong national feeling was combined with economic and social grievances.

Stolypin approached the problem of restoring order with the same common-sense, no-nonsense attitude which he applied to other problems and issues. On the one hand, he used firm measures which sometimes circumvented regular judicial procedure. On the other hand, he attempted to eliminate some of the causes of discontent, principally by implementing agrarian reforms. In addition, he condemned excessive repression. Throughout his administration his orders to firmly and decisively quash disorders were linked with orders to avoid undue severity, and he was willing to relax repressive measures when he believed the situation warranted it. Finally, he endorsed improvements in the courts and the dispensation of justice, although we shall see that, like the other reform proposals which he sponsored, these were not as far-reaching as they might have been.

Stolypin's classic statement on the government's dual responsibility to achieve order and reform was presented in a speech to the Duma, June 8, 1906, in which he affirmed that "power cannot be considered an end. Power is a means for safeguarding life, tranquility and order; therefore while condemning absolute rule and arbitrariness, it is impossible not to consider as dangerous impotence in a government."[9] He went on to emphasize, however, that it was the "obligation of the government—the sacred responsibility of the government—to preserve tranquility and lawfulness, the freedom not only to work, but to live, and . . . [the] order necessary for the growth of the very widest reform." During this summer the government was indeed busily revamping and approving reform proposals.

The prescription for an adroit blend of reform and repression was reiterated in Stolypin's circular to governors and other provincial officials on September 15, 1906. He first ordered local officials to attend to the needs of the local peasantry, the primary target for agitators, by facilitating land sales and transfer of land to them, and to inform them of government plans to ease their situation. (The agrarian reform measures were implemented by the government in the late summer and fall of that year.)

At the same time, local officials were to warn peasants of the consequences of seizing or destroying *pomeshchik* land[10] and they were to arrest local agitators, collect proof for their prosecution, and in the event of armed insurrection call upon the army for aid. Stolypin reminded these officials that professional unions of engineers, teachers, and lawyers, and workers' unions, were almost without exception regarded as revolutionary according to the law of March 4, 1906. Even those societies which were registered had to be closely supervised. Governors were given the right to stop the activity of a society and request the administrative board (the collective body which assisted the governor) to abolish it. Private meetings of legal societies could take place without the presence of government officials, but public meetings, even when they were permitted, required the presence of a government representative who had the power to judge the legality of speeches and activity. Stolypin stressed that according to criminal law an entire society was liable to be prosecuted for the criminal acts of one of its members. After a terrorist attack, local authorities were to establish the identity of the "fighting group" (armed cadres of revolutionary parties) and "liquidate them immediately, even if by administrative exile" (exile without court trial of the accused).[11]

During Stolypin's first year in office the government issued several new restrictive regulations. A decree of August 8, 1906, raised the penalty for distribution of antigovernmental propaganda among the armed forces from three to six years. A bill prohibiting persons under police surveillance from being recruited into the army was promulgated on November 6, 1906.[12] On December 19, 1906, Stolypin urged that the rule allowing police to use arms only in self-defense be abolished and that they be governed by army regulations when dealing with unruly crowds.[13]

The chief suppressive device of the first year of Stolypin's administration and that which earned him the most criticism was the application of martial law and use of the field courts martial. These courts were established at the request of the civil or military authority of a city or province. According to the procedure of the courts, civilians were to be tried within twenty-four hours after their apprehension, proceedings were secret, death sentences—which were forbidden by ordinary law—were imposed, sentences had to be carried out within twenty-four hours after imposition, and there was no defense and no appeal.[14]

During the time the courts martial existed, from August 19, 1906, until April 21, 1907, 1,102 persons were executed under their provisions, 127 were sentenced to hard labor, 7 were exiled, and 21 acquitted. Under the provisions of the naval courts martial 42 were executed, 202 were sentenced to hard labor, and 443 were jailed, all under the general charge of insurrection. The courts were most active in the Baltic provinces, Poland, the Caucasus, and Ekaterinaslav province.[15]

The proposal for the courts martial was introduced to the Council of Ministers on August 17, 1906, just a few days after the attack on Stolypin, by the Minister of War, who claimed that regular procedure was too slow at a time when "criminal activity had reached such staggering proportions and threatened universal destruction and anarchy."[16] There is no record of Stolypin's opinion on the courts in this meeting, and V. I. Gurko, Assistant Minister of Internal Affairs for a time under Stolypin, has suggested that perhaps Stolypin was not the originator of the idea of the courts martial, noting that he, Stolypin, had been requested by the Tsar to implement this measure.[17] Indeed, there is a letter from Nicholas to Stolypin dated August 14, 1906, asking the Council of Ministers to report on appropriate measures to stop sedition and restore order and suggesting that only the establishment of exceptional law would achieve these ends.[18] Stolypin himself stated cryptically, in an interview with an American correspondent early in 1907, that "exceptional measures" were "a cross" which he had to bear "against his will." He claimed that he had inherited these measures from his predecessors and while they could not be "legally abolished they must be continued. I and the other ministers," Stolypin acknowledged, "are only executors, not legislators. We are condemned to wait."[19]

On the other hand, in this same interview he defended the courts to the correspondent who criticized them as incompatible with the rights guaranteed by the manifesto of October 17—stressing that the turmoil which wreaked the country had to be suppressed by exceptional measures.[20] In the same spirit, there is a letter from Stolypin to Nicholas dated December 3, 1906, urging the Tsar not to accede to an official's request for leniency for Nicholas' would-be assassin and reminding Nicholas that, given the situation in Russia, it was unfortunate but true that "only the execution of a few could stave off a sea of blood." Thus, Nicholas could not afford to be kind.[21] Furthermore, in an interview with Sir Donald MacKenzie Wallace in December 1908, Stolypin seemed to accept responsibility for the courts, stating that he had established them to expedite justice and that cases remaining after they had been abolished had also been handed over to military courts, as regular tribunals were not competent to handle serious political crimes.[22]

Even so, during this first critical year Stolypin opposed unnecessary or unduly harsh repression. On July 13, 1906, before the courts martial were instituted, he sent a circular to local officials, urging them to "direct in the most decisive manner and without hesitation the institutions subordinate to you . . . . Disorders and revolutionary attempts must be repressed without any feebleness and with all legal means." But he reminded them "the struggle is not against society but against the enemies of society. Repression of the masses cannot be approved. Acts not supported by laws or imprudent acts, exciting spirits rather than tranquilizing them, will not be tolerated."[23]

This warning was repeated in the circular of September 15, in which Stolypin advised local officials to refrain from "acts cruel and for personal gain . . . or measures not warranted by the circumstances."[24] Early in 1907 he complained to the press that many officials, who had "deserted" the year before, had undergone a "change of heart" and, reassured by firm authority in the central government, were employing power with unnecessary severity.[25]

More important, although he publicly refused to accede to the Second Duma's request that the courts martial be abolished before their natural expiration date of April 20, 1907, he actually was willing to discard widespread usage of the courts early in 1907. On February 6, 1907, a few weeks before the Second Duma was convened, he privately proposed to the Council of Ministers that the courts be abolished immediately by a circular and they be abolished formally by ukase the day before the Duma met. Nicholas would not agree to the ukase, although he approved of a private circular limiting the courts' activity.[26] As a result, on February 9 Stolypin sent a confidential circular to governors and other administrative personnel, urging them to refrain from use of the courts because the revolution had diminished somewhat and their continued existence would cause friction between the Duma and the government.[27]

Some areas of the country remained under martial law for several years—the Baltic provinces until September 1908, Baku, Odessa, Kharkov, and Ekaterinaslav province until July 1908, and the Caucasus and Poland until July 1909. Even after that, Tiflis and one district in Poland remained under martial law.[28]

The rest of the empire was placed under extraordinary or reinforced protection, the second-lightest and lightest degrees of exceptional law.[29] Like martial law, but to a lesser extent, these two forms of exceptional law gave quasi-judicial authority to administrative officials and concomitantly often dispensed with regular judicial procedures. In a state of extraordinary protection, the chief commander, governor general, or governor was permitted to issue so-called obligatory regulations. These regulations were not to concern matters covered by criminal law. Violations of the obligatory regulations could be punished in the administrative order by a fine not exceeding 2,000 rubles or three month's imprisonment. In a state of reinforced protection money fines for violation of obligatory regulations were lower, but the term of imprisonment was the same.

According to the new police regulations being drafted in the Ministry of Internal Affairs in 1907, police officers were allowed to punish summarily infractions of obligatory regulations by a fine of fifty rubles and could exact the same punishment for disturbances of peace and order if, in their opinion, the offense was punishable by a fine not exceeding fifty rubles.[30]

In a state of extraordinary protection, the chief commander of a district could transfer certain crimes or whole categories of crime to military courts. These were only slightly different from the courts martial. The accused could employ counsel, call witnesses, and appeal. However, the judges were not trained jurists, the trial was held in camera, and death sentences could be imposed.[31]

Under both states of exceptional law, local officials had power to dismiss personnel of zemstvos and municipal dumas who were appointed, not elected. The police could hold persons whom they considered dangerous to public security in custody for two weeks, without consulting judicial authorities; they could censor mail and conduct house searches at all times.[32]

Under both states of exceptional law, local administrative officials had the power to banish persons guilty of political offenses to Siberia, without trial. It was commonly held that the term "political offense," for which this punishment was applied, was loosely interpreted.[33] In 1907 the number of persons exiled by criminal and military courts for political reasons exceeded the figure of 1906 by 35 percent. The total of those banished by administrative authorities without trial, however, was 70 percent more in 1907 than in 1906. Most of these exiles were sent to remote areas of Archangel'sk, Astrakan, Vologda, and Tobolsk.[34] There was an appreciable decrease in the use of administrative banishment during the latter years of Stolypin's administration. In 1907 there were 24,275 exiles, in 1909 there were 17,102, and as late as February 1910, there were still 12,272 exiles. In 1906, 7,677 persons were banished by administrative authorities, whereas in 1909 only 1,991 were banished.[35] Nevertheless, the government had no intention of abolishing this procedure. An official pronouncement of 1909 stated that for the years 1910 to 1912 administrative exiles would be sent alternately to Yenesei and Irkutsk provinces.[36] Sir Arthur Nicolson also reported in 1909 the existence in St. Petersburg of a sort of court of the star chamber. Apparently, a special commission composed of representatives of the ministries of Justice and Internal Affairs had the right to arrest any person, from any part of Russia, for political offenses and banish him to Siberia.[37] This information was hearsay, however, and there is no further evidence to corroborate it.

Reinforced protection could be proclaimed for one year and could be renewed by the Ministry of Internal Affairs. Extraordinary protection was established for six months and could also be continued by order of the ministry.

Moderate liberals such as Minister of Foreign Affairs A. P. Izvolsky and A. I. Guchkov, Octobrist leader in the Third Duma, as well as the observer Sir Arthur Nicolson, had approved of the courts martial in 1906 and 1907.[38] By 1908 and 1909, however, the moderate Octobrist party, not to mention the Kadets and parties to their left, very much opposed the renewal of exceptional law. In July and August 1908, Guchkov, Stolypin's friend and supporter, and Baron Alexander Meyendorff, Stolypin's cousin and an Octobrist member of the Third Duma, spoke against exceptional law and administrative banishment.[39] In 1909 the moderate right in the Duma introduced a resolution urging the government to abolish exceptional law as a form of administration not compatible with a time of peace.[40]

Stolypin, however, believed exceptional measures were still necessary in 1908. In December of that year he told MacKenzie Wallace that "revolutionary elements were not . . . entirely suppressed" and alluded to "hooliganism" and even a plan for a "coup on the highest personages in the Empire" on which the government had secret information. He believed that it might take as long as five years before real improvement could be achieved.[41] In February 1908, in a letter for M. A. Gazenkampf, the assistant head of the St. Petersburg military district, Stolypin emphasized that military courts and other exceptional measures were necessary as long as revolutionary currents and disorder lasted. He rebuked Gazenkampf for too great leniency, explaining that laxness both increased crime rates and had an unfavorable psychological effect on the masses—when laws were properly enforced after a period of leniency, people would think them unduly harsh.[42] Robberies, Stolypin advised Gazenkampf, must be "unmercifully extinguished, for they were more numerous in 1908 than in 1905."[43]

Stolypin was particularly concerned about assassination of policemen. He informed Gazenkampf that they "dangerously demoralized the police, whose moral support, in view of the onerous duty they had undertaken, was the responsibility of the government."[44] In 1908, he requested 1 million rubles from the state treasury—the same amount granted in 1907—for pensions for widows and orphans of policemen assassinated during that year.[45] He also requested that the police force in Moscow be strengthened to equal that in St. Petersburg in order to combat disruptive forces.[46]

During the period 1908-1911 there was ample evidence to prove that the government needed to employ some exceptional measures to preserve itself from revolutionary onslaughts. British Foreign Office reports in 1908 and 1909 contained accounts of terrorist assassinations, revolutionary activity among the armed forces, discoveries of caches of bombs and revolutionary literature, and armed robbery in St. Petersburg, Moscow, and Kiev, as well as in Poland and in the Caucasus.[47] Official statistics listed 1,820 killed by terrorists and 2,083 wounded throughout the empire during 1908, the majority of these being policemen.[48] Throughout 1909 and 1910, current literature still discussed the danger of revolutionary agitation in the army,[49] and in 1911 newspapers reported the finding of a revolutionary printing press, secret explosive factories, and stacks of revolutionary literature in St. Petersburg.[50] There were enough student demonstrations in 1910 and 1911 to convince moderate rightists like A. A. Bobrinsky that student-led revolution was imminent.[51]

Nevertheless, it is interesting to note that the proposal for the establishment of exceptional law, which affirmed that this law was "a temporary measure introduced during wartime or in cases of internal disturbance when the regular authority of administrative institutions seemed insufficient for guaranteeing state order and public security," was introduced to the Council of Ministers for discussion in February 1907 by Makarov, an Assistant Minister of Internal Affairs, and not by Stolypin.[52] Furthermore, there is no record of Stolypin's defending it before the Council of Ministers as he defended the reform measures he introduced at the same time.

Stolypin did uphold one aspect of exceptional law—the practice of allowing policemen to summarily punish small infractions of obligatory regulations. During discussion by the ministry in 1907 of a proposal introduced by the Ministry of Justice on reform of the *volost'* courts, Minister of Justice I. G. Shcheglovitov criticized the practice of giving purely judicial functions to administrative officials, particularly the police, and pointed out the danger of increasing police supervision over matters immediately affecting the individual.[53] Stolypin, in opposition, claimed that most people preferred to pay a police-imposed fine rather than go through troublesome judicial proceedings. Moreover, he complained, judicial officials had been evading their duty and were not prosecuting violations of obligatory regulations, which made it difficult for administrative officials to maintain public order. In order to give obligatory regulations sufficient force, police had to be able to impose penalties. However, he stressed, this would no longer be permitted when the bill on personal inviolability, being drafted by the Ministry of Internal Affairs, was put into effect.[54]

In any case, although Stolypin maintained that some exceptional law was necessary after 1908, he also ordered, as he had with regard to the courts martial, that the provisions of exceptional law not be applied beyond their need. In September 1909, in a circular to provincial authorities, he urged that capital punishment be used as infrequently as possible because the country had become more tranquil. In districts under exceptional law, he wrote, only especially grave cases were to be submitted to military tribunals; other cases were to be dealt with by ordinary civil courts.[55] In the same year the Committee of State Defense, established in 1905 for defense of the state from internal enemies, was abolished.[56]

In 1910 Stolypin sent a circular to governors and municipal authorities clarifying the purpose and limitations of obligatory regulations which they were permitted to issue under the terms of exceptional law. He stressed that obligatory regulations were intended only to protect state order and public security (*gosudarstvennago poryadka i obshchestvennoi bezopasnosti*) and were not to touch matters covered by criminal law or frivolous matters such as traffic regulations, theater ticket scalping, billiard parlor usage, the playing of harmonicas, the sale of untinned samovars and kosher meat, swimming too close to steamships, shaking carpets from windows and balconies, and so on.[57]

Two special areas of governmental concern were the press and secondary schools and universities. Preliminary censorship had been abolished in 1905, but in his circular of September 1906 Stolypin reminded local officials that under a state of exceptional law editors could be prosecuted and printing presses closed for consistently printing "tendentious" articles, or for reproducing a criminal or revolutionary appeal unless accompanied by criticism.[58] A proposal of December 1906 increased the list of topics which the press was forbidden to discuss and set punishment for praise of criminal acts from two to eight months' imprisonment, arrest not exceeding three months or a fine not higher than 500 rubles. The Council of Ministers maintained that punishments for such matters were more severe in western European countries.[59]

According to this proposal of 1906, editors were to be prosecuted through court procedure. However, under a state of extraordinary protection, governors general, governors, and municipal prefects could summarily suspend or prohibit the publication of newspapers, and editors could be summarily fined 4,800 rubles or imprisoned for a term not exceeding three months. In a state of reinforced protection, printing establishments could be closed by the police. A governmental proposal of March 1908 asked for greater enforcement of the law punishing praise of criminal activity in speech or in the press.[60]

Throughout 1907 and 1908 numerous liberal editors were fined and publications were confiscated for articles dealing with the general state of affairs in the country, for criticism of corruption in the Naval Department, and for the reprinting of Leo Tolstoy's condemnation of capital punishment.[61] Simultaneously, official papers withheld or falsified news derogatory to the government. It was impossible, official British observers in Russia insisted, to obtain statistics on the number of executions for certain periods or information on such matters as the mutiny in the Preobrazhensky regiment, student unrest in 1910, or the ministerial crisis of April 1909.[62] Printed material from abroad was censored and often reached the addressee blacked out, or "caviared" as local slang termed it.[63] A congress of book-sellers and publishers, permitted to meet in St. Petersburg in 1909 for the first time in Russian history, claimed that booksellers had been sent to prison for selling books arbitrarily declared illegal. Editors were liable to be prosecuted two to three years after their offenses were registered.[64] Stolypin's introduction into the Duma of a proposal which would have permitted Duma members to receive printed matter from abroad free of duty and censorship resulted in a torrent of criticism of the government's treatment of the press.[65]

Nevertheless, the press during Stolypin's term of office was freer than it had ever been before. In St. Petersburg and Moscow in 1909 there was outspoken criticism of the government, and the proceedings of the Duma were freely reported and reproduced.[66] A. S. Izgoev, the liberal journalist, criticized both the government's prohibition of a Social Democratic newspaper and the poor condition of the provincial press, but he stated that in St. Petersburg and Moscow during Stolypin's administration newspapers and journals were freer than at the time of Plehve and were able to print what their editors thought. He even saw the beginning of the expression of public opinion.[67]

A good indication of freedom of the press was *Knizhnaya letopis* (Chronicle of Books), a biweekly compilation of books and journal articles. For the years 1907 to 1911, *Knizhnaya letopis* recorded publication of rightist, reactionary works, but also editions of Marx and other socialist writings, as well as a sizable number of books and articles by liberal authors, dealing with such controversial topics as abolition of capital punishment, establishment of constitutional rights, increasing the budget rights of the Duma, criminal punishment for agents provocateur, the Azef affair, the capability of judges, and legality in Russia.[68]

An equally good indication of the status of the press during Stolypin's administration was Izgoev's own book, *Russkoe obshchestvo i revolyutsiya* (Russian Society and Revolution), a critique of the government which would not have been allowed in a condition of strict censorship.

As far as the universities were concerned, those which had been closed due to revolutionary activity on their premises were reopened and granted autonomy during the summer of 1906. The office of inspector, a governmental official who was to supervise the university, was abolished; responsibility for administration and preserving order henceforth was vested in a council of professors called pro-rectors, elected by the faculty from among themselves and confirmed by the Minister of Education.

In his circular of September 1906 Stolypin acknowledged the autonomy of the universities, but gave the police extensive power to supervise and interfere if they suspected revolutionary activity.[69] A ministerial proposal of April-May 1907 again recognized the principle of autonomy in the universities and gave professors authority to judge the lawfulness of student societies and meetings. However, the right of the police to ascertain the legality of these societies and to interfere with or stop their activities also was confirmed.[70]

During 1907 the police arrested several revolutionary groups on university premises. Nevertheless, in the opinion of British observers there was good rapport between the universities and the government until the appointment of A. N. Schwarts to the post of Minister of Education at the end of 1907. Schwarts had been hated in Poland for his repressive policies there. However, Stolypin approved his appointment because he believed the previous Minister of Education, Kaufman, had been too lenient.[71] Some elements of Schwarts' policy, such as clarification of university autonomy, had been discussed in the Council of Ministers during 1907.[72]

After assuming his new post, Schwarts imposed a series of restrictive measures on the universities. In January 1908 he abolished the Institute of Faculty Officers, a student organization. In August 1908 the Council of Ministers approved the issuance of residence permits to students, limiting their places of residence. In September Schwarts initiated the publication of two decrees, one prohibiting female students from attending universities and the other requiring all professors belonging to hostile political associations either to resign their memberships or their faculty positions. Since the Kadet party and all parties to its left were hostile, this struck a powerful blow at the academic community. In October 1908 Schwarts asked the Senate to issue a rule clarifying (and possibly restricting) the autonomy of the universities.[73]

The result was an outburst of student strikes. Schwarts tried to force continuation of lectures, without much success. Students were expelled, several leading professors were dismissed, and general interference in student life continued during 1909, and from 1910 to 1911 under Schwarts' successor, L. A. Kasso.

Was there justification for the strictures which the government put upon the universities? Discussion in the Council of Ministers and British Foreign Office reports from 1907 to 1911 testified to a substantial number of student demonstrations of a revolutionary character, instances of revolutionary activity in student dormitories, and terrorist methods of intimidating students unsympathetic to the revolutionary cause. One of the requirements for joining the Institute of Faculty Officers, the organization suppressed by Schwarts, was profession of extreme left political beliefs; most of the officers of that society were Social Democrats.[74] A middle-of-the-road student, Fedyushin, recalled in an article published in 1914 that the universities also were rent by conflicts between leftist and extreme-right student groups.[75]

In some respects Stolypin seemed to take, a priori, a conservative view toward student participation in politics. In 1908, in an interview with Fedyushin and his student group, he advised students to stay out of politics and emulate German students, whom he had observed in his travels to the West, by professing loyalty to the regime.[76] A bit grumpily, he complained to Sir George Buchanan in 1911 that "the Government . . . could not accord to a number of hot-headed youths the right which no other Russian subject possessed of holding meetings without the sanction of competent authorities." He went on to cite specific instances of questionable activity on the part of university groups: professors' councils allowed meetings to be held "at which subversive doctrines were preached," and revolutionary groups were attempting to "organize a fresh revolutionary movement through the agency of the students." He stated that in his opinion universities were almost the only field left to the "machinations" of the revolutionary groups, as the "peasants were contented and the army would no longer lend an ear to their propaganda." In any case, he believed that the government could not permit the universities to return to the turbulent days of 1905, but he hoped that normalcy would be achieved in a short time.[77]

Despite Stolypin's stern attitude toward university students and faculty, he was not entirely unsympathetic. In 1907 he reproved the Governor of Kiev for closing the university of that city, stipulating that such a measure was to be used only in the gravest cases.[78] Fedyushin portrayed Stolypin as a very warm person who enjoyed personal contact with moderate students.[79] At least one of Schwarts' proposals, the prohibition of women students in universities, contradicted Stolypin's earlier statements on the subject and was cancelled some weeks after it appeared.[80]

In addition to suppressing revolutionary disorder, the government, during Stolypin's administration, undertook some positive measures in the judicial area. A very significant proposal was that on reform of the local courts. Although it had been included in the government program for the Second Duma, it was left unexamined by that body, and thus was introduced to the Third Duma in 1909. This proposal offered great benefit to the peasant in particular. Peasants were to be removed from the jurisdiction of special class *volost'* courts and the *zemskie nachal'niki* and made subject to the regular judicial authorities. According to the proposal, *volost'* courts and the office of *zemskii nachal'nik* were to be abolished, and all jurisdiction for lesser matters was to be trusted to an elected justice of the peace,[81] as before 1889, although in fact the authority of this personage was curtailed somewhat by the existence of exceptional law.

A more limited improvement was the bill on conditional release, passed by the Duma in 1908 and by the State Council in 1909. This provided for release of prisoners before completion of their sentences after certain conditions had been fulfilled. The Minister of Justice happily predicted that the bill would affect from 20,000 to 40,000 of the 178,000 persons then in prison. However, the bill was not to be applied to political prisoners.[82] The condition of the prisons, it might also be noted, was undergoing review in the Council of Ministers' meetings during 1908 and 1909.

In 1906 administrative immunity, which had barred prosecution of officials for criminal acts committed while on duty, was removed, and in 1907 the Council of Ministers approved a bill extending this proposal to lower officials both appointed and elected. Gendarmes, however, were exempt from this regulation,[83] and as noted in the preceding chapter, qualifications somewhat limited the effectiveness of this provision insofar as administrative officials were concerned.

Two abortive proposals indicate that the government was attempting to some extent to implement the guarantee of civil rights promised by the October Manifesto. The most important of these proposals was that on personal inviolability drafted by the Ministry of Internal Affairs. During 1907 Stolypin had assured the Council of Ministers that when this bill on personal inviolability was passed administrative officials would be deprived of their quasi-judicial powers.[84] Throughout the Second Duma period and the first session of the Third Duma, he alluded to the judicial guarantees contained in this bill. When it finally appeared in the Duma in 1909 it met a shocked reception. On the one hand, the proposal established a modicum of civil rights: it specified instances in which police could circumvent judicial authorities in exercising their right of search, required that police have search warrants, and stipulated that persons held under arrest be released within twenty-four hours or brought before judicial authorities. On the other hand, the bill allowed the gendarmerie to retain their right of conducting special inquests (although these were under the supervision of the prosecutor, an official with judicial standing), and most amazing of all, the proposal stated that it was not to be put into effect in areas under exceptional law.[85] As a result, Baron Meyendorff declared that the bill proposed conundrums which could not be solved,[86] and the Duma rejected the bill, terming it paralyzed by its own provisions.[87]

The second abortive proposal was that on deferred punishment, introduced to the Duma at the end of 1909. According to its provisions a person who had committed a first offense, punishable by not more than sixteen months' imprisonment or a fine of not more than 500 rubles, might have his punishment deferred at the discretion of the court. The Kadets and Octobrists approved the bill, but the ministry decided it could not incorporate their amendments that political offenders be allowed deferred punishment, that the offender retain his personal rights during probation, and that the decision to defer punishment be made by a jury.[88] Thus the bill was scuttled.

From this review it appears that Stolypin's policy of repression was, of necessity, somewhat ambivalent. On the one hand, he was committed to forceful suppression of violence in order to preserve the government. On the other hand, he did not wish to institute a police state in Russia. His policies, therefore, fluctuated, at times resulting in greater harshness than at other times. For example, probably one of the worst features of the system was the practice of administrative banishment. In contrast, although the press was restricted, it seems to have been freer than in the past. The confusion also was reflected in the judicial reforms proposed during Stolypin's administration. However, as head of the government during a time of internal stress, it seems that Stolypin had little choice but to forcefully maintain law and order.

Notes

1. Originally printed in *Pravitel'stvennyi vestnik*, reprinted in Great Britain, Public Record Office, Foreign Office (hereafter cited F. O.) 371, vol. 726, no. 21149, June 3, 1909, and *ibid.*, vol. 732, no. 23026, June 15, 1909, p. 5.

2. F. O. 371, vol. 318, no. 578, January 3, 1907; *ibid.*, no. 2263, January 17, 1907; *ibid.*, no. 3774, January 30, 1907; *ibid.*, no. 5245, February 14, 1907.

3. Maria Petrovna von Bock, *Vospominaniya o moem ottse, P. A. Stolypine* (New York: Chekhov Publishing House, 1953), p. 144; Alexandra Stolypine, *L'homme du dernier Tsar* (Paris: Redier, Librairie de la Revue Française, 1931), pp. 58-61.

Maria Bock gave the figures twenty-five killed and thirty wounded. I have used figures cited by later historians.

4. F. O. 371, vol. 128, no. 31315 (no. 492), September 7, 1906.

5. F. O. 371, vol. 128, no. 30508, September 10, 1906.

6, F. O. 371, vol. 126, no. 23116, July 3, 1906; *ibid.,* no. 24878, July 10; F. O. 371, vol. 127, no. 27544, August 6, 1906; *ibid.,* no. 34609, October 1, 1906; F. O. 371, vol. 128, no. 25029, June 28, 1906; *ibid.,* no. 29155, August 15, 1906; F. O. 371, vol. 318, no. 18927, June 6, 1907: F. O. 371, vol. 324, no. 19456, June 12, 1907; *ibid.,* no. 21266, June 24, 1907.

7. Geroid Tanquary Robinson, *Rural Russia Under the Old Regime* (New York: Macmillan, 1961), pp. 176, 203.

8. Bertram D. Wolfe, *Three Who Made a Revolution* (Boston: Beacon Press, 1957), pp. 389, 393.

9. *Gosudarstvennaya Duma: Stenograficheskie otchety,* 1906, sessiya I, zasedanie 23, p. 1129.

10. "Tsirkulyar predsedatelya Soveta Ministrov P. A. Stolypina ot 15 sentyabrya 1906 g. general gubernatoram, gubernatoram i gradonachal'nikam," *Krasnyi arkhiv,* 32 (1929), pp. 163-68.

11. *Ibid.,* pp. 164-74.

12. *Osobyi zhurnal soveta ministrov* (hereafter cited *Osobyi zhurnal;* there were three volumes annually after 1906), 1906, no. 40.

13. "O predostavlenii chinam uezdnoi politseiskoi strazh rukovodstvovat s pravilami, postanovlennymi otnositelno upotrebleniya oruzhiya voiskami pri podavlenii bezporyadkov," *Osobyi zhurnal,* 1906, no. 186, p. 2.

14. The law establishing the courts-martial is contained in *Polnoe sobranie zakonov Rossiikoi imperii, Sobranie tretie,* March 1, 1891-December 31. 1913 (St. Petersburg, 1906), p. 184, Law no. 28255.

15. Alfred Levin, *The Second Duma* (New Haven: Yale University Press, 1940), p. 262.

16. "Po voprosu ob uchrezhdenii voenno-polevykh sudov," *Osobyi zhurnal,* 1906, no. 27.

17. Vladimir Iosifovich Gurko, *Features and Figures of the Past,* trans. Laura Matveev (Stanford, California: Stanford University Press, 1939), p. 499.

18. "Perepiska N. A. Romanova i P. A. Stolypina," *Krasnyi arkhiv,* 5 (1924), 103-104. The Tsar emphasized his issuance of the previous July 9 which had announced that violators of the law would be subjected to the Tsar's will.

19. Quoted in P. A. Tverskoi, "K istoricheskim materialam o pokoinom P. A. Stolypinim," *Vestnik evropy,* no. 4 (April 1912), p. 188.

20. *Ibid.*

21. "Perepiska N. A. Romanova i P. A. Stolypina," *Krasnyi arkhiv,* 5, p. 105.

22. F. O. 371, vol. 519, no. 44381 (no. 584), December 14. During a defense of gendarme investigation in 1907, Stolypin stated unequivocally that the rights of the individual must yield when they conflicted with the rights of the state. "O dopolnenii deistvuyushchikh postanovlenii ustava o voinskoi povinnosti," *Osobyi zhurnal,* 1907, vol. 2, no. 226, pp. 4-5.

23. Quoted in French in F. O. 371, vol. 127, no. 26844 (no. 482), July 26. 1906.

24. "Tsirkulyaṭ predsedatelya Soveta Ministrov P. A. Stolypina ot 15 sentyabrya 1906 g. general gubernatoram, gubernatoram i gradonachal'nikam," *Krasnyi arkhiv,* 32, p. 167.

25. Quoted in P. A. Tverskoi, "K istoricheskim materialam o pokoinom P. A. Stolypinim," *Vestnik evropy*, no. 4, pp. 195-96.

26. Aleksei Andreevich Polivanov, *Iz dnevnikov i vospominanii po dolzhnosti voennogo ministra i ego pomoshchika, 1907-1916* (Moscow: Vyshii voennyi redaktsionnyi sovet, 1924), pp. 18-19.

27. *Osobyi zhurnal*, 1907, vol. 1., no. 55, February 9.

28. F. O. 371, vol. 513, no. 23188, July 1, 1908; *ibid.*, no. 33408, September 28, 1908; F. O. 371, vol. 726, no. 37482, October 7, 1909; F. O. 371, vol. 732, no. 26021, July 8, 1909.

29. Moscow was moved to the lightest form of exceptional law, reinforced protection, in July 1909. St. Petersburg remained in the state of extraordinary protection. F. O. 371, vol. 726, no. 17581, May 6, 1909; F. O. 371, vol. 732, no. 28887, July 22, 1909.

30. "O preobrazovanii mestnago suda," *Osobyi zhurnal*, 1907, vol. 1, no. 38, January 19 and 23, pp. 6-7; "Po proektu isklyuchitelnago polozheniya," *Osobyi zhurnal*, 1907, vol. 1, no. 49, February 2 and 6, p. 3.

31. "Po proektu isklyuchitelnago polozheniya," *Osobyi zhurnal*, 1907, vol. 1, no. 49, pp. 2-4; F. O. 371, vol. 732, no. 23026, July 15, 1909.

32. *Ibid.*

33. F. O. 371, vol. 513, no. 25035, July 15, 1908. As an example of administrative banishment, we may cite the case of Mme. Perelishin, wife of a marshal of nobility in Kostroma, who was exiled for gathering her peasants to talk on nonpolitical matters. Sir Bernard Pares in F. O. 371, vol. 512, no. 30901, September 4, 1908, p. 9.

34. Richard Seymour in F. O. 371, vol. 513, no. 14255, April 22, 1908. The statistics were provided by the Department of Police.

35. F. O. 371, vol. 979, no. 8697, March 6, 1910. The statistics, obtained from Zuev, director of the Department of Police, were included in the budget request of the Ministry of Internal Affairs.

36. F. O. 371, vol. 726, no. 37482, October 7.

37. F. O. 371, vol. 732, no. 23026, July 15.

38. Izvolsky to Nicolson, quoted in F. O. 371, vol. 513, no. 31318, September 7, 1908; Guchkov, quoted in F. O. 371, vol. 128, no. 31324, September 10, 1906; Nicolson, in F. O. 371, vol. 318, no. 571, January 1, 1907.

39. F. O. 371, vol. 513, no. 30065, August 26; *ibid.*, vol. 512, no. 25036, July 16. Other critics included Maklakov (Kadet) and Uvarov (Octobrist), F. O. 371, vol. 512, no. 17775, May 18, 1908, and Leo Tolstoy and others in the Duma, F. O. 371, vol. 513, no. 28449, August 14, 1908.

40. F. O. 371, vol. 726, no. 9777, March 11. The moderate right was composed mainly of Octobrists.

41. F. O. 371, vol. 519, no. 44381 (no. 584), December 14, 1908.

42. "Pismo P. A. Stolypina na imya Nikolaya Nikolaevicha ot 10 fevralya 1908 g.," *Krasnyi arkhiv*, 19 (1926), pp. 217-21.

43. *Ibid.*, p. 220. Prince Nikolai Nikolaevich was the commander of the St. Petersburg military district.

44. *Ibid.*

45. Ministerstvo vnutrennikh del. Department politsii. Proekty i predpolozheniya. Bill no. 56956, November 1, 1907, pp. 1-4. Also, Bill no. 54246, August 8, 1909, "Ob assignovanii v rasporyazhenie Ministra vnutrennikh del na 1910, 250,000 r. na vydachu posobii chinam politsii obshchei politsii i otdelnago korpusa zhandarmov."

46. *Osobyi zhurnal*, 1908, vol. 3, no. 311, October 21, p. 2.

47. 1908: F. O. 371, vol. 513, no. 12600, April 8; *ibid.*, no. 14255, April 22; Pares,

in *ibid.*, vol. 512, no. 30901, September 4, p. 10; *ibid.*, vol. 513, no. 31810, September; *ibid.*, vol. 513, no. 23408, September 23; *ibid.*, no. 37068, October 28; *ibid.*, no. 38892, November.

1909: F. O. 371, vol. 726, no. 2214, January 14; *ibid.*, no. 13608, April 8.

48. Nicolson, in F. O. 371, vol. 726, no. 21149, June 3, 1909; corroborated, F. O. 371, vol. 732, no. 23026, June 15, 1909.

49. *Knizhnaya letopis* (St. Petersburg: Glavnago upravleniya po delam pechati), 1909-1910, *passim.* The *Knizhnaya letopis* was a biweekly compilation of books and journal articles recently published.

50. Sir George Buchanan, in F. O. 371, vol. 1213, no. 9071, March 6, 1911.

51. "Dnevnik A. A. Bobrinskogo," *Krasnyi arkhiv,* 26 (1928), pp. 140-41, 3, 5, 9 dekabrya.

52. "Po proektu isklyuchitelnago polozheniya," *Osobyi zhurnal,* 1907, vol. 1, no. 49, p. 1.

53. "O preobrazovanii mestnago suda," *Osobyi zhurnal,* 1907, vol. 1, no. 38, pp. 9-12.

54. *Ibid.*, pp. 8-9. The rest of the ministry supported Stolypin, affirming the expeditiousness of the measure. Although in some aspects they made the provisions of the bill slightly more lenient, in others they strengthened it.

55. Quoted in F. O. 371, vol. 732, no. 34767, September 4, 1909.

56. F. O. 371, vol. 726, no. 34157, September 9, 1909. In that year the governor generalship of the Baltic provinces also was abolished. *Osobyi zhurnal,* 1909, vol. 1, no. 29.

57. "Tsirkulyarnoe obrashchenie P. A. Stolypina k gubernatoram i gradonachal'nikam—o stremleniyakh tsentral'noi vlasti v otnoshenii vnutrennei politiki," *Gosudarstvennaya deyatel'nost' predsedatelya soveta ministrov, stats sekretarya, Petra Arkad'evicha Stolypina,* ed. E. Verpakhovsky (St. Petersburg: Izdanie sostavitelya, 1911), part 1, pp. 52-54.

58. Tsirkulyar predsedatelya Soveta Ministrov P. A. Stolypina ot 15 sentyabrya 1906 g. general gubernatoram, gubernatoram i gradonachal'nikam," *Krasnyi arkhiv,* 32, pp. 179-80.

59. "Ob ustanovlenii ugolovnoi otvetstvennosti za voskhvalenie prestuplenykh deyanii v rechi ili pechati," *Osobyi zhurnal,* 1906, no. 159, December 1, p. 5.

60. *Osobyi zhurnal,* 1908, vol. 3, no. 91, March 11.

61. F. O. 371, vol. 513, no. 26870, July 29, 1908; *ibid.*, vol. 726, no. 4150, January 28, 1909; *ibid.*, no. 23081, June 17, 1909.

62. F. O. 371, vol. 318, no. 20735, June 20, 1907; *ibid.*, vol. 513, no. 28449, August 14, 1908; *ibid.*, vol. 1213, no. 56, December 28, 1910. The crisis of April 1909 will be discussed below in chapter 6, pp. 167-68.

63. F. O. 371, vol. 976, no. 159, February 2, 1910.

64. F. O. 371, vol. 726, no. 28892, July 29, 1909.

65. *Gosudarstvennaya Duma: Stenograficheskie otchety,* tretii sozyv, sessiya II, zasedanie 36, January 20, 1909.

66. Nicolson, in F. O. 371, vol. 732, no. 23026, June 15, 1909.

67. *Russkoe obshchestvo i revolyutsiya* (Moscow: Izdanie zhurnala "Russkaya mysl," Tovarishchesto tipografii A. I. Mamontova, 1910), pp. 103-104.

68. *Knizhnaya letopis, passim.*

69. "Tsirkulyar predsedatelya Soveta Ministrov P. A. Stolypina ot 15 sentyabrya 1906 g. general gubernatoram, gubernatoram i gradonachal'nikam," *Krasnyi arkhiv,* 32, pp. 177-78.

70. "Po proektu pravil o studencheskikh organizatsiyakh i ob ustroistve sobranii v stenakh vysshikh uchebnykh zavedenii," *Osobyi zhurnal,* 1907, vol. 1, no. 162, April 19 and May 29.

71. "Iz perepiski P. A. Stolypina s Nikolaem Romanovam," *Krasnyi arkhiv,* 30 (1928), p. 81; "Perepiska N. A. Romanova i P. A. Stolypina," *Krasnyi arkhiv,* 5, p. 117. Both letters are dated December 22, 1907.

72. "Po proektu pravil o studencheskikh organizatsiyakh i ob ustroistve sobranii v stenakh vysshikh uchebnykh zavedenii," *Osobyi zhurnal,* 1907, vol. 1, pp. 2-8.

73. F. O. 371, vol. 513, no. 8956, March 11, 1908; *ibid.,* no. 28449, August 14, 1908; *ibid.,* no. 33408, September 23, 1908; *ibid.,* 35230, October 8, 1908; *Osobyi zhurnal,* 1908, vol. 3, no. 225, August 12.

Alexander Nikolaevich Schwarts was lecturer at Moscow University for some time after 1875. In 1900, he become *popechitel'* or trustee of the Riga school district. Shortly thereafter, until his appointment as Minister of Education, he served as trustee of the Warsaw school district.

74. In March 1907 Stolypin complained to the Council of Ministers of revolutionary activity in student dormitories, and although he stressed that the universities had been granted autonomy, he presented a proposal which would impress upon rectors their duty to eliminate such activity and tighten police control over dormitories. "Obizdanii pravil dlya podderzhaniya poryadka v obshchezhitiyakh pri uchebnykh zavedeniyakh," *Osobyi zhurnal,* 1907, vol. 1, no. 95, March 3 and 16, pp. 1-2.

On December 16, 1910, the Council of Ministers agreed to repress the disorders in the higher educational institutions in Odessa with all severity. Polivanov, *Iz dnevnikov i vospominannii po dolzhnosti voennogo ministra i ego pomoshchika,* p. 10; "Po proektu pravil o studencheskikh organizatsiyakh i ob ustroistve sobranii v stenakh vysshikh uchebnykh zavedenii," *Osobyi zhurnal,* 1907, vol. 1, no. 162, p. 5; Gurko, *Features and Figures of the Past,* p. 419.

For the British assessment of student revolutionary activity: 1907: F. O. 371, vol. 318, no. 17054, May 23; *ibid.,* no. 26798, August 15; *ibid.,* no. 40302, December 18. 1908: F. O. 371, vol. 513, no. 7145, February 26; Rowland Smith, in *ibid.,* no. 8956, March 11; *ibid.,* no. 10741, March 25; *ibid.,* no. 33396, September 19; Nicolson, in *ibid.,* no. 35230, October 8. 1909: Garnett, in F. O. 371, vol. 726, no. 39168, October 21. 1910: F. O. 371, vol. 981, no. 43984, November 30. 1911: Buchanan, in F. O. 371, vol. 1213, no. 56, December 28, 1910; Buchanan, in *ibid.,* no. 9071, March 6, 1911.

A student version of the problem in the universities is given by K. Fedyushin, "Petr Arkad'evich Stolypin i studenty," *Istoricheskii vestnik,* no. 5 (May 1914), pp. 534-35.

75. Fedyushin, "Petr Arkad'evich Stolypin i studenty," *Istoricheskii vestnik,* no. 5, p. 536.

76. *Ibid.,* p. 534.

77. As quoted in F. O. 371, vol. 1213, no. 9071, March 6, 1911.

78. "Po voprosu o zakrytii vysshikh uchebnykh zavedenii kak meri bor'bu s studencheskimi bezporyadkami," *Osobyi zhurnal,* 1907, vol. 2, no. 328, November 9.

79. Fedyushin, "Petr Arkad'evich Stolypin i studenty," *Istoricheskii vestnik,* no. 5, pp. 533-35.

80. F. O. 371, vol. 513, no. 40797, November 23, 1908.

81. "O preobrazovanii mestnago suda," *Osobyi zhurnal,* 1908, vol. 1, pp. 2-4.

82. F. O. 371, vol. 512, no. 10742, March 26, 1908; *ibid.,* no. 21300, June 8, 1908; F. O. 371, vol. 726, no. 7977, February 25, 1909.

83. "Ob izmenenii poryadka proizvodstva del o prestuplenykh deyaniakh po sluzhbe," *Osobyi zhurnal,* 1907, vol. 1, February 9.

84. "O preobrazovanii mestnago suda," *Osobyi zhurnal,* 1907, vol. 1, p. 9.

85. *Gosudarstvennaya Duma: Stenograficheskie otchety,* Tretii sozyv, sessiya III, zasedanie 17, November 13, 1909, cols. 1863-1866.

86. F. O. 371, vol. 726, no. 44314, December 2, 1909.

87. The Duma sent the bill to a committee but it never reappeared. F. O. 371, vol. 726, no. 45982, December 20, 1909.

88. F. O. 371, vol. 726, no. 42641, November 18, 1909.

Chapter 5:
Stolypin and the Non-Russian
Nationalities of the Empire

As Minister of Internal Affairs, Stolypin had special jurisdiction over the non-Russian nationalities of the empire. Excluding the Jews, who have been discussed in a preceding chapter, the chief non-Russian nationalities within the empire were the Poles, the Finns, and the Caucasian peoples.

There are several commonly repeated appraisals of Stolypin's nationality policy which do not bear up under scrutiny. One is that his policy was somehow unjustified. Another is that it was oppressive for the non-Russian nationalities which it affected. A third is that it was devised to gain the support of the Nationalist party, a fairly strong, conservative power bloc in the State Duma, the State Council, and the country at large, which developed after 1908 and 1909 and whose support Stolypin needed after he lost that of more middle-of-the-road groups at about the same time.

Actually, Stolypin's nationality policy, save for one measure,[1] was neither unreasonable, nor unduly harsh. Furthermore, it was not devised to appeal to the Nationalist party, for Stolypin was adamantly concerned about fostering Russian interests in the borderlands as early as 1907. His program simply coincided with the thinking of a vociferous segment of the Russian population.

Basically, Stolypin viewed the position of the non-Russian nationalities with the same cold realism with which he appraised his relationship to the Tsar. First, he considered the Caucasus, Finland, even

Poland, parts of the empire for all practical purposes. The people inhabiting these areas thus were subject to the authority of the Russian government within the boundaries prescribed by law. In the event that the relationship between the non-Russian peoples and the Russian government were not spelled out, ultimate authority rested with the Russian government as a result of its sovereignty. The inhabitants of the borderlands, if historically Russian, and the area itself, since it constituted historically Russian soil, were even more closely tied to the central government. Since the empire was a Russian empire, Russian interests must be protected and a certain amount of universality of language, education, and military and governmental organization must be preserved or, in some cases, enforced where it had not been. Second, in his opinion his policies were a reaction to increasing nationalism, even anti-Russian tendencies, on the part of the non-Russian peoples of the empire. In other words, to him his policies were self-defensive.

In some cases Stolypin overreacted to the threat to the empire's integrity, in some cases he did not. But his imperialistic and chauvinistic outlook was both logical and characteristic of the age in which he lived. Indeed, he justified the Russian government's authority over Finland, in particular, by examples of the contemporaneous colonialism or imperialism practiced by western European countries. Even so, Stolypin's treatment of the national groups varied as to whether they lived on ancient Russian land (the Poles in the western provinces), whether they once had existed as an independent state (the Poles in Poland), whether they had always existed and been conquered by Russia as the province of another country (the Finns), or whether the people in question were engaged in indiscriminate violence (the Caucasian peoples).

The Poles in Tsarist Poland

Russia had acquired portions of Poland in the partitions of the late eighteenth century. In 1815 at the Congress of Vienna she received roughly four-fifth's of Prussian Poland, which was christened the Kingdom of Poland or the Congress Kingdom. The kingdom enjoyed a certain amount of autonomy, with separate governmental institutions and an army, until 1832. At that time, owing to the insurrection of 1830-31, the Poles lost their army and the ringleaders of the revolt suffered reprisals, although to a large extent the Poles retained control of their separate governing bodies. After the insurrection of 1863, the special governmental institutions were abolished; the Russian judicial system of 1864, minus the institution of the jury, was introduced; and the University of Warsaw, which had been restored to the Poles during the hectic months of the early '60s, was made a Russian institution. The Catholic church was curtailed. The peasants benefited, receiving freeholds for which they made no direct redemption payments, as did the peasants in the empire.[2] Polish nobles after 1864 put aside for a generation hopes and plans for independence, and concentrated on economic improvement. In the early twentieth century the population of Poland was over 11 million.

Stolypin adopted a carrot and stick policy toward the Poles in Tsarist Poland, or Privislinskii *krai* as he termed it. On the one hand, the government met the unrest in Poland, which had flared up in 1905 and continued through 1908,[3] with strong measures. Martial law was imposed. The Polish School Association (Maciez Polska) was closed by the governor general in late 1907. As a result, Poles boycotted Russian schools and attacked students and professors of Russian schools in Warsaw.[4] In late 1908 Polish schools were closed for several days.[5] Polish representation in the Russian State Duma was reduced by the electoral law of June 3, 1907.[6]

On the other hand, although Stolypin regarded Poland as part of the empire, he recognized the separateness of Polish culture. He intended to institute self-government in Poland in the summer of 1906, in line with improvements planned for the internal provinces.[7] The Council of Ministers referred to plans for the introduction of zemstvos into Poland until 1909. At that time the idea was discarded. However, in the fall of 1909 Stolypin brought to the *Sovet po delam mestnago khozyaistva* for discussion a proposal for the implementation of municipal self-government in Poland. He referred to the bill as giving Polish cities "the full dimension of the rights of self-government which Russian cities possessed," due the Poles because of "their distinctive culture." However, this self-government, Stolypin warned, was not to be turned into a "weapon of political struggle or a means of attaining political autonomy," but was to be subordinate to the "Russian state idea."[8]

The 1909 version of the bill did not contain the anti-Polish and anti-Jewish provisions included in the law passed by the Duma in 1913. In Stolypin's original bill both the Polish and the Russian language were to be allowed for internal business; Russian was required for communication with the Russian government. Jews were not to be disenfranchised, although Jewish representation was limited. Voters in municipal elections were to be organized in three curiae: Russian, Jewish, and other. Jews were allowed only one-fifth of the representation in the municipal duma, despite the fact that they constituted a majority of the urban population. Stolypin explained unabashedly that these provisions were necessary in order to prevent Jews from predominating in the city administration.[9]

Although Stolypin's Polish municipal government bill discriminated unfairly against Jews, its provisions for insuring Russian representation were not unjust. Since suffrage qualifications were based on property and payment of city taxes, and since Russians in Poland did not usually own land, the bill permitted apartment renters the right to vote after paying a city tax.[10] In fact, this measure was very similar to one proposed in Stolypin's municipal government bill of 1907 for the internal provinces.

The Poles in the Western Provinces

To the east of Poland lay the western provinces of Russia: Kovno, Vilna, Grodno, Minsk, Mogilev, Vitebsk, Volhynia, Podolia, and Kiev, with a combined population of about 21 million. This region occupied the same position in Russo-Polish relations as did Alsace-Lorraine between Germany and France. If anything, the situation was more confused due to a greater multiplicity of languages and religions.

Throughout the Kievan era the area had been governed by Russian princes and was, therefore, part of the loosely federated Kievan Russian state. But Lithuanian and Polish rulers began acquiring the territory in the fourteenth century, during the last period of Mongol rule. When Russia regained control over the territory in the eighteenth century, it had been a part of Lithuania-Poland for several centuries, and Polish language and customs and the Catholic religion had exerted great influence.

In the early twentieth century the western provinces were extremely heterogeneous in terms of language, religion, and national consciousness. Poles were a definite minority in all these provinces according to statistics of the 1897 census based on mother tongue (see appendix to this chapter). They amounted to no more than 10 percent of the total population in any province. So-called Great Russians also were in the minority, amounting to no more than 13 percent of the population in

Vitebsk, the province of their greatest concentration. Lithuanians amounted to 68 percent of the population in Kovno and 17 percent in Vilensk. Ukrainians enormously predominated in Volhynia, Kiev, and Podolia, their percentage of the population in these provinces ranging from 70 to 80 percent. Belorussians predominanted in Minsk, Mogilev, Vitebsk, and Vilensk and amounted to 44 percent of the population of Grodno. Jews comprised from 12 to 17 percent of the population of all the provinces. Germans amounted to over 5 percent of the population of Volhynia and a tiny fraction of the population of Kovno.[11]

The policy which Stolypin formulated for the western provinces reflected his tripartite appraisal of the situation. He believed that, first, the territory and the Belorussian and Ukrainian population of these areas were historically Russian; second, the Poles wielded (and would continue to wield, if zemstvos were introduced) extraordinary economic and political power in relation to their percentage in the population; and third, the Poles were attempting to Polonize the western provinces, to increase their cultural influence and wean the populace from the Russian government, an attempt which the Russian government must suppress. Stolypin's object was to contain or decrease Polish influence and to simultaneously strengthen Russian influence in response to Polish aggressiveness. His policy, thus, was a response to Polish dominance or Polish threats to the integrity of the empire—to him not an aggressive policy. Furthermore, it was mitigated by two further considerations. Stolypin maintained he was not hostile to Poles per se[12] and recalled his close relationship with Poles while Governor of Grodno to prove his contention. In addition, he sensibly realized that the government needed the wealth and expertise of the Polish magnates in the western provinces and his proposals for these provinces were adapted accordingly.[13]

Stolypin sponsored three bills affecting the Poles in the Polish-Russian borderlands. One, the Kholm province bill, was almost totally unjustified. The other two measures, the bill to prolong the terms of members of the State Council from the nine western provinces and the zemstvo bill for the six southwestern provinces, were in no way unfair to the Poles in these areas.

In the Kholm province bill, the government proposed to divorce the eastern *uezdy* of Sedletsk and Lyublinsk provinces of Tsarist Poland and unite them more firmly with western Russia. The proposal had justification only on the basis of Russian settlement of the area during the Kievan period. It had very little or no justification on the basis of the ethnic groups then existing in the region.

A proposal to form a separate Kholm province from the eastern *uezdy* of Sedletsk and Lyublinsk provinces had first been raised after the Polish revolt of 1863. The question was reopened in 1902, but left undecided. Among the Orthodox in the area there was a feeling that the October Manifesto gave the Catholic church a stronger position than it had had formerly, and in late 1905 some 50,000 Orthodox signed a petition, brought to the Tsar by a delegation led by a bishop, asking for the formation of a special Kholm province, and if this were infeasible, annexation of the Kholm area to Grodno and Volhynia provinces. The request was left in abeyance by the Council of Ministers when it was discussed in the spring of 1906.[14]

In the proposal which Stolypin introduced for discussion by the Council of Ministers in January 1907, the eastern *uezdy* of Sedletsk and Lyublinsk provinces were to be joined to contiguous Russian provinces. In the 1909 proposal, a special Kholm province was to be created from these *uezdy*. Otherwise, the terms of both proposals were similar. The new Russian area was clearly a hybrid. It was to remain in the Warsaw military district, and the Napoleonic civil law code and criminal court procedure without sworn witnesses were to be retained. Taxation also was to remain on the tax foundations of Privislinskii *krai*. The justice-of-the-peace courts, however, were to be subordinate to the district courts of Vilensk and Kiev *gubernii*, and the city administration and other administrative institutions were to be subordinate to the governors and administrative agencies of Grodno and Volhynia *gubernii*. The Julian calendar was to be restored, and the Kholm episcopal see was to retain its present boundaries.[15]

These terms were included in the 1909 version of the project. In addition, in the 1909 bill it was stipulated that schools in the area were to be put under the Kiev school district; there were certain discriminatory regulations against Poles acquiring land; and there were provisions for special privileges for would-be Russian landowners and for peasants transferring from Polish to Russian estates.[16]

Although it has been claimed that Stolypin's nationalistic policies resulted from an attempt to secure the support of conservative elements after the ministerial crisis of 1909,[17] his most vigorous defense of the Kholm proposal in the Council of Ministers occured in 1907. He insisted that the government had to separate the Kholm area from Tsarist Poland for two reasons, first, because the Poles were inundating the inhabitants with Polish-Catholic propaganda, trying to destroy national consciousness in Russians who were living in what was ancient Russian land, and second, since the ministry was planning to institute zemstvos in Tsarist Poland, if the Kholm area were not removed from Poland, its Russian inhabitants would be subordinated politically as well as economically to Polish influence. He considered the matter so urgent that he suggested that it be enacted under the terms of article 87 of the Fundamental Laws while the Duma and the State Council were not in session.[18]

Justification for the Kholm province proposal was not very sound. For example, while the Council of Ministers insisted that by scrupulously dividing *uezdy* only those areas predominantly Russian on the basis of language and religion would be included in the new province, in actuality in the new Kholm province there were destined to be more Catholic (310,677) than Orthodox (304,885), as well as 114,410 Jews and 28,436 others.[19] The ministry dismissed this problem with the theory that perhaps as many as one-third of the Catholics in the area had been coerced into joining that religion and would probably return to the Orthodox church when again on Russian soil. Even if they did not, the ministry claimed that by "tribal descent" and language they were Russian, and thus had only their religion in common with the Poles.[20]

The second justification for the proposal was that it was a prelude to the instituting of zemstvos in Tsarist Poland.[21] This argument was destroyed when the ministry decided in 1909 to postpone the introduction of zemstvos.

Did the vulnerability of Poland in the event of war with Germany affect the government's policy toward the Kholm region? In December 1908 the British consul in Warsaw reported that there was great concern in local papers about the increase and new political character of German colonization in Poland, particularly in the western provinces near the German border. Although there had always been German settlers in Poland, the new colonists appeared to have taken possession of the best rivers, the largest fortresses, and the most important towns and railroads. Indeed, *Deutsche Erde* had commented that "these German colonies in Poland ought to be the subject of our most tender care." According to the consul, the Governor General of Poland had remarked that if Germany invaded Poland Russia would not be able to defend it. Existing fortresses in Poland were obsolete and the Russians would be forced to retire behind the Kovno-Brest line of fortresses. It was also alleged that the Polish leader Dmowski believed that Poland would be the objective of a hostile move by Germany.[22]

The Kholm proposal, of course, antedated the foregoing report, and there is no statement by Stolypin or by the ministry on the necessity to divorce the Kholm area from Poland because of possible German occupation of Poland. Nevertheless, Stolypin and the government were apprehensive about German colonization in the western Russian provinces, if not in Poland proper. In October 1910 Stolypin presented the Duma with a government proposal prohibiting land buying by foreigners in Volhynia, Podolia, and Kiev. The preface of the proposal stated that, whereas in 1860 there were 2,443 foreign families in these provinces, by 1890 there were 200,000 foreigners, due to an increase of colonization during these years amounting to 128 percent. German colonists in Volhynia alone, according to the proposal, held 1,890,000 acres, or 12 percent of the nonmunicipal land in the province. The government stated that in view of the facts cited it had designed the bill to protect the southwestern frontier provinces from a "peaceful invasion."[23]

In contradistinction to the Kholm province proposal, two other proposals affecting Poles in the western Russian provinces were eminently reasonable, insofar as the Poles were concerned. The first of these was the proposal to prolong the terms of representatives from the western provinces to the State Council; the second was the zemstvo bill.

The bill to alter representation from the western provinces in the State Council originated with thirty-three council Nationalists led by D. I. Pikhno. The Nationlist party had been formed in 1908-1909. Its party platform contained many progressive ideas, such as maintenance of a representative form of government, supervision of the administrative sector by the Duma and the State Council, reform of the law courts, improvement of peasant and general agricultural conditions, and the establishment of old age pensions and working-men's compensation. It also stressed the "unity and indivisibility of the Russian Empire and predominance of Great Russians in all parts of the Empire," reinforcement of the country's military strength, freedom of belief but supremacy of the Orthodox church, extension of Great Russian interests, universal education based on "religion and patriotism," and continuation of the disabilities on the Jews.[24]

By 1910 the Nationalists numbered 105 in the Duma and when cooperating with the Octobrists formed an almost certain majority.[25] In the opinion of British observers in Russia they were the only serious contenders against the right and far right parties for influence over the Tsar. D. I. Pikhno apparently enjoyed Nicholas' special favor; in

1907 he had been recommended for a post as assistant minister. It was also rumored that Nicholas read with special interest the Nationalist paper the *Kievlyanin.*[26]

It is difficult to ascertain how much influence the Nationalists had upon Stolypin's policy.[27] Stolypin's defense of the Kholm province proposal in 1907 showed a concern for promoting Russian interest in the western borderlands and historically Russian territory dating before the advent of the Nationalist party. However, Stolypin subsidized the party, spoke with gratification of its support of the government in 1910,[28] and accepted the Nationalist proposal for introducing Russian representation into the delegation to the State Council from the western provinces.[29]

The Nationalists had a great deal of justification for asking for change in the representation in the State Council from the western provinces. As Stolypin emphasized in speeches to the Duma in 1909 and 1910, Poles constituted only about 4 percent of the total population in the nine western provinces and from 1.03 to 6.16 percent in the six southwestern provinces. Yet all nine representatives to the State Council from the western provinces were Poles, a situation which he considered "abnormal and unjust."[30]

The Nationalists had proposed that the western area be divided into three sections, each section electing one Polish and two Russian members of the State Council. Stolypin preferred to institute zemstvos in which representation would be weighted in favor of the Russian population. Elections to the State Council were to be held on the same bases as to the zemstvos, thus insuring Russian representation. It was estimated that implementation of zemstvos would take about one year. For this reason, the Ministry of Internal Affairs proposed that the terms of present members of the State Council be postponed for one year.[31] The Duma finally accepted the proposal after substituting the clause, "elections will be called after one year."[32]

Stolypin justified the practice of prolonging terms of members of representative bodies by examples from eighteenth century England, nineteenth century France, and turn-of-the-century Russia. The project itself he termed necessary to aid the 15 million Russians in the area.[33]

The western zemstvo bill marked the culmination of Stolypin's Polish policy, though the bill did not originate with Stolypin. The idea of introducing zemstvos into the western provinces had been discussed in government circles since their institution in the internal provinces in the 1860s. The topic had been raised in the meetings of the Grodno

committee for the needs of local agricultural industry, over which
Stolypin presided as governor in 1902-1903. At that time, it will be
recalled, he had squelched discussion of the issue on the grounds that
it was not among the topics which the committee had been charged to
consider.

By an ukase of April 2, 1903, quasi-zemstvos had been instituted in
the six southwestern provinces. These were called the *gubernskie
komitety* and *upravy po zemskogo khozyaistva.* The members were
appointed by the government and were considered personnel of the
Ministry of Internal Affairs. The work of these quasi-zemstvos was
the same as that of the zemstvos in the internal provinces and their
budget struggles with the Ministry of Finance were also identical.[34]
Due to their organization, however, the "zemstvos" on the provincial
level played the key roles in these western provinces, whereas the *uezd*
zemstvo was the most vital zemstvo institution in the internal
provinces.

Despite the success of many of their undertakings, according to
Professor A. V. Zenkovsky, head of the economic and accounting
section of the Kiev *guberniya* "zemstvo," members of the quasi-
zemstvo organizations of the southwestern provinces desired elected
zemstvos. However, the bulk of the large landowners in the area were
Polish and would predominate in the new zemstvos if the electoral
qualifications established for the zemstvos in the internal provinces
were used. Thus, according to Zenkovsky, the members of the quasi-
zemstvos desired lower property qualifications and separate Polish
curiae.[35] In 1906, according to Stolypin, Kryzhvitskii, the governor
general of the northwest *krai,* brought him a petition from the
populace asking for the introduction of zemstvos into that area.[36]

In 1904 the ministry began working on a bill for the establishment
of zemstvos in the western provinces. It was almost enacted in 1906,
under the terms of article 87 of the Fundamental State Laws.[37] The
Octobrist and rightist factions in the Duma presented petitions for
elective zemstvos in the western provinces in May and June 1908, and
the question arose again in the Duma during a discussion on the
introduction of zemstvos into Siberia and the Caucasus in 1909. The
ministry began working out the final version of the western zemstvo
bill during the summer of 1909.[38]

According to the bill, which was finally presented to the Duma in
1910, zemstvos were to be introduced into the six southwestern
provinces. They were not to be introduced into the three northwestern
provinces because there was a dearth of Russians there. The zemstvos

were to be classless, but electors were to be divided into two curiae, Polish and non-Polish. The percentage of representation allotted to each group was decided by adding the percentage of land held by the group to its percentage in the population and dividing the sum by two. The amount of land or other immovable property required for voting was lowered by one-half, giving the possibility of increased representation to peasant smallholders, though not to communal peasants, whose representation was limited to one-third of the *uezd* zemstvo and who were excluded from the provincial zemstvo. The majority of the *uprava* or "executive board" of the zemstvo could not be Polish and the chairman of the school board was required to be Russian. Certain officials (the local chairman of the Department of State Domains, the local manager of the Peasant Bank or officials empowered by him, and representatives from the Holy Synod) were barred from the zemstvo chairmanship or from participation in the *uprava*. Members of the clergy were permitted to vote in zemstvo elections, but Jews could neither vote nor be elected.[39]

Although the western zemstvos, according to this proposal, were to have a nationalistic character not present in the internal zemstvos, the proposal was more than generous to the Poles, being as they were in an absolute minority in the southwestern provinces.[40] In fact, Stolypin revealed that at one time the government had considered proportional representation in the western zemstvos, which would have reduced Polish representation considerably, compared to that provided by the zemstvo bill. The government had abandoned the idea of proportional representation, however, because it might possibly lead to a "flare up of old national hatreds" and also because it would deprive the zemstvos of cultured elements.[41] (It will be recalled that democratization of the zemstvos—while preserving the influence of "cultured" members—was also a problem for Stolypin with regard to the internal provinces.)

Stolypin's defense of the zemstvo bill in the *Sovet po delam mestnago khozyaistva* in October 1909 emphasized the by now familiar theme that, although Russians predominated numerically in the southwestern provinces (it was clear from this that Stolypin regarded Ukrainians as historically Russian), Poles predominated economically, thus necessitating government protection of the Russians.[42] His defense of the zemstvo bill in the Duma in 1910 sounded the equally familiar corollary that the bill was an antidote for Polonization in ancient Russian lands which had been taken by the Poles in the fourteenth century. He admitted that harsh measures had been levelled on the Poles during the time of Catherine II and Alexander II after the revolution of 1863. However, during the reign of the present Tsar, Stolypin claimed, the government had proffered friendship to the Poles living in the area, and the Poles had spurned this and had engaged in nationalistic disturbances led by priests, particularly by Bishop Ropp (Stolypin's former friend). The bishop had spoken openly about "forming a regiment of the local inhabitants . . . [and] about autonomy not only for Tsarist Poland, but for other regions. Polish societies had begun quickly to paint the western *krai* in Polish colors. Agricultural societies turned into Polish societies . . . it was stated that Polish culture was superior to Russian and that Poles enjoyed a special position in the southwest *krai.*"[43] Russian landowners who attempted to cooperate with the Poles and petitioned that restrictions on them be abolished were repudiated by the Poles.[44]

The zemstvo bill affected primarily Polish magnates, a fact which led the Soviet historian A. Ya. Avrekh to argue convincingly that Stolypin promoted the zemstvo bill not only for nationalistic purposes, but to bolster peasant smallholders in the area.[45] His thesis is substantiated by a discussion which took place in the Council of Ministers in November 1910 on measures which ought to be taken to protect Russian interests in the *volost'* self-government[46] which the ministry was planning to introduce in the six southwestern provinces, as well as in the internal provinces. In that discussion, held in camera and thus exempt from the need for popular appeal, the ministers claimed that they had never differentiated between Russian and Polish peasantry in the southwestern provinces, but had depended upon both. The measures which the ministry was contemplating to protect Russian interests in the *volost'* were, thus, a departure from usual governmental policy.[47]

Despite this change of policy, Stolypin had taken into account the fact that the low cultural-educational level of the Russian peasants in the southwest region necessitated Polish cooperation in local self-government. As a consequence, although he admitted that he believed that in addition to the establishment of Russian and non-Russian curiae for *volost'* elections certain posts in the *volost'* ought to go to persons of "Russian Orthodox" extraction, he pointed out that this stipulation would cause practical difficulty, because in most *volosti* there was a lack of qualified people. Limiting certain posts to Russians, he acknowledged, might mean that those posts would remain unoccupied.[48]

To summarize Stolypin's attitude toward the Polish question, we may state the following: he regarded the different groups of Poles in the empire differently. He was firm but sympathetic to the Poles in Tsarist Poland, and though he could not consider divorcing them from the empire, he was willing to allow them a small amount of self-government. He had no reasonable basis for his support of the Kholm proposal, except for remote Russian ownership of the territory. He did, on the other hand, have a rational basis for the proposal to change representation in the State Council from the western provinces and for the western zemstvo bill, despite the fact that it earned him a great deal of opprobrium. (The political repercussions of the zemstvo bill, which were enormous, are examined in Chapter 6.) The government was concerned about German infiltration in the western provinces, but nationalistic rather than strategic considerations were most important to Stolypin.

Stolypin's Attitude toward Finland

In 1906, Finland had a population of just under 3 million. Russia had acquired Finnish territory through peace treaties in 1721 and 1743, but the bulk of Finland was annexed by the Treaty of Fredrikshamn, September 17, 1809. The government of Finland, organized shortly after this treaty, was called the Imperial Senate of Finland. It consisted of a supreme court, comprising ten or half the members of the Senate, and ministries, comprising another ten members. Members of the Senate were Finns, appointed by the Tsar. There was also a procurator, whose duty was to supervise the legality of the courts and the actions of government figures and the Minister State Secretary for Finnish Affairs, who submitted Finnish business to the Tsar and who resided in St. Petersburg. Finally, there was a Governor General of Finland, who presided at Senate meetings and served as commander-in-chief of the Russian forces in Finland. With one exception, all governors general of Finland were Russians.

Finland had a separate customs organization, monetary system, and postal service from the 1860s. The Diet, the Finnish parliament (which Stolypin called the Seim),[49] really began to function only after 1869. By a statute of 1906 it became a unicameral legislature, members of which were elected for three-year terms on the basis of proportional representation and almost universal suffrage.[50]

Russo-Finnish relations during Stolypin's administration, as described in reports of the British ambassador, British consuls, and other observers in Russia, were a nearly constant stream of bitter conflicts—over Finnish military contributions to imperial defense, rights of the Diet, aiding and abetting of Russian revolutionaries by the Finns, attacks on the Russian government by the Finnish press, plans to change the gauge of Finnish railroads to match Russian railroads, and so on.[51]

The basic cause of these conflicts was the antithetical view of Finland's position in the empire held by Stolypin and the Russian government on the one hand and by Finnish jurists and the Finnish Senate and Diet on the other. The Finnish position was perhaps best summarized in the report of the Finnish members of the Kharitonov commission of 1909 and in the several petitions sent to the Tsar by the Senate and the Diet during the years 1908 to 1910.

The key points of the Finnish position were that Finland had a well-defined autonomy, that she was governed by the Tsar in the capacity of a constitutional monarch (referred to as *Velikii knyaz* in Russian sources, and in English translations as Grand Duke) in conjunction with Finnish institutions, and that she was free from interference from Russian institutions or individuals other than the Tsar-Grand Duke. This meant that Finland was not subject to the Council of Ministers, the Duma, or the State Council. Derived from this view of Finland's position in the empire was the theory that the Finnish Diet had the right to legislate matters which concerned both Finland and the empire.

The Finns substantiated their conception of Finland's position in the empire by reference to Alexander I's promises, made several times during 1808 and 1809, to uphold the Finnish constitution. This constitution, the Finns claimed, was composed of two eighteenth century Swedish laws, the *Forma pravleniya* (Form of Government) of 1772 and the *Akta soedineniya i bezopasnosti* (Act of Union and Security) of 1789. These laws stipulated that the monarch could not publish new laws, exact new levies, or abolish old laws without agreement of the people's representatives, a term the Finns interpreted to mean the Diet. The Senate and the Diet emphasized the separateness of Finland from the empire by various trade treaties, made during the nineteenth century, which referred to Finland as a separate economic entity.

Finnish jurists found modern affirmation of the right of the Diet to have decisive voice in matters which concerned Finland, and conversely, prohibition of interference in Finnish matters by the Council of Ministers, the Duma, and the State Council, in articles 31 and 75 of the Diet statute of 1906. Article 31 referred to matters which could be decided by the Grand Duke without agreement of the Diet; article 75 referred to matters which the Grand Duke was bound to resolve in conjunction with the Diet. These latter matters included changes in the *Forma pravleniya* or *Akta soedineniya i bezopasnosti* and other special laws.[52]

Stolypin informally refuted the Finnish point of view in interviews with Sir Arthur Nicolson in March and August 1908. He stressed, first, that Finland was part of the Russian Empire and that its government was subordinate to the Russian government.

There was not the slightest intention to curtail the rights and privileges of Finland, but there were certain Imperial questions which must be decided by the Imperial Government and the Imperial Duma. Finland was not an independent country, linked to Russia only by a simple personal union, nor was it even in the position of Hungary. The Imperial questions to which he alluded were the necessary junction, for strategical reasons, of Finnish and Russian railway systems, the posts, telegraphs and also the military.[53]

He went on to cite a list of grievances committed by the Finns against the Russian government. One was their refusal to pay for exemption from personal military service, which now would necessitate recruitment for the Russian army in Finland. Permitting the Finns to have an army of their own would be "too dangerous." A second was Finnish protection of Russian revolutionaries. "It was in Finland that conspiracies were hatched and . . . that the revolutionaries took refuge," Stolypin asserted.[54]

He reiterated emphatically his view of Finland's position in the empire in August 1908, railing against the Diet, whose "pretensions were really excessive," and calling the Finns a "stubborn, hard-headed race . . . obstinate in their opinions. They could not admit the fact that they were an integral part of the Empire, with a liberal autonomy as regards local affairs but they desired to be treated as a separate and independent state, bound by a purely personal union to Russia. This was contrary to all the arragements which had been made between the two countries."[55]

Nicolson informed the Foreign Office that "M. Stolypin, I think, has some justification for this point of view."[56]

The formal and fullest expression of Stolypin's views on Finland was contained in an official paper, the *Ob"yasnitel'naya zapiska,*[57] accompanying the so-called Law of June 17, 1910. It ought to be noted at the outset that the ideas contained in the *Ob''yasnitel'naya zapiska* were neither original nor unique to Stolypin. They were held by the rest of the ministry, with the possible exception of Kokovtsov and Izvolsky,[58] as well as by many Russian jurists of the day. They were contained in all the reports on the discussion of Finnish matters held by the Special Council for Finnish Affairs and by the Council of Ministers (both of which were usually chaired by Stolypin) and in the report of the Russian contingent of the Kharitonov commission.

The opening theme of the *Ob''yasnitel'naya zapiska* was that Finland was an integral part of the Russian empire with internal autonomy limited by and dependent upon the Tsar-Grand Duke. The proof of this, according to the document, rested upon several bases. First, Finland had been conquered by Russian troops in 1808-1809 and at that time did not exist as a separate state but as a province of Sweden.[59] Russian conquest was legalized by several treaties, but chiefly by the Fredrikshamn Treaty of 1809. This internationally recognized document referred to Finland as a province (*guberniya*) henceforth in the "property and firm ownership (*sobstvennosti i derzhavnom oblidanii*) of the Russian empire."[60] There were also statements by Alexander, some in his correspondence with Napoleon, referring to Finland as a "province."[61]

Some Finnish jurists at the time believed that the Börgo Diet, a representative group of Finns assembled by Alexander I in 1809, indicated that the Finns had entered into a contractual relationship with the Russian government. Stolypin rejected this theory on the basis that the Diet was merely advisory and that the Finns had no authority from their former sovereign, the Swedish king, to engage in a contract. In fact, Stolypin pointed out, many of those at Borgo had already sworn allegiance to the Russian Tsar.[62] Stolypin's cousin Baron Alexander Meyendorff believed that Stolypin was influenced by the famous Russian jurist N. M. Korkunov's theory that there was no bilateral obligation underlying Finland's rights and that the unilateral promises of the Russian sovereign were not binding.[63] As we know, Stolypin was influenced by Korkunov in regard to local self-government and may have been influenced in regard to Finland as well. However, as has been pointed out, Stolypin's ideas on the Finnish question were also commonly held within the Russian government.

Stolypin emphasized that Finland's position as part of the empire was confirmed in modern times by article 2 of the Fundamental State Laws of 1906, which plainly termed Finland as an "indivisible part of the Russian empire," albeit governed on the basis of special institutions in her internal matters.[64]

Flowing from the above reasoning, Finland's autonomy, Stolypin maintained, was a free gift of a generous Tsar[65] and it could, because of Finland's place within the empire, extend only to internal Finnish matters. Furthermore, and most important, the imperial government, on the basis of its sovereignty, could decide what constituted internal Finnish matters and what constituted statewide matters—issues which, although they also concerned Finland, could not be left exclusively to Finnish institutions. "To the Russian state authority (*vlast*)," Stolypin stated in the *Ob"yasnitel'naya zapiska*, "belongs the right over Finland of state supremacy (*Derzhavnago Verkhovenstva*) and on the strength of this right all questions general for Finland and other parts of the Russian state must be decided by the activity of Russian laws; local Finnish resolutions concern exclusively her internal matters. . . . [66] The Russian supreme power, on the basis of the sovereignty belonging to it, has full and unquestioned right to establish and define local Finnish self-government."[67]

Stolypin repudiated the notion that the *Forma pravleniya* and *Akta soedineniya i bezopasnosti* could have bearing on the present Diet's rights because at the time they were issued the Finnish Diet did not exist; the term "people's representatives" alluded to the Swedish Riksdag to which the Finns sent representatives.[68]

He also rejected the theory that articles 31 and 75 of the Diet statute of 1906 had bearing on the role which the Diet ought to play in the legislating of matters of imperial concern, on the grounds that the Diet statute dealt only with the Diet as a purely Finnish institution, not with the Diet in its wider context as an institution within the empire. Articles 31 and 75 covered matters which the Tsar-Grand Duke could decide independently and which he had to decide jointly with the Diet, but these matters had never been explicitly defined.[69]

Even Finnish jurists accepted the overlordship of the Tsar-Grand Duke. It was the authority of the Council of Ministers, the Duma, and the State Council which they resisted. Stolypin, on the contrary, emphasized that according to articles 7 and 86 of the Fundamental State Laws of 1906, the Tsar's legislative power was shared by the Council of Ministers, the Duma, and the State Council.[70]

As in regard to the government's policy in the western provinces, Stolypin claimed that the government's treatment of Finland was dictated partially by a need for self-defense. From the 1860s, according to Stolypin, the Diet had begun enacting laws on taxation, the establishment of local self-government, military service, and monetary reform—matters which were within the jurisdiction of the central government. Furthermore, the Finns had advanced proposals for a new form of government which would have turned Finland into a separate state united to Russia by a "precarious union" like that which formerly existed between Norway and Sweden.[71] In the *Ob"yas-nitel'naya zapiska* Stolypin alluded several times to the "militant separatism" of the Finns.

He concluded his argument on the reasonableness of the Russian government's right to legislate matters which affected the empire as a whole and to decide what constituted such matters with an analogy to the governments of other countries, including the Austrian Empire, the German Empire, the Swiss Confederation, the British Empire, and the United States of America.[72] In 1911, as we shall see, the government also published a comprehensive comparative study of the kind and number of matters handled by the central and local legislative bodies in eleven countries.[73]

Stolypin hoped to resolve the constitutional conflict between the Finnish and Russian governments by enacting two measures. The first was the Ordinance of May 8, 1908,[74] and the second was the Law of June 17, 1910. The Ordinance of May 8 stipulated that henceforth Finnish business destined for the Tsar was to be submitted to the Council of Ministers and then forwarded to the Tsar, instead of being sent directly to the Tsar by the Minister State Secretary for Finnish Affairs. Stolypin considered this provision necessary because, in his opinion, allowing the Minister State Secretary exclusive authority to report Finnish business to the Tsar encouraged the isolation (*obosoblennost*) of Finland and made the empire dependent upon the Minister State Secretary.[75] He also emphasized that the Council of Ministers, after its reconstitution in 1906, was the chief coordinating agency of all administrative and legislative institutions in the empire, thus requiring all important matters to be filtered through it.[76]

The Council of Ministers issued a lengthy analysis of Finland's position in the empire which prefigured that contained in the *Ob"yasnitel'naya zapiska.*[77] When the Finnish Senate and Diet petitioned the Tsar to abolish the Ordinance of May 8,[78] the Council of Ministers recommended that he reject the request on the basis that these institutions, having only local jurisdiction, could not review a state law.[79] While Stolypin maintained this opinion, he later was willing to simplify it by allowing the Finnish Senate to give its opinions on a Diet bill prior to its being sent to the Council of Ministers and to the Tsar.[80]

The Law of June 17, 1910, was to be the final solution to the Finnish problem. Although it was entitled the Proposal of the Chairman of the Council of Ministers, it had been in the making long before Stolypin entered the central government. Five committees had grappled with the problem of what constituted purely Finnish legislation and could be handled by the Diet and what concerned the whole empire and thus must be under the jurisdiction of the central government.[81] From one of these committees had come the Regulation of February 3, 1899.

The Regulation of February 3, however, did not define explicitly which subjects were to come under Finnish and imperial legislation. Both the Finns and the Russian government believed that the boundaries of Finnish and imperial legislation ought to be established by means of a detailed list of subjects under the jurisdiction of each. Thus, following an imperial command, the Council of Ministers discussed the problem in the summer of 1907 and decided that on the basis of articles 2, 7, and 86 of the Fundamental State Laws of 1906 Finnish legislation ought to be limited exclusively to internal affairs of the principality. All other matters ought to be handled by the State Duma and the State Council.[82] There were further discussions on the issue in the Special Conference on Finnish Affairs in December 1908[83] and February 1910[84] and in the Council of Ministers in February 1910,[85] as well as in the Kharitonov commission of 1909,[86] the Russian members of which actually drafted the Law of June 17, 1910, defining the spheres of Finnish and Russian legislation.

The Law of June 17, 1910, was divided into three parts. The first section listed nineteen subjects which were to be handled by the Russian government, either in the form of laws passed by the Duma and the State Council or as regulations (*postanovlenii*) issued by the Council of Ministers and approved by the Tsar. These matters included Finnish participation in state expenditures and taxation, military service and other duties connected with state defense, rights of Russians in Finland, the use of the state language in Finland, rights and responsibilities of imperial institutions and officials situated in Finland, execution in Finland of sentences or decisions of imperial courts, guarantee of state interests in establishing general policies of education in Finland, the activity of societies and companies operating in other parts of the empire as well as in Finland, customs and tariff regulations, the monetary system, the post, rights of foreigners, trademarks, the press and importation of prohibited publications, railroads necessary for state defense, and general religious policy.[87] The first section also dealt with questions of succession and maintenance of the royal family.

The second and third sections regulated Finnish representation in the Duma[88] and the State Council and the reimbursement of representatives. Emphasizing Finland's position as part of the empire, representation was to be from the population at large, rather than from the Diet. The ministry believed that it had been shown that representation from local parliaments to a central legislature had a divisive effect on the country.[89] Special representation was provided for Russians living in Finland, because general representation, according to the law, was based on Diet electoral laws. Since Russians in Finland had no representation in the Diet, without special representation in the Duma and the State Council they would have been denied representation altogether.[90]

The arguments for the reasonableness of this law, presented in the various conferences, committees, and meetings of the Council of Ministers where it was considered,[91] sometimes carrying explicit statements by Stolypin, sometimes indicating his tactic approval, were almost identical to the sentiments expressed in the *Ob''yasnitel'naya zapiska*. The culminating argument for the law was the publication of a comparative list of subjects handled by central and local legislatures in various European countries, Canada, Australia, the United States, and South American countries. The publication, issued in 1911 by the Government Printing House, under whose auspices it is not certain, was entitled *Sravnitel'nyi perechen predmetov razrezhaemykh v poryadke obshchegosudarstvennago zakonodatel'stva po osnovnym zakonom stran s tsentral'nym i mestnym zakonodatel'stvami* (A Comparative List of Subjects Decided in the Order of State Legislation according to the Fundamental Laws of Countries with Central and Local Legislation).[92] From the legislation of the eleven countries which were analyzed,[93] it appeared that the matters which were to be handled by the Duma and the State Council according to the Law of June 17 were about equal in number and type to matters handled by the Congress of the United States and less than those within the jurisdiction of the central legislatures of Germany, Switzerland, and the South American countries.

The law of June 17 was greeted with a storm of protest in Finland and disapproval in Sweden, Germany, England, and other countries.[94] Even in Russia, there was strong opposition to it. During discussion of the law in the Duma on May 9 and 10, 1910, large numbers of disapproving Kadets and parties to their left, marched out of the hall,[95] so that the passage of the bill in no way indicated unanimous support. V. N. Kokovtsov had objected to the Ordinance of May 8 and the Law of June 17 during the meetings of the Council of Ministers.[96] He publicly expressed his disapproval to the British ambassador after the bill's passage.[97] Witte also was strongly critical, although the gist of his criticism was that rather than issue such a law he would have used the strong measures available to suppress Finnish revolutionaries.[98]

Suppression of Finnish revolutionary activity did not seem to be a crucial issue in Stolypin's sponsorship of the Law of June 17. Rather, his motive appeared to be stubborn insistence upon asserting the Russian government's legal rights in the case.

After his point had been proved, Stolypin was extremely prudent in applying the law, as defenders of the law had intimated he would be.[99] When the law was rejected by the Finnish Diet,[100] Stolypin refused to consider the institution of another Russo-Finnish commission to review the law, on the grounds that the matter had already been entirely illuminated. And after six such commissions, it was indeed evident that Finnish and Russian views were irreconcilable. However, he did acknowledge that the law would be implemented gradually and would not lead to immediate replacement of Finnish laws.[101]

In fact, the first two issues in which the principles of the Law of June 17 were applied were matters about which there could be little or no contention to the position that they were of imperial concern. These involved Finnish participation in imperial defense and the rights of Russians living in Finland.[102]

Friction over Finland's participation in imperial defense had come to a head several years before Stolypin's administration. In 1901 an imperial manifesto decreed that the special Finnish army of 6,000 troops would be abolished and Finnish soldiers would serve with Russian troops under Russian regulations. A mass protest greeted this order—over 50 percent of the Finnish troops failed to show up in the spring of 1902. In 1905, therefore, it was decreed that instead of compulsory military service the Finns would pay an annual sum of 10 million marks. In May 1907 it was reported from Helsinki that the Finns were resisting this payment, but the Diet finally decided to remit 20 million marks for both 1906 and 1907 in October of that year. In the opinion of the British consul in Helsinki, Charles Cooke, the Finns had "got off very easily."[103]

The Finnish Senate and the Diet began to resist the military payment bill on constitutional grounds during 1908 and 1909.[104] They contended that it violated the fundamental laws of Finland because the Diet had not been allowed to vote on the establishment of the credits per se, but only on the amount to be paid.[105]

The Minister of War reminded the Council of Ministers that it would be dangerous to arm the Finns because of their doubtful loyalty, and that the percentage of "aliens" in the Russian army already amounted to 25 percent. He stated that he believed, furthermore, that the rank and file Finns disliked military service.[106]

The Diet was dissolved in April 1908, upon recommendation of the Council of Ministers, in part because it resisted the military payments bill. The Diet was reconvened in the summer of that year, after elections, and prorogued again in November. The Diet again rejected the military payment bill late in 1909.

At this point, Stolypin opposed the suggestion of the Governor General of Finland that the money be taken without the Diet's consent from the Million and State funds—Finnish funds accessible only to the Tsar.[107] He suggested instead that a second request be made of the new Diet which was to be convened in the spring of 1910. He wished to avoid offending the Diet, but he also had practical motives. If the Diet agreed to levy temporary taxes for defense payments, the state and million funds could be allocated for other purposes.[108] When the new Diet also rejected the payments, he agreed with Governor General Zein that this should not immediately lead to closure because of the mild manner in which the Diet had acted.[109]

Nevertheless, Stolypin was irritated by the obstinacy of the Finns. In a related discussion in the Council of Ministers in late 1909 and early 1910 on the building of barracks for increased Russian troops in Finland, he stressed that the Finns should take a feasible part in shouldering the expenses of state defense because they had been freed from personal military service. He considered the barracks a matter of state defense and subject to state legislation. He suggested that half the payment for the barracks (about 5 million rubles) be taken in the order of administrative legislation from the million fund.[110]

Kokovtsov believed, on the contrary, that the Finns would have trouble paying for the barracks,[111] and the Council of Ministers finally decided to obtain the money from the state treasury, for fear that demanding it from the Finns would worsen Russo-Finnish relations.

In a discussion held on April 27, 1910, the Council of Ministers, including Stolypin but excluding Kokovtsov, approved the Minister of

War's plan to purchase land for the barracks through a third party, rather than resorting to the procedure of eminent domain. The Council of Ministers hoped that this method would bring the land more cheaply.

In any case, the Law of June 17 established that the question of military payments was a state matter, in which the Finns could have a say through their representatives in the Duma and the State Council, but over which the Diet could have no decisive voice.

The second issue to which the Law of June 17 was applied involved the granting of equal rights to Russians living in Finland. Russian citizens living in Finland did not have the right to participate in city or rural self-government, although they paid local taxes. University requirements were more stringent for Russians living in Finland than for Finns, and Russians were limited in the practice of medicine— although Finnish doctors in the empire were not. Russians living in Finland also were limited in engaging in business or shipping.[112]

Stolypin felt that equalization of the rights of Russians living in Finland with those of the Finns was urgent.[113] Nicholas ordered Stolypin to prepare a bill on equal civil rights[114] and such a bill was drafted in 1910 by Governor General Zein. In the same year, the Finnish Senate worked out a proposal permitting Russians to vote in Finnish *obshchina* (urban and rural) self-government.[115]

Stolypin's stand on the position of the Orthodox church in Finland, in contrast to his stand on the issues cited above, seemed unduly stringent. He and the Council of Ministers as a whole opposed a bill issued by the Finnish Senate which proposed that minors be allowed to convert from Orthodoxy to the Evangelical Lutheran faith. The ministry's involved brief contended that the bill violated earlier laws on conversion and discriminated against the Orthodox church.[116] On two occasions, Stolypin championed individual Orthodox churches in their conflict with Finns. He stated in one instance that if a certain governor permitted such harassment he would be replaced by a "person more responsive to state needs."[117]

Stolypin's treatment of the Diet was a special case, which shall be examined momentarily. His other policies dealing with the points of conflict between Finland and the Russian government do not seem oppressive or motivated by plans for Russification of Finland.

His position on the language question was that Russian should be used for communication between Finnish and imperial governmental institutions in order to expedite business and unify the empire.[118] There are no official records of his advocating that Russian be used in internal proceedings of the Finnish government.

From 1890 to 1905 the Russian government had tried to make the Russian language mandatory in Russo-Finnish governmental communication. Prior to that time official business had been conducted in Swedish, due to lack of knowledge of Russian—or for that matter Finnish—on the part of Finnish officials. However, the Council of Ministers contended that the Finnish governor general had abrogated the regulations on this subject without its knowledge. In 1909-1910 the Special Conference on Finnish Affairs and the Council of Ministers, both of these bodies usually presided over by Stolypin, recommended that the governor general work out a proposal for "immediate communication between Finnish and imperial governmental institutions and officials in the state language."[119]

The fragmentary evidence of Stolypin's thoughts on education in Finland reflect his conviction that strong separatist currents existed there. In the spring of 1911, for example, he expressed approval of Minister of Public Education Kasso's proposal to upgrade Russian schools in Finland, especially in Karelia, to counteract Finnish separatist and pan-Finnish influence.[120] Stolypin advocated in particular the establishment of a teacher training college in Finland.[121]

At about the same time, he opposed the appointment of a Finnish clergyman for the teaching of religion to Finns in Russian educational institutions because the man had "leftist leanings" (he belonged to the Young Finn party) and had an "inimical attitude" toward Russia. He suggested instead the appointment of a Lutheran pastor of German extraction, loyal to the empire.[122]

Of course, in addition to separatist movements within Finland, Stolypin feared revolutionary threats to the imperial capital itself. The Assistant Minister of War, A. A. Polivanov, has described the worried meetings of the Council of Ministers during 1909 on the possibility of revolutionary violence in Finland and the precautions which ought to be taken for protection of St. Petersburg.[123] Records of the meetings of the Council of Ministers during 1908 and 1909 display elaborate plans for suppressing insurrection in Finland.[124]

Stolypin was particularly angry about articles in the Finnish press calling for revolution and criticizing himself and Assistant Governor General (later Governor General) Zein.[125] He blamed the state of the press in Finland on the fact that the Finnish Senate had abolished the post of censor, on the laxity of judicial officials, and on the inadequacy of the Finnish criminal code.[126] He reminded the governor general that although preliminary censorship had been abolished, other forms of censorship still were to be implemented.[127] Relying on administrative rather than legislative regulation, as was his wont, Stolypin proposed that the Finnish Senate work out a supplement to the Finnish criminal code providing for prosecution of newspaper editors for scurrilous articles, to be in effect until the Diet published laws on the subject.[128]

Because he believed that that situation in Finland was volatile[129] and the Finnish police had been lax,[130] Stolypin advocated granting imperial police officials special rights of arrest, search, and seizure in Finland. It must be noted, however, that these measures were to be applied to Russians, not Finns, and were to be undertaken only when no Finnish policemen were present or when they refused to perform the duty. Imperial police were to be present when Finnish police arrested or searched the homes of Finns.[131]

The Diet seems to have been regarded by Stolypin not only as a Finnish institution, but like the Duma, a popular institution, which could be dismissed if it interfered with the government program. Dissolution of the Diet in 1908[132] was preceded by dissolution of the Second Duma. Plans for early closure of the Diet in 1911[133] nearly coincided with prorogation of the Duma and the State Council during the so-called zemstvo crisis. At this time Stolypin reminded Governor General Zein that the Diet need be closed prematurely only if some objectionable matters were discussed in plenary session, not in committees.[134] The Russian government's treatment of the Diet may have been considered undue interference in Finland and undue limitation of her autonomy, but the government dissolved the Diet over issues which it considered of imperial significance, such as the Diet stand on military defense payments.

Two minor issues of conflict between Stolypin and the Finns illustrate graphically the divergent viewpoints of the Russian government and Finnish political writers as well as Stolypin's rather consistent policy of attempting to deal with the Finns as fairly as possible while insuring imperial interests. Stolypin advocated that the centennial celebration of Finland's incorporation into the empire be held in September 1909, on the anniversary of the signing of the Fredrikshamn treaty, the date on which the Swedish King Gustav IV Adolphus "renounced the sovereign rights belonging to him over the Finnish *guberniya.*" The Finns insisted that the centennial celebration be held in March 1909, on the anniversary of the convocation of the Börgo Diet. In Stolypin's opinion they distorted facts, wrongly believing that with the calling of the Börgo Diet, Tsar Alexander I "of blessed memory" created an independent state.[135] Stolypin supported Nicholas' proposal that a chapel be built in Finland, in memory of the centennial anniversary of the Fredrikshamn peace treaty; however, he maintained that the Russian treasury should defray the costs of the chapel because it had "state patriotic" significance.[136]

To summarize, it appears that the Russo-Finnish conflict which continued during Stolypin's administration was the result of two diametrically opposed views—that of the Russian government on the one hand and that of Finnish jurists on the other. Both of these views could be convincingly substantiated due to the existence of contradictory laws and unclear policy pronouncements of previous Russian rulers. The situation was aggravated by the salutary neglect accorded to Finland by the Russian government during the nineteenth century and by the threat of revolution in Russia to which the Finns contributed by harboring Russian revolutionaries or by actually conspiring against the Russian government.

It is true that Stolypin's policy was to emphasize the Russian government's overlordship of Finland and to curtail the Finnish government and the Diet when he felt they had overstepped their lawful boundaries. But it can be contended that he ruthlessly suppressed Finnish rights and culture only if one accepts the Finnish point of view.

The Caucasian Peoples

It has been claimed that Stolypin "distrusted all Armenian political groups" and feared and suppressed nationalism in the Caucasus.[137] But from the major source of evidence we have concerning Stolypin's views on the Caucasus, he was as distressed about general violence and disorder in the area as he was about separatist activity. Stolypin's views on the Caucasian situation must be distilled chiefly from his letter of April 11, 1908, to the Caucasian Governor General Vorontsov-Dashkov.[138]

Nearly three-fourths of the fifteen-page letter—the first three-fourths—is devoted to castigating murder (terrorist activity led to 1,239 deaths in 1907, 50 murders having been committed in broad daylight in April of that year), extortion, vigilante justice, violence directed by Armenians toward Molokanes and other minority groups, strikes, and the collusion of police and local administrative officials with both revolutionary and right-wing groups.

One of these rightist groups was part of the Armenian national society, the Dashnaktsutyun.[139] Armed and outfitted with bombs, it demanded payoffs from local merchants and summarily fined or jailed individuals.[140] The desperate merchants of Tiflis not only tried to buy the group off, but formed protective organizations of their own to defend themselves against robbery and violence.[141] Only toward the end of his letter to Vorontsov-Dashkov did Stolypin warn the governor general that the Dashnaktsutyun was an Armenian national revolutionary society which trained its leaders in a special Bulgarian military school.[142]

Stolypin's primary concern in the Caucasus, then, seems to have been the terrible havoc there, which affected the local citizenry as well as the state apparatus. Though he probably did not want the empire to lose the Caucasus, only a hint of this attitude is recorded in the last two pages of his lengthy letter to Vorontsov-Dashkov.

Conclusion

Stolypin's promotion of Russian national interests was the unifying factor in his relationship with the national minorities in the empire. Otherwise, his policies differed according to the national minority in question and had considerable variance as to their rationale and justification. His proposal for the separation of the Kholm area from Russian Poland was the one policy based on emotional and nearly irrational considerations. His proposals regarding the Poles in the western provinces, while perhaps not politically judicious, could be justified on the basis of the percentage of Poles in the population.

Although Stolypin compared his Finnish policy with policies in modern federated states such as Germany and the United States, his Finnish policy actually was conservative. It was directed toward the reestablishment of Russia as the multinational empire it had been in the early and middle nineteenth century and in no way took into account the modern force of self-determination of national minorities.

To some extent Stolypin's nationality policies were influenced by nationalistic sentiment in the country at large and by the need to gain support from the newly established Nationalist party, but his views at least on the western provinces had been formulated, by his own admission, in the early years of his provincial career and expressed several years before the formation of the Nationalist party.

Appendix to Chapter 5

NATIONALITIES IN THE WESTERN PROVINCES

Province	Great Russian	Ukrainian	Belorussian	Total Russian	Polish	Lithuanian	German	Jewish
				Percentage According to Mother Tongue				
Vilensk	4.90		56.05	61.05	8.10	17.49		12.71
Vitebsk	13.29		52.95	66.26	3.38			11.69
Volhynia	3.50	70.09		73.73	6.16			13.20
Grodno	4.62	24.47	44.22	71.20	10.08		5.73	17.20
Kiev	5.88	79.20		85.25	1.93			12.09
Kovno	4.70	.10	2.44	7.27	9.03	68.28		13.72
Minsk	3.90	.47	76.00	80.37	3.00		.10	16.00
Mogilev	3.44		82.39	85.93	1.03			12.06
Podolsk	3.28	81.26		84.54	2.30			12.20

Source: *Pervaya vseobshchaya perepis' naseleniya Rossiiskoi imperii, 1897: Obshchii svod po imperii rezultatov razrabotki*, ed. N. A. Troinitskii (St. Petersburg: Ministerstvo vnutrennikh' del', 1905), vol. 2, table 13, pp. 20-22, 28, 30.

Note: Percentages are based on the 1897 census, the last census before 1910. Nationalities which constituted less than 1 percent of the population have not been included.

Notes

1. See the Kholmskii krai proposal, pp. 115-117 below.

2. Hugh Seton-Waton, *The Russian Empire* (Oxford: Clarendon Press, 1967), pp. 281-89, 409.
Apparently, Napoleonic law was retained. See the Kholmskii krai proposal, p. 116 below.

3. The unrest in Poland was described in British diplomatic reports, Great Britain Public Record Office, Foreign Office (hereafter cited F. O.) 371. For 1906: vol. 127, nos. 26850, 29740; vol. 128, nos. 31114, 29727, 28583. 1907: vol. 318, no. 578, (January), no. 11899 (April), no. 26798. 1908: vol. 513, no. 28449 (August). The unrest consisted of assassinations of officials and simple murders, robberies, and strikes. The number of assassinations, murders, and robberies was quite high.

4. F. O. 371, vol. 512, no. 453, January, 1908, Consul Clive Bayley to Sir Arthur Nicolson.

5. F. O. 371, vol. 512, no. 3251, December 9, 1908, Consul Bayley to Nicolson.

6. The intent was to secure a harmonious parliament. Stolypin told Nicolson in August 1907 that the Poles "had adopted a hostile attitude to the Government in the last Duma, and encouraged the elements of disruption," and he added that he "intended to show them that the Government could not be terrorized into granting Polish autonomy." F. O. 371, vol. 326, no. 29515, August 16.
For the Polish point of view, or to be more accurate the outlook of the Polish leaders in the Duma, on the entire Polish problem during Stolypin's administration see Edward Chmielewski's *The Polish Question* (Knoxville: University of Tennessee Press, 1970).

7. Stolypin to Nicolson, F. O. 371, vol. 128, no. 30374, September 7, 1906.

8. Quoted in *Gosudarstvennaya deyatel'nost predsedatelya soveta ministrov, stats sekretarya, Petra Arkad'evicha Stolypina*, ed. E. Verpakhovsky (St. Petersburg: Izdanie sostavitelya, 1911), part 1, pp. 22-23, 25.

9. *Ibid.*, pp. 23-24.

10. *Ibid.* The governor also was given control over municipal self-government, as in the internal provinces.

11. See the statistical table in the appendix to this chapter.

12. *Gosudarstvennaya Duma: Stenograficheskie otchety,* Tretii sozyv, sessiya III, zasedanie 103, May 7, 1910, col. 779.

13. See p. 122 below.

14. "Po voprosu o vydelenii vostochnykh uezdov Sedletskoi i Lyublinskoi gubernii (Kholmskaya Rusi) iz sostava Privislinskago kraya," *Osobyi zhurnal soveta ministrov* (hereafter cited *Osobyi zhurnal;* there were three volumes annually after 1906), 1907, vol. 1, no. 5, January 3, pp. 1-3.

15. *Ibid.,* pp. 4-5; "Po proektu Ministerstva vnutrennikh del vydelenii iz sostava Privislinskago kraya vostochnykh chastei Sedletskoi i Lyublinskoi gubernii, s obrazovaniem iz nikh osoboi Kholmskoi gubernii," *Osobyi zhurnal,* 1909, vol. 1, no. 10, January 13, pp. 4-7, 9-10. In some areas appointed justices of the peace remained after 1889.

16. *Osobyi zhurnal,* 1909, vol. 1, no. 10, pp. 7-9.

17. See chapter 6, below, pp. 167-68.

18. *Osobyi zhurnal,* 1907, vol. 1, no. 5, pp. 5-6. This was echoed by the Council of Ministers in 1909, *Osobyi zhurnal,* 1909, vol. 1, no. 10, pp. 10-11. The ministry emphasized that the purpose of the proposal was to save Kholm Russia from denationalization.

19. *Osobyi zhurnal,* 1909, vol. 1, no. 10, p. 5. In the remaining Lyublinsk province there were to be 783,077 Catholics, 46,397 Orthodox, 174,752 Jews, and 17,537 other.

20. *Ibid.,* p. 12.

21. *Osobyi zhurnal,* 1907, vol. 1, no. 5, pp. 3-4.

22. F. O. 371, vol. 512, no. 3251, December 8, 1908.

23. F. O. 371, vol. 981, no. 39169.

24. Description of the Nationalist party by Sir Bernard Pares, F. O. 371, vol. 979, no. 30164, August 22, 1910; *ibid.,* no. 20071, May 30, 1910; *ibid.,* vol. 1217, no. 29095, July 24, 1911; and by Sir Arthur Nicolson, *ibid.,* vol. 978, no. 5082, February 5, 1910.

25. Nicolson, in F. O. 371, vol. 978, no. 5082.

26. F. O. 371, vol. 326, no. 23525, July 9, 1907; Pares, in *ibid.,* vol. 979, no. 19549, May 28, 1910.

27. In general, British reports from Russia contained the theory that Stolypin had developed his nationalistic proposals to obtain the support of the Nationalists after he lost some Octobrist support due to the naval general staff crisis of 1909. Of course, they admitted he was a nationalist in his own right. See also Chmielewski's similar opinion on this issue, as discussed in Chapter 6, below, p. 169.

28. Sir George Buchanan, in F. O. 371, no. 46, December 18, 1910. See also Chapter 2, above, p. 32. Stolypin also expressed appreciation for Octobrist support of the government at this time. Sir George Buchanan, *ibid.*

29. Bill on the extension of the terms of representatives from the western provinces to the State Council, Ministerstvo vnutrennikh del, Department obshchikh del, osobye deloproizvodstvo, no. 14521, May 8, 1909.

30. *Gosudarstvennaya Duma: Stenograficheskie otchety,* Tretii sozyv, sessiya II, zasedanie 123, May 30, 1909, col. 2751.

31. Bill no. 14521, *passim.*

32. *Gosudarstvennaya Duma: Stenograficheskie otchety,* Tretii sozyv, sessiya II, zasedanie 123, May 30, 1909, cols. 2831, 2762.

33. *Ibid.,* cols. 2750-57, 2761-62.

34. A. V. Zenkovsky, *Pravda o Stolypine* (New York: Vseslovyanskoe Izdatel'stvo, 1957), pp. 195-96, 206-11.

35. *Ibid.,* pp. 212-13.

36. *Gosudarstvennaya Duma: Stenograficheskie otchety,* Tretii sozyv, sessiya III, zasedanie 103, May 7, 1910, çols. 812, 733.

37. *Ibid.* Also, Stolypin to the *Sovet po delam mestnago khozyaistva,* October 6, 1909, quoted in *Gosudarstvennaya deyatel'nost . . . Petra Arkad'evicha Stolypina,* part 1, p. 18.

38. *Gosudarstvennaya Duma: Stenograficheskie otchety,* May 7, 1910, cols. 733-37.

39. A verbatim text of the zemstvo law is quoted in "O rasprostanenii deistviya polozheniya o zemskikh uchrezhdeniyakh v Vitebskuyu, Volynskuyu, Kievskuyu, Minskuyu, Mogilevskuyu i Podolskuyu gubernii," *Osobyi zhurnal,* 1911, vol. 1, no. 61, March 12. The ukase to the Senate and the text of the law are preceded by a discussion of the Council of Ministers. The text of the law also is quoted in Zenkovsky, *Pravda o Stolypine,* pp. 285-302.

40. In his speech to the Duma, May 15, 1910, Stolypin stressed that the zemstvos with this electoral basis were not being introduced into Tsarist Poland, but into six provinces in which Poles averaged 4.2 percent of the total population. Poles amounted to about 7.9 percent of the population in Volhynia province and to about 2.3 percent of Podolia province. *Gosudarstvennaya Duma: Stenograficheskie otchety,* Tretii sozyv, sessiya III, zasedanie 109, col. 1391.

41. *Gosudarstvennaya Duma: Stenograficheskie otchety,* May 7, 1910, col. 776.

42. *Gosudarstvennaya deyatel'nost . . . Petra Arkad'evicha Stolypina,* part 1, pp. 22-23, October 15, 1909; also, pp. 16-19, October 6, 1909.

43. *Gosudarstvennaya Duma: Stenograficheskie otchety,* May 7, 1910, cols. 789-96.

44. *Ibid.*

45. "Vopros o zapadnom zemstve i bankrotstvo Stolypina," *Istoricheskie zapiski,* 70 (1961), pp. 61-112.

46. The *volost'* was the primary, all-peasant level of self-government. For Stolypin's proposals for *volost'* self-government in the thirty-four internal provinces, see Chapter 3, above, pp. 67-69.

47. "Po predstavleniyu Ministerstva Vnutrennikh Del ot 4 Noyabrya 1910 goda (po Zemsk. Otd.), o nekotorykh meropriyatiyakh k ograzhdeniyu interesov russkago po proiskhozhdeniyu naseleniya v budushchikh volostyakh gubernii Yugo-Zapadnago i Severo-Zapadnago kraya," *Osobyi zhurnal,* 1910, vol. 3, no. 186, November 16, pp. 1-2.

48. *Ibid.*

49. In Russian sources the term "Diet" is rendered "Seim." Therefore, I have used the common English translation "Diet" when referring to the Finnish parliament in the text, but have retained the term "Seim," where apropos in the notes.

50. In April 1907 the Finnish Diet of 200 members included the following composition of its major political parties: Socialists, 78 seats, Old Finns, 57 seats, Young Finns, 26 seats, Swedish party, 24 seats. F. O. 371, vol. 322, no. 13661, April 22, 1907, Charles Cooke.

51. In general, British diplomatic reports, particularly Nicolson's, were sympathetic to the Russian government in its conflicts with Finland and to the government's constitutional theories regarding Finland. For example, the British reported instances in which the Finns antagonized the Russian government: Svinhufud's speech to the throne, F. O. 371, vol. 515, no. 28443, August 13, 1908 (Svinhufud was the speaker of the Finnish Diet); Nicolson on the Finnish press, *ibid.,* vol. 515, no. 7130, February 22, 1908, and no. 28440, August 17, 1908; the Finnish government acting as the head of an independent state, *ibid.,* vol. 515, no. 23180, June 29, 1908, and *ibid.,* no. 31799; harboring revolutionaries, F. O. 371, vol. 515, no. 30053, August 31, 1908; on independent military activity, *ibid.,* no. 17771, May 19, 1908. General statement from one of these reports: "Though the Finns affect to be unconscious of having afforded any reason for the policy now adopted by Russia, as a matter of fact they never miss an opportunity of rendering themselves obnoxious to the Russian authorities" *ibid.,* no. 28440.

52. Finland, National Archive (Valtionarkisto) KKK (Fund of the Governor General of Finland) (hereafter cited Valtionarkisto, KKK), osasto II/ 18 *ch.* 1, Seim petition to Nicholas II (untitled in Russian translation), April 4, 1910, pp. 6, 13-16, 18-20. The eighteenth century laws are quoted in Valtionarkisto, KKK, osasto II/18 *ch* II, Duma komissiya: Doklad #389 po vnesennomu Predsedatelem Soveta Ministrov zakonoproektu o poryadke izdaniya kasayushchikhsya Finlyandii zakonov i postanovlenii obshchegosudarstvennago znacheniya (hereafter cited Duma komissiya: Doklad #389). Articles 31 and 75 are quoted in Duma komissiya: Doklad #389, pp. 206, 218.

53. F. O. 371, vol. 515, no. 122, March 3, 1908.

54. *Ibid.*

55. F. O. 371, vol. 519, no. 30064, August 27, 1908, p. 2.

56. *Ibid.*

57. The full title was *Ob''yasnitel'naya zapiska k proektu Predsedatelya Soveta Ministrov o poryadke izdaniya kasayushchiksya Finlyandii zakonov i postanovlenii obshchegosudarstvennago znacheniya,* n.d. (circa April 4, 1910) (hereafter cited *Ob''yasnitel'naya zapiska*), in Valtionarkisto, KKK, osasto II/18 *ch.* II.

58. Kokovtsov expressed sympathy for the Finnish position several times during meetings of the Council of Ministers. Izvolsky thought the law of June 17 was unwise in the political situation which then exicted in Europe and the Far East. "O poryadke napravleniya Finlyandskikh del kasayushchikhsya interesov Imperii," *Osobyi zhurnal,* 1908, vol. 1, no. 96, January 22 and May 14, pp. 11-12; "Po proektu pravil o poryadke izdaniya kasayushchiksya Finlyandii zakonov i postanovlenii obshchegosudarstvennago znacheniya," *Osobyi zhurnal,* 1910, vol. 1, February 22, pp. 19-22; Aleksei Andreevich Polivanov, *Iz dnevnikov i vospominanii po dolzhnosti voennogo ministra i ego pomoshchika, 1907-1916* (Moscow: Vysshii voennyi redaktsionnyi sovet, 1924), p. 95.

59. *Ob''yasnitel'naya zapiska,* pp. 9-10, 29, 35.

60. *Ibid.,* p. 2. In a letter to Nicholas in February 1909, Stolypin stressed the fact that the Swedish King had renounced his sovereign rights to Finland and they had been transferred to Alexander I, Finland's new ruler. Valtionarkisto, KKK, osasto I 3/25, "Po voprosu o prazdnovanii stoletnyago yubileya zavoevaniya Finlyandii," pp. 2-3.

61. *Ob''yasnitel'naya zapiska,* pp. 5-6.

62. *Ibid.,* pp. 6-8.

63. Baron Alexander Meyendorff, "A Brief Appreciation of P. Stolypin's Tenure of Office," p. 6 of chapter on "Agrarian Problems"; MS, Russian Archive, Columbia University. Written 1932-1947.

During discussion of the Finnish measures in the Duma, however, Meyendorff greatly criticized Stolypin. Ben-Cion Pinchuk, *The Octobrists in the Third Duma* (Seattle: University of Washington Press, 1974), p. 122.

64. *Ob''yasnitel'naya zapiska,* p. 18.

65. *Ibid.,* pp. 10, 29-30.

66. *Ibid.,* pp. 10, 22-23.

67. *Ibid.,* p. 30.

68. *Ibid.,* pp. 53-54.

69. *Ibid.,* pp. 54, 56. At an earlier time, Stolypin agreed with the Council of Ministers that the Tsar had the right to transfer matters from the category of Seim legislation to that of administrative-economic. Valtionarkisto, KKK, osasto 8-2-*D,* Council of Ministers, *Spravka o Vysochaishem Reskrite 24 Avgusta/6 Sentyabrya 1909 o delakh, otnosyashchikhsya k oblastu administrativnago zakonodatelstva. Nachalo urazvitie stogo voprosa,* p. 8.

70. *Ob''yasnitel'naya zapiska,* p. 56.

71. *Ibid.,* pp. 10-12.

72. *Ibid.,* pp. 27, 32, 63-68. Stolypin even saw the principle of state supremacy in British parliamentary versus colonial legislation.

73. See below, p. 130. Nicolson supported Stolypin's and the Russian government's theories on the position of Finland in the empire. In 1908 he wrote: "The Russian Government considers Finland as a component part of the Empire but with special local autonomy. The Finns consider Finland a separate state connected with Russia by merely a personal union. The latter thesis is clearly untenable, if it be borne in mind that after Finland had been conquered by Russia, the Treaty of Fredrikshamn (1809) transferred to the Emperor all the rights of the King of Sweden over Finland . . .

"The most recent reference to Finland is in the Fundamental Laws of the Empire, 23 April 1906: 'The Russian State is one and indivisible. The Grand Duchy of Finland, which forms an indivisible part of the Russian Empire is in its internal affairs . . .' It would appear that Finland should, strictly speaking, be considered as a component part of the Russian Empire, with full autonomy as regards its local affairs.

"The decision as to which are local and which are Imperial Affairs, however, will be a difficult problem to solve.

"Russia, as the predominant partner, should go as far as her own interests permit in the way of conciliation." F. O. 371, vol. 515, no. 31802, September 2, 1908.

In August 1908 Nicolson wrote: "It is evident also . . . that some machinery must be created to give the Imperial Government a voice in deciding whether a particular matter is or is not of Imperial interest." F. O. 371, vol. 515, no. 28443, August 13.

Another British report on the Russo-Finnish constitutional conflict stated: "The same sort of difficulty would arise for us, if Ireland had a Parliament." F. O. 371, vol. 515, no. 28443, 1908. And another: "Sensible people in Finland have realized for some time past that the present state of things could not continue indefinitely." F. O. 371, vol. 515, no. 17771, O'Beirne.

74. The ordinance of 1908 was never passed by the State Duma and the State Council and so, technically it was not called a law but the "polozhenie Soveta Ministrov o poryadke napravleniya Finlyandskikh del, kasayuchikhsya interesov Imperii."

Geoffrey Hosking describes the Octobrists' raising the Finnish question, which led to the Ordinance of 1908, and ultimately to the Law of June 17, 1910, in the first session of the Third Duma. *The Russian Constitutional Experiment, Government and Duma, 1907-1914* (New York, London: Cambridge University Press, 1973), pp. 108-109.

75. "O poryadke napravleniya Finlyandskikh del kasayushchikhsya interesov Imperii," *Osobyi zhurnal,* 1908, vol. 1, no. 96, January 22 and May 14, pp. 12-13. As an example, Stolypin pointed out that a new form of government proposed for Finland had come to his attention only accidentally. There was no provision for the Council of Ministers taking action if the Minister State Secretary failed to send them a matter which they considered of state significance.

76. *Ibid.,* pp. 13-14.

77. That is, that Finland was a constituent (*sostavnaya*) part of the Russian empire, called *"krai"* in most laws, and stipulated thus in article 2 of the Fundamental State Laws of 1906. "O poryadke napravleniya Finlyandskikh del kasayushchikhsya interesov Imperii," *Osobyi zhurnal,* 1908, vol. 1, no. 96, January 22 and May 14, pp. 17-18; "Po vozbuzhdennomu Imperatorskim Finlyandskim Senatom khodataistvu o peredoklad Ministrom Stat-Sekretarem Vysochaishe otklonnago po dokladu Soveta Ministrov vsepoddanneishago predstavleniya Senata ot 6/19 Iyunya 1908 goda," *Osobyi zhurnal,* 1909, vol. 1, no. 55, April 14, p. 5; "Po vsepoddanneishemu adresu Finlyandskago Seima ob izmenenii poryadke napravleniya Finlyandskikh del," *Osobyi zhurnal,* 1909, vol. 2, no. 129, September 15, pp. 5-9.

The Council of Ministers claimed that the Diet had been dissolved in 1908 through its own fault and that the delayed bills about which the Diet complained (see note 78 below) were not within its jurisdiction. The Finnish budget, of course, had been delayed because of the dissolution of the Diet.

78. The Finnish Senate and the Diet voiced opposition to the Ordinance of May 8 in several declarations during 1908 and 1909. The Senate and the Diet claimed the ordinance was unconstitutional because Finnish fundamental laws had been changed without approval of the Diet. The Diet also claimed that the ordinance allowed the Council of Ministers to stifle or delay reform measures, such as checks on the activity of governmental officials, laws on freedom of the press and union (based on ukases of 1906), a bill for compulsory universal education, and the Finnish state budget. The

Senate asked for a return to the procedure of 1891 and a mixed Russo-Finnish commission to review questions which concerned Finland as well as the empire. Valtionarkisto, KKK, osasto II 4/47, Finnish Senate to Tsar Nicholas II, June 19, 1908, pp. 5-7; *ibid.*, Finnish Senate to Tsar Nicholas II, February 25, 1909, pp. 2-5; Valtionarkisto, KKK, II 4/8-3-*b*, Diet petition to the Tsar, June 30, 1909, pp. 8-11.

79. Valtionarkisto, KKK, II 4/47, *Zhurnal* vysochaishe uchrezhdennago osobago soveshchaniya po delam Velikago Knyazhestva Finlyandskago, no. 8, October 30, 1908, "O peredach na peresmotre sostavlenoi is russkikh i finlyandskikh chlennov Komissii Vysochaishe utverzhdennago, 20 Maya 1908 goda, polozheniya Soveta Ministrov o novom poryadke napravleniya Finlyandskikh del," pp. 4-5; "Po vozbuzhdennomu Imperatorskim Finlyandskim Senatom khodataistvu o peredoklad Ministrom Stat-Sekretarem Vysochaishe otklonnago po doklady Soveta Ministrov vsepoddanneishago predstavleniya Senata ot 6/9 Iunya 1908 goda," *Osobyi zhurnal,* 1909, vol. 1, no. 55, April 14, p. 6; "Po vsepoddanneishemu adresu Finlyandskago Seima ob izmenenii poryadke napravleniya Finlyandskikh del," *ibid.,* 1909, vol. 2, no. 129, September 15, pp. 11-12.

80. Valtionarkisto, KKK, osasto II 4/76, Stolypin to Governor General Bekman, December 13, 1908, pp. 1-2, and July 27, 1909, pp. 1-3; also Stolypin to Governor General Zein (Bekman's successor), November 18, 1909.

81. Project of Finnish Governor General Court F. L. Heiden, 1891; conference of N. Kh. Bunge, October 1892-January 1893; conference of Grand Duke Michael Nikolaevich, 1899; committee under the chairmanship of N. S. Tagantsev, November 1904-October 1905; conference of Count D. M. Sol'sky, February-March 1906.

82. Valtionarkisto, KKK, osasto II 4/23 *ch.* I, *Zhurnal* Vysochaishe uchrezhdennago osobago soveshchaniya po delam Velikago Knyazhestva Finlyandskago (hereafter cited *Zhurnal* vysochaishe uchrezhdennago osobago soveshchaniya), no. 14, December 29, 1908. "Ob uchrezhdenii russko-finlyandskoi komissii dlya sostavleniya proekta pravil o poryadke izdaniya kasayushchikhsya Finlyandii zakonov obshchegosudarstvennago znacheniya," pp. 19-20.

83. *Ibid.* This conference served as a steering committee for the Kharitonov commission.

84. Valtionarkisto, KKK, osasto II/18 *ch.* I, *Zhurnal* Vysochaishe uchrezhdennago osobago soveshchaniya, no. 20, February 21, 1910, "Po voprosu soobshchenii na zakluchenie Finlyandskago Seima zakonoproekta o poryadke izdaniya kasayushchikhsya Finlyandii zakonov obshchegosudarstvennago znacheniya."

85. "Po proektu pravil o poryadke izdaniya kasayushchiksya Finlyandii zakonov i postanovlenii obshchegosudarstvennago znacheniya," *Osobyi zhurnal,* 1910, vol. 1, February 22.

86. Valtionarkisto, KKK, osasto II/18 *ch.* I, *Zhurnal* Vysochaishe uchrezhdennoi komissii dlya vyrabotka proekta pravil o poryadke izdaniya kasayushchikhsya Finlyandii zakonov obshchegosudarstvennago znacheniya, zasedaniya June 16, October 30, December 7 and 8, 1909.

The commission was composed of five Russian and five Finnish members under the chairmanship of P. A. Kharitonov, member of the State Council, State Controller, Senator, and Privy Councilor. The project for the law was worked out by the Russian majority, *ibid.,* pp. 13-24. The dissenting Finnish opinion, *ibid.,* pp. 27-29, contended that the Finnish Fundamental Laws were being changed without agreement of the Diet, claimed that representation provided for Finns in the Duma and State Council did not project Finnish interests, and asked for abolition of the Ordinance of May 20, 1908.

87. Section I, article II. Valtionarkisto, KKK, osasto II/18 *ch.* I. Odobrennyi Gosu-

darstvennym Sovetom i Gosudarstvennoi Dumoi zakon o poryadke izdaniya kasayush-chikhsya Finlyandii zakonov i postanovlenii obshchegosudarstvennago znacheniya, 6 pp.; and 1910 Sbornik postanovlenii Velikago Knyazhestva Finlyandskago, no. 45, odobrennyi Gosudarstvennym Sovetom i Gosudarstvennoi Dumoi i vysochaishe utverzhdennyi zakon 1097 o poryadke izdaniya kasayushchikhsya Finlyandii zakonov i postanovlenii obshchegosudarstvennago znacheniya, 7 pp.

The draft law, approved by the Council of Ministers, is in "Po proektu pravil o poryadke izdaniya kasayushchiksya Finlyandii zakonov i postanovlenii obshche-gosudarstvennago znacheniya, *Osobyi zhurnal,* 1910, vol. 1, February 22.

The text of the bill as worked out by the Duma committee (in meetings of April 27, 29, 30 and May 6, 1910) is on pp. 45-52 of Duma komissiya: Doklad #389. Comparison of the bills introduced by the Council of Ministers to the Duma and worked out by the committee is in *ibid.,* pp. 53-72.

88. The Council of Ministers decided that it was not mandatory for the Finnish members of the Duma to be present for a bill concerning both Finland and the empire to become law. The Duma omitted this clause from the final version of the bill. *Ob"yasnitel'naya zapiska,* pp. 70-72. *Zhurnal* vysochaishe uchrezhdennago osobago soveshchaniya, no. 14, December 29, 1908, p. 30.

89. *Zhurnal* vysochaishe uchrezhdennago osobago soveshchaniya, no. 14, December 29, 1908, pp. 26-29; *Zhurnal* vysochaishe uchrezhdennoi komissii dlya vyrabotka proekta pravil, 1909, p. 56.

90. *Ob"yasnitel'naya zapiska,* p. 74. The Duma committee also deleted this clause.

91. See above notes 83-86.

92. Valtionarkisto, KKK, osasto II/18, *ch.* II (Gosudarstvennaya tipografiya).

93. The countries under comparison were the following: Germany (Constitution, 1871), Austria (Constitution, 1867), Hungary (Law of 1868), Switzerland (Constitution, 1874), the United States (Constitution, 1787), Mexico (Constitution, 1857), Argentina (Constitution, 1860), Brazil (Constitution, 1891), Australia (Act of 1901), Canada (Act of 1867), Venezuela (Constitution, 1904).

94. Nicolson, in F. O. 371, vol. 970, no. 15173, April 28, 1910; *ibid.,* no. 17010, May 13, 1910.

95. O'Beirne, in F. O. 371, vol. 976, no. 21886.

96. See above, note 58.

97. O'Beirne, in F. O. 371, vol. 976, no. 23867, June 29.

98. *Ibid.*

99. *Ibid.*

100. Play by play description of debate on the bill by the Diet is contained in Valtionarkisto, KKK, osasto II/18 ch. I, in six long telegrams from Governor General Zein to Stolypin, April 24 and 25, 1910.

101. *Zhurnal* vysochaishe uchrezhdennago osobago soveshchaniya, no. 20, February 1, 1910, p. 4.

102. F. O. 371, vol. 976, no. 32991, September 5, 1910.

103. F. O. 371, vol. 725, no. 37481, October 6, 1909. British observers in Russia thought the Finnish military contribution of the equivalent of £400,000 per annum from a Finnish national budget of £5 million was a very moderate demand. F. O. 371, vol. 738, no. 39173, October 25, 1909.

104. F. O. 371, vol. 976, no. 37481, p. 2.

105. Valtionarkisto, KKK, osasto II 4/8-2-y, Report of the Imperial Finnish Senate to the Tsar, September 25, 1909 (untitled in the Russian translation), pp. 3-4; *ibid.,* Diet presentation to the Tsar, November 16, 1909, pp. 3-6, 7-8.

106. "O nekotorykh merakh, svyazannikh s izdaniem zakona 17 Iyunya 1910 goda ob obshchegosudarstvennom zakonodatel'stve," *Osobyi zhurnal,* 1910, vol. 2, no. 150, July 3, pp. 6-7.

107. Valtionarkisto, KKK, osasto II 4/8-2-*y,* Governor General Bekman to Stolypin, November 1, 1909. Bekman advocated dissolving the Diet if it rejected the bill on money payments in lieu of military service.

108. *Ibid.,* Stolypin to Governor General Zein, November 27, 1909.

109. Valtionarkisto, KKK, osasto II, 8-2-*A,* Governor General Zein to Stolypin, May 16, 1910; Stolypin to Zein, May 17, 1910.

110. "Po voprosu o postroike v Finlyandii kazarm dlya russkikh voisk," *Osobyi zhurnal,* 1910, vol. 1, no. 3, December 1, 1909, and January 19, 1910, pp. 2-3, 6-8, 9-12.

111. *Ibid.,* pp. 5-6.

112. Valtionarkisto, KKK, osasto II/II-2 *ch.* I, Duma Kommisiya [šic] po napravleniyu zakonodatel'nykh predpolozhenii: Doklad #123 po zakonoproektu ob uravnenii v pravakh s Finlyandskimi grazhdanami drugikh russkikh poddannykh, pp. 2-3.

Nicolson sympathized with the attempt to equalize the rights of Russians living in Finland with those of native Finns. F. O. 371, vol. 515, no. 31802, September 2, 1908.

113. Valtionarkisto, KKK, osasto II 4/42, *Zhurnal* Vysochaishe uchrezhdennago osobago soveshchaniya, no. 17, May 23, 1909, "Ob uravnenii v Finlyandii prav russkikh urozhentsev s pravami mestnikh grazhdan," pp. 2-4, 7.

114. "O nekotorykh merakh svyazannikh s izdaniem zakona 17 Iyunya 1910 goda ob obshchegosudarstvennom zakonodatel'stve," *Osobyi zhurnal,* 1910, vol. 2, no. 150, July 3, p. 5.

115. *Zhurnal* Vysochaishe uchrezhdennago osobago soveshchaniya, no. 17, May 23, 1909, p. 6; "Po voprosu ob uravnenii v pravakh s Finlyandskimi grazhdanami drugikh russkikh poddannykh," *Osobyi zhurnal,* 1910, vol. 2, no. 156, August 3; Valtionarkisto, KKK, osasto II/II-2 *ch.* I, Governor General Zein to Stolypin, November 11, 1910.

Persons who resided in Finland less than one year or who were affiliated with the military were not to be granted this right. *Ibid.,* Governor General Zein to P. A. Kharitonov, November 25, 1910.

Jews and gypsies, although the number of the latter were insignificant, were not to be given equal rights with other Russians in Finland. Duma komissiya: Doklad #123, p. 8.

Of course, Stolypin also firmly upheld a law of 1900 checking transfers of Russians to Finnish citizenship. Nobles and governmental personnel automatically became Finnish citizens if they entered Finnish governmental service. Other classes, however, had to apply for Finnish citizenship. Stolypin reminded the governor general that only in exceptional cases were the Minister State Secretary for Finnish Affairs and the Governor General of Finland permitted to petition the Minister of Internal Affairs (Stolypin) and then the Tsar for such applications. "Po voprosu o perechislenii russkikh urozhentsev v Finlyandskoe grazhdanstvo," *Osobyi zhurnal,* 1909, vol. 2, no. 169, December 1, pp. 3-8; Valtionarkisto, KKK, osasto II/16, Stolypin to the governor general, January 6, 1910.

116. The Orthodox Bishop of Finland and Vyborg and the Chief-Procurator of the Holy Synod, who were far more zealous in promoting Orthodoxy among the Finns than Stolypin was, accused the Lutheran pastors in Finland of trying to convert Orthodox en masse. Valtionarkisto, KKK, osasto II/3-2, Archbishop of Finland and Vyborg to Governor General Gerard, June 30, 1906; *ibid.,* Chief-Procurator of the Holy Synod to

Gerard, October 12, 1906; *ibid.*, Perevod otnosheniya Khozyaistvennago Departmenta Imperatorskago Finlyandskago Senata k gospodinu Vr. i. d. Finlyandskago General-Gubernatora, August 1, 1907.

Criticism of the Finnish Senate's bill in Valtionarkisto, KKK, osasto II/3-2, Stolypin to Governor General Zein, February 11, 1910; *ibid.*, Chief-Procurator of the Holy Synod to Stolypin, May 12, 1910; *ibid.*, Stolypin to the Minister State Secretary for Finnish Affairs, A. F. Lanhof, February 11, 1910; *ibid.*, *Spravka* k otnosheniyu Ministra Stats-Sekretarya Finlyandii ot 24 Fevralya (9 Marta) 1910 za no. 460 po voprosu o voznikayushchikh dlya detei posledstviyakh perekhoda ikh roditelei iz pravoslavnago v evangelichesko-lyuteranskoe ospovedanie (ot 1 Avgusta 1907). Sostavlena kantselyareyu Soveta Ministrov, pp. 1-6; *ibid.*, Minister State Secretary Lanhof to Stolypin, February 24, 1910; *ibid.*, Doklad po kantselyarii Finlyandskago General-Gubernatora po voprosu a voznikayushchikhsya, March-April, 1910, pp. 1-7; *ibid.*, letter of the Council of Ministers (signed by Kokovtsov) to the Minister State Secretary of Finland, April 4, 1910.

117. Valtionarkisto, KKK, osasto II 4/65, Archbishop of Finland and Vyborg to Governor General Bekman, July 17, 1907 and January 21, 1908; *ibid.*, Stolypin to Bekman, September 13, 1908; *ibid.*, Chief-Procurator of the Holy Synod to the Council of Ministers, August 10, 1908; *ibid.*, Bekman to Stolypin, January 7, 1909; *ibid,* Stolypin to Governor General Zein, February 11, 1910.

In one instance cited above the building plans of a town conflicted with parish property rights. In a second instance, a monastery asked for protection from harassment of local Finns, Valtionarkisto, KKK, osasto I 1/XLIII, Stolypin to Governor General Zein, December 2, 1909; *ibid.*, Chief-Procurator of the Holy Synod to Stolypin, November 4, 1909; *ibid.*, Governor General Zein to P. D. Ol'khovsky, commander of the 22nd Army Corps, December 7, 1909.

See Stolypin's statement in *ibid.*, Stolypin to Governor General Zein, December 23, 1909.

118. Valtionarkisto, KKK, osasto II/26, *Zhurnal* vysochaishe uchrezhdennago osobago soveshchaniya, no. 24, November 13, 1910, "Po voprosu ob ustanovlenii mezhdu pravitel'stvennymi uchrezhdeniyami i dolzhnostnymi litsami Finlyandii i prochikh chastei Imperii neposredstvennykh snoshenii na obshchegosudarstvennom yazyke," p. 15.

119. *Ibid.*, pp. 18-19; "Po voprosu ob ustanovlenii mezhdu pravitel'stvennymi uchrezhdenniyami i dolzhnostnymi litsami Finlyandii i prochikh chastei Imperii neposredstvennykh snoshenii na obshchegosudarstvennom yazyke," *Osobyi zhurnal,* 1911, vol. 2, no. 145, July 12. Use of the Russian language in official communication was declared a matter for state legislation by the Law of June 17, 1910.

120. There were thirty-six Russian schools in Finland, fifteen of which were in Karelia.

121. Valtionarkisto, KKK, osasto II/5-5, Stolypin to Zein, July 30, 1911; *ibid.*, Stolypin to L. A. Kasso, July 30, 1911.

122. Valtionarkisto, KKK, osasto I/57-10, report of Stolypin: O prepodavanii zakona Bozhiya vospitannikam-finlyandtsam, obuchayushchimsya v nekotorykh russkikh uchebnykh zavedeniyakh, circa January 21, 1911, pp. 2-4.

123. Polivanov, *Iz dnevnikov i vospominanii po dolzhnosti voennogo ministra i ego pomoshchika, 1907-1916,* pp. 82-88.

124. Valtionarkisto, KKK, osasto I/LVIII-3, Soveshchanie po voprosu o merakh na sluchi vozniknoveniya bezporyadkov v Finlyandii, October 5, 1909, pp. 1-3; *ibid.*, Stolypin to the Finnish Governor General, January 23, 1910; "Po voprosu o merakh na

sluchi bezporyadkov v Finlyandii, *Osobyi zhurnal,* 1910, vol. 1, December 1, 1909, 16 pp.; F. O. 371, vol. 759, March 3, 1908.

125. Valtionarkisto, KKK, IX-3, Stolypin to Governor General Bekman, December 28, 1908; also, osasto II 4/7-2-*ch.* III, Stolypin to Bekman, March 10, 1908.

Articles from the Finnish press are contained in Valtionarkisto, KKK, IX-3 and osasto II 4/7-2-*ch.* III.

126. Valtionarkisto, KKK, 7-4, Stolypin to Governor General Gerard, December 20, 1907, and Stolypin to Gerard, January 18, 1908; Valtionarkisto, KKK, IX-3, Stolypin to Governor General Bekman, December 28, 1908; Valtionarkisto, KKK, osasto II 4/7-2-*ch.* III, Stolypin to Bekman, September 18, 1908, pp. 1-3.

127. Valtionarkisto, KKK, 7-4, Stolypin to Governor General Gerard, December 20, 1907, pp. 1-2.

128. Valtionarkisto, KKK, osasto II 4/7-2 *ch.* III, Stolypin to Governor General Bekman, September 18, 1908, p. 2; *ibid.,* Stolypin to Bekman, May 5, 1909.

129. Valtionarkisto, KKK, XXVI, letter of the Finnish Governor General to the Governor of Vilna province, December 1907-January 1908; *ibid.,* Stolypin to Minister State Secretary Lanhof, February 1, 1908.

130. *Ibid.,* Stolypin to Minister State Secretary Lanhof, February 1, 1908.

131. Valtionarkisto, KKK, XXVI [Comparison of] Proekt Ministra Vnutrennikh del'—Proekt Finlyandskago General-Gubernatora.

132. See above, p. 132. The Diet was closed because it vetoed a Senate bill which approved measures the Russian government was taking in Finland to squelch revolutionary activity and because it opposed money grants for defense. "Po voprosu o rospuke nyne sobrannago ocherednago Finlyandskago seima," *Osobyi zhurnal,* 1908, vol. 1, no. 59, March 18, pp. 1-6.

Two committees of the Diet—the Ekspeditsionaya and the Poverochnaya—continued to operate for several months after dissolution, mainly taking care of unpaid bills. Stolypin argued that such activity was legitimate only after normal closure. Valtionarkisto, KKK, osasto II 4/8-4, Stolypin to Governor General Bekman, March 29, 1908; *ibid.,* Bekman to Stolypin, April 22/25, 1908; *ibid.,* Stolypin to Bekman, April 16, 1908; *ibid.,* Stolypin to Bekman, April 25, 1908; *ibid.,* Memorandum of the Economic Department of the Imperial Finnish Senate, May 18, 1908; *ibid.,* Bekman to Stolypin, June, 1908, pp. 2-3.

133. Plans for closing the Diet prematurely in 1910 are in Valtionarkisto, KKK, osasto II/8-6, Stolypin to Governor General Zein, February 8, 1910; *ibid.,* Zein to Stolypin February 10, 1910; *ibid.,* Zein to Nicholas II, n.d.; *ibid.,* Zein to Minister State Secretary, May 2 and 15, 1910.

134. Zein pointed out that premature closing of the Diet, rather than dissolution, would give the government more time before convocation of the next Diet, according to the rules for dissolution and closure. Valtionarkisto, KKK, osasto II/8-6, Zein to Stolypin, February 17, 1911; *ibid.,* Zein to Stolypin, February 10, 1911; *ibid.,* Stolypin to Zein, February 10, 1911; *ibid.,* Zein to Stolypin, April 14, 1911; *ibid.,* telegram from Stolypin to Zein, April 1911.

135. Valtionarkisto, KKK, osasto I 3/25, Stolypin to Nicholas II, "Po voprosu o prazdnovanii stoletnago yubileya zavoevaniya Finlyandii," February 20, 1909, pp. 2-3.

136. Valtionarkisto, KKK, osasto II 4/65, Stolypin to Governor General Bekman, August 22 and 24, 1909; *ibid.,* Stolypin to Kokovtsov, May 6, 1911.

137. Hugh Seton-Watson, *The Russian Empire, 1801-1917,* p. 670.

138. "Pismo predsedatelya Soveta Ministrov i ministra vnutr. del P. A. Stolypina na

imya namestnika na Kavkaze gr. I. I. Vorontsova-Dashkova ot 11 aprelya (st. st.) 1908 g. No. 64885," and "Bor'ba s revolyutsionnym dvizheniem na Kavkaze v epokhu stolypinshchinu," *Krasny arkhiv,* 34 (1929), pp. 187-202.

139. *Ibid.,* p. 194.
140. *Ibid.,* p. 192.
141. *Ibid.,* p. 194.
142. *Ibid.,* pp. 200-201.

Chapter 6:
Stolypin and the Parliament

The First and Second Dumas

On October 17, 1905, in the midst of revolution, Nicholas had given the Russian people a parliament, the State Duma. Thus began Russia's eleven-year experiment with popular participation in the legislative process. The liberals were ecstatic; this was the moment of which they had dreamed. At last Russia could stand with other enlightened nations of the world. Nicholas, and conservative and reactionary elements at court and throughout the country, had varying emotions, ranging from apprehension to abhorrence of the new parliament. Almost immediately after the declaration establishing the Duma had been issued, Nicholas retreated, narrowing both the representation and the jurisdiction of the Duma. Therefore, when Stolypin assumed office the Duma was neither genuinely representative nor did it have full legislative power.[1] Nevertheless, it was the closest approximation to a representative legislature which Russia had ever had, and there were many who believed the Duma would evolve into a full-fledged parliament.

Stolypin did not wish to return to the old order. Neither however, did he wholly endorse popular participation in the legislative process. He always considered the Duma a peripheral entity, an appendage to the administration, which might advise the administration and ratify its measures, but not check or direct it.

He disapproved of an elected legislature not on principle, but for practical reasons. First, he believed that a chief prerequisite for it, namely, a stable and enlightened electorate, was lacking. In the only record we have of Stolypin's views on the Duma prior to 1906, he intimated that the peasants' economic and educational level would have to be raised before they would be able to participate in enacting legislation.[2] This opinion did not change. In August 1907 he told the British Ambassador Sir Arthur Nicolson that "political life and parliamentary ideals were enigmas to the enormous majority of the nation, ignorant and unlettered as they were," and harking back to the theory of Montesquieu espoused by Catherine II, he added that "it was impossible to govern a vast Empire like Russia on the lines of advanced Western Nations."[3]

Even so, an experiment with a representative legislature might have been acceptable to Stolypin had not Russia, recently emerged from a disastrous and costly war, been suffering from agrarian problems and revolutionary turmoil. In addition to forceful authority, Russia needed improvements in her social, economic, and administrative sectors. Stolypin was willing to tolerate the Duma only insofar as it fit in with his scheme for bettering the country.

The factor which finally decided Stolypin's attitude toward popular participation in the legislative process during the First and Second Dumas was the conduct of these bodies, which appeared to Stolypin destructive of the peace and incapable of constructive legislation.

The First Duma, which opened in the Winter Palace on April 27 and then reconvened in the Tauride Palace, the yellow and white classical structure which Catherine II had built for her lover Potemkin, was dominated by the Kadet party. It immediately adopted the Kadet program: amnesty for political prisoners, obligatory alienation of private estates, a ministry responsible to the Duma, universal and direct suffrage, abolition of the State Council, repeal of exceptional law, abolition of the death penalty, and administrative reform.[4] The Duma presented this program, which was obviously more liberal than the government would accept, more as an ultimatum than a request. It greeted ministers' speeches, including that of Stolypin on aid to famine-stricken areas, with boos and cat-calls. The extreme left parties used the Duma as a forum in which to proclaim anti-governmental and revolutionary slogans.[5] The Duma accomplished little constructive legislation. At its untimely demise on July 9, 1906, it had finished considering only two bills: one for aid to areas suffering from crop failure and another for abolition of the death penalty.

The government, under the leadership of I. L. Goremykin, was equally hostile. Ministers ignored Duma sessions and, with the exception of A. P. Izvolsky, Minister of Foreign Affairs, waited from the beginning for an occasion to dissolve the Duma.[6] The opportunity finally came in May when the Duma "appealed to the people" over the authority of the government to await a land reform based upon compulsory expropriation.

Stolypin, who had arrived in Petersburg nearly simultaneously with the opening of the Duma, exhibited a certain amount of tolerance toward the new parliament. According to the recollections of Minister of Finance V. N. Kokovtsov, Stolypin feared that one of the deputies might hurl a bomb, yet he favored a "watch and wait" policy.[7] To Sir Arthur Nicolson, Stolypin contended on the eve of the Duma's dissolution that it was not surprising that "violent and inflammatory language was being used in the Duma. Tongues had recently been loosened and it was inevitable that orators should revel in their newly acquired liberty of speech."[8]

On the other hand, he admitted that he had been critical of the Duma in its early sessions[9] and that finally he had urged the Tsar to dissolve the Duma, although the latter did not like the idea.[10] Stolypin was in favor of dissolution for two reasons. First, he considered the Kadet program unrealistic and even dangerous:

A complete amnesty was impossible, for not only would dangerous elements be let loose upon society, but the immunity of criminals would encourage others to commit similar crimes. A general expropriation of land, irrespective of any consideration, would be unjust and economically ruinous. It was scarcely the moment to abolish the death penalty when police officers and others were being daily shot down. . . . As to equality of rights for all, this no doubt was a question which to the European mind seemed an elementary right. But in Russia, in view of the backward state of education and of the traditional antipathy of the Russian for the Jew, the question must be dealt with cautiously.[11]

Second, he felt that the Duma was usurping the government's authority, confusing governors and other local officials as to where their allegiance lay and even "carrying out an active revolutionary propaganda in the provinces."[12] He himself had "felt the reins were slipping out of his hands," and that if the administrative and social disintegration to which he had alluded continued much longer "he could not be responsible for maintenance of order."[13] In general, he insisted that his "own ideal was the British Constitution, but it was impossible to cast Russia at once into that mold. In some years she might reach that goal, but sudden and impetuous changes would work ruin."[14]

This wariness of popular representation, at least as it had manifested itself in the First Duma, and the social and political disorganization which existed in Russia during the summer and fall of 1906, determined Stolypin's policy in the eight months before the scheduled opening of the Second Duma. Having been appointed Chairman of the Council of Ministers at the same time the Duma was dissolved, Stolypin's chief goals were two: to secure and maintain the government's, and particularly, his own power, and to inaugurate important measures before the Duma was back in session.

On one level, strengthening the government's power meant the enactment of various repressive measures. On another, it meant rejecting any possibility of a partnership between the Kadets and the government; and, practically, it meant curbing the Kadets. The institution of a responsible ministry, dominated by the Kadets, had been suggested before the dissolution of the First Duma by V. F. Trepov, a member of the court circle. The Tsar appointed Stolypin to confer with P. N. Miliukov, one of the Kadet leaders, on this matter. Negotiations took place both before and after dissolution. Miliukov insisted upon implementation of the Kadet program as a basis for agreement and requested four chief ministries—including Stolypin's own—and chairmanship of the Council of Ministers for the Kadets. Octobrists were to be named to two other posts, there was a possibility that Izvolsky would remain Minister of Foreign Affairs, and the Tsar was to have the prerogative of selecting the Naval, War, and Court ministers.[15]

Stolypin would have none of this. In addition to his opposition to the Kadet program he became convinced, through his discussions with Miliukov and because of party policy after the dissolution, that the Kadets were irresponsible. In one of his interviews with Miliukov, Stolypin asked what the Kadet leader would do, should he become Chairman of the Council of Ministers, if the Kadet program were implemented and, taking advantage of the laissez-faire situation, more extreme revolutionary parties attempted to overthrow the government and establish a socialist republic. According to Stolypin, Miliukov answered that he would "shoot down the anarchists freely, more freely than Stolypin himself."[16] After the dissolution, the Kadets and some members of parties to their left went to Vyborg, part of the province of Finland. There they issued a manifesto which called upon the Russian people to refuse to pay taxes and send recruits to the army until the new Duma should be convened. The Vyborg Manifesto actually would have had little practical effect, and the Kadets originally intended it to be merely a proclamation of passive resistence. However, they yielded to the radical parties present and made it more vociferous.[17] The Kadets continued to flirt with violent, revolutionary groups. In August 1906, in the midst of daily terror, mostly perpetrated by the Socialist Revolutionaries, the Kadet paper *Rech* published an article calling for continued cooperation between the Kadets, the Social Democrats, and the Socialist Revolutionaries.[18]

Stolypin opposed a Kadet cabinet also because he claimed that if they assumed power and then failed, due to their "doctrinaire views" and subservience to the "Left Wing of the Chamber," the Tsar would be forced to ask more radical groups, who formed the largest bloc in the Duma after the Kadets, to form a government, thus resulting in the ultimate "ruin of the dynasty and of the country."[19]

Stolypin's distrust of the Kadets further led him to interfere in their campaigns for the Second and Third Dumas. The Kadets who had taken part in the Vyborg proceedings were disqualified from taking part in the elections for the Second Duma. This meant that 120 out of 169 possible Kadet candidates were forbidden to run. In addition, in August 1906 Stolypin forbade the Kadets to hold a meeting in which they were to draw up their program for the following year.[20] In August 1907 he likewise refused to allow the Kadets to hold a party congress. Kadets were barred from both membership and employment in the zemstvos. According to Kokovtsov, Stolypin condoned intimidation practices against the Kadets on the part of local officials, and there is at least one instance in which he approved the dismissal of a Kadet zemstvo president who had refused to list the political affiliation of zemstvo members.[21] Kadet newspapers also were hard hit by administrative fines during the election campaigns.[22]

While Stolypin repudiated the Kadets, he did attempt to draw more moderate liberals into the government. He succeeded in having the Tsar dismiss the two most reactionary ministers, A. S. Stishinsky, Minister of Agriculture, and A. A. Shirinsky-Shikhmatov, Chief Procurator of the Holy Synod. They were replaced by the more liberal B. A. Vasilchikov and P. P. Izvolsky, brother of the Minister of Foreign Affairs. In addition, both before and after the Duma's dissolution Stolypin carried on negotiations with leading Octobrists for the formation of a so-called Cabinet of Public Men, that is, a cabinet including persons who had never held positions in the bureaucracy. It must be noted that the idea of a Cabinet of Public Men, as well as that of a Kadet cabinet, had originated with the Tsar or his entourage and not with Stolypin.

The individuals whom Stolypin was to conscript into the cabinet included A. I. Guchkov, N. N. Lvov, D. N. Shipov, Prince G. E. Lvov, A. F. Koni, and Count Heyden. Guchkov and N. N. Lvov were leading Octobrists and personal friends of Stolypin. Guchkov was an industrialist from a sectarian family, later became president of the Third Duma, and remained on close terms with Stolypin nearly to the end of Stolypin's tenure. N. N. Lvov had worked with Stolypin in Saratov, although their friendship later terminated. Shipov was an ex-Kadet and zemstvo leader from Moscow. Prince Lvov, who became head of the Provisional Government in 1917, was chairman of the all-zemstvo union. Koni was a distinguished jurist.

The Octobrists were moderate reformers who had separated from the Kadets by accepting the October Manifesto of 1905. Their platform for the Second Duma acknowledged that Russia was a hereditary, constitutional monarchy. Supreme authority was vested in the Tsar. However, his power was limited by the Fundamental Laws. The Duma and the State Council had equal power, but the Duma ought to have certain privileges in financial legislation. The Octobrists were proponents of equal and direct suffrage for all over twenty-five who had fulfilled a residency requirement. They supported direct elections in towns, but approved two curiae, landowner and peasant, for elections held in rural areas. They considered ministers liable to impeachment either by the crown or by a motion of the Duma and the State Council. They agitated for freedom of the press, speech, meetings, and association, and for equal rights for women.

The Octobrists' political views obviously were more liberal than Stolypin's, but their proposals for social and economic improvement were very similar to his. They repudiated expropriation of estates and regarded the establishment of separated farmsteads as a solution to the agrarian problem. In addition, like Stolypin they advocated cash credits for peasants, the establishment of agricultural schools, model farms, dissemination of agricultural techniques, and the distribution of public land to peasants. Believing that social welfare was the responsibility of the government, they campaigned for accident and sickness compensation, old age pensions, and a minimum working day. They advocated legalizing trade unions and the establishment of tribunals for arbitration of strikes and disputes between labor and management. They strove for social reform, including equal rights for Jews—which was beyond what Stolypin approved—and also for free, compulsory primary education. Unlike Stolypin, they desired more freedom for private initiative in founding schools.[23]

Despite personal friendships and the similarity of many of their views, Stolypin and the public men failed to reach an agreement on a coalition cabinet. The public men stipulated that they be given half the ministerial posts, that a new Duma be convened immediately and legislative proposals dealing with the most pressing problems in the country and the rights promised in the October Manifesto be submitted to it, and that capital punishment be suspended until the legislative chambers sanctioned it.[24]

To Stolypin, abolition of the death penalty, in the face of terror, was as unacceptable when proposed by the Octobrists as by the Kadets. As for immediate convocation of a Second Duma which would be entrusted with the enactment of necessary reforms, Stolypin did not believe the Duma could either control revolutionary, terrorist groups or achieve improvement. What was necessary was a sovereign but paternalistic authority. "For the present the firmness of the State authority is necessary, unhampered by unjust criticism or by the short-sighted proposals of people who form opinions without being in touch with the facts." The government would owe its authority only to the "projected reforms without retreating a single step."[25] Of course, Stolypin himself had to remain at the head of this government, for "he saw clearly what measures were required" and was convinced that "the government would be able without delay to grant to all classes of the population what they really needed."[26]

From their side, the public men also had reason to reject the coalition cabinet. They could not agree to join if their program were not accepted. In addition, they were fearful of compromising their careers by entering the government.[27] Finally, Shipov, for one, believed his entering the government would be futile because he lacked a following in the Duma.[28]

Collapse of the discussions on the formation of either a Kadet cabinet or a Cabinet of Public Men left Stolypin free to initiate both repressive and reform measures on the responsibility of the government alone. Under his auspices the ministry approved fifty-eight temporary laws on the basis of article 87 of the Fundamental State Laws of 1906, which gave the government the power to enact necessary measures while the Duma was not in session. Most of these measures were inconsequential; of far greater importance were the manifold reform proposals which ministers were readying to present to the Second Duma. However, among the temporary measures were the extremely significant agrarian regulations; the decree establishing the courts martial; regulations punishing sedition in the army, universities, the press, and speech; and six reforms concerning the Old Believers, sectarians, and non-Orthodox Christians.

Following the procedure established by article 87, these measures later were introduced to the Second Duma for confirmation. However, it is obvious that once these measures—particularly the agrarian measures and the courts martial, which would have the greatest repercussions—had been put into operation their reversal by the Second Duma would have been difficult or would have had little effect.

Disapproval of these temporary measures, particularly the agrarian reforms, without prior sanction of the Duma was voiced within the Council of Ministers by Minister of Finance Kokovtsov and by Prince Vasilchikov and Prince Obolensky of the Ministry of Internal Affairs. They contended that the next Duma was not so distant that the government could not wait until the Duma assembled. Stolypin, however, justified the use of article 87 to implement the agrarian laws on the grounds that Russia was in a state of crisis and that it was more efficient to implement the laws through the ministry rather than through the Duma.[29]

The final problem to which Stolypin had to attend before the next Duma met was the election for this Duma. In this matter his policy was to prevent opposition parties from gaining a majority. Thus, while he issued a circular to governors and local authorities in February 1907 stipulating that, barring antigovernmental propaganda, the elections were to proceed in complete freedom,[30] this was not the case. It is true that some of the irregularities which took place during the Duma election apparently were committed or allowed by local officials without Stolypin's knowledge or approval.[31] And it is also true that some restrictions issued by Stolypin in August and October 1906 had been promulgated by the Senate in March 1906. These included the regulations prohibiting administrative personnel from becoming directors of political parties of any complexion or chairmen of their committees.[32] Nevertheless, Stolypin not only restricted the Kadets but also subsidized parties to their right in order to achieve a moderate Second Duma.[33]

He did not succeed. The Second Duma was composed of 65 Social Democrats, 34 Socialist Revolutionaries, 15 Narodnik Socialists, 100 Labor Deputies, 22 deputies of reactionary persuasion, 40-50 unaffiliated deputies (mostly priests and peasants who voted with the right), 92 Kadets, and some representatives of the national minorities in the empire. The largest group of the latter were the Poles, number-ing 47 seats. They often voted with the Kadets.

The most comprehensive description of the Second Duma, Alfred Levin's *The Second Duma,*[34] graphically portrays the dissension which racked the Duma almost from the beginning. The extreme left parties, which had boycotted the First Duma, clashed with the extreme right parties in the Second Duma and used the Duma floor as a proscenium on which to deliver revolutionary speeches. The Kadets were now cast as mediators between left and right, and although they desperately attempted to save the Duma, they also antagonized the government.[35] They continued to demand forced alienation of land, although they later added a clause specifying that there be "just" compensation. They refused to support a resolution of the right condemning terror, although Stolypin personally appealed to Miliukov to do so. They pressed for abolition of the courts martial, despite the fact that the courts were to expire legally two months after the Duma had begun.[36] Like the First Duma, the Second accomplished no constructive work. It did not even consider one of the most important items, the state budget, and even the Kadets criticized the leftist deputies for being unprepared for committee work.

Stolypin made some conciliatory gestures toward the Second Duma. Believing that one of the mistakes of the Goremykin government had been its failure to present the First Duma with a progressive, concrete program,[37] Stolypin introduced the impressive body of reform proposals which the government had worked on during the fall and winter of 1906-1907 for Duma debate. He also attended Duma meetings, which Goremykin and his cabinet had rarely done, and showed himself to be a dynamic orator. He held discussions with the Kadets and moderate liberals on certain matters, urging them, for example, to consider the budget, in order to ward off dissolution.[38]

On the other hand, he annoyed the Duma by rigorously enforcing a regulation of August 1905 which stipulated that non-Duma members be refused admittance to Duma sessions. A guard and crew of gendarmes were posted at the entrance to the Duma chanbers and the chief of the stenographic department was excluded twice by mistake. Stolypin also sent officious notes to the Duma president, F. A. Golovin.[39]

Part of the problem, of course, was simply inexperience on both the part of the Duma and the government. The Kadets naively expected immediate realization of the sort of political system which England had taken centuries to produce. The government was equally unsure about how to handle the parliament. Not only was this obvious from its overt actions, but behind the scenes it debated in December 1906, for instance, whether the Second Duma ought to be considered an extension of the First or a new Duma with bills discarded by the First submitted to it again in original form. The ministry finally decided to resubmit the bills in a shortened form.[40]

Stolypin's overriding concern was to prevent the Duma from disrupting the country or impeding the government's plans for moderate reform. As early as September 1906 he had warned Nicolson that if the Duma were composed of a majority of extreme parties, he would not hesitate to recommend dissolution.[41] On April 9 he complained to the Tsar that his visit to the Duma had left him with the impression of dullness and greyness; the Duma was "rotting on its stem." The committees had not engaged in work because of "lack of preparation and the inability to work in general."[42] A week later he informed Nicholas that if the Duma did not approve the new draft of recruits it would be dissolved.[43] However, the Duma was not dissolved until June 3, 1907, as a result of its refusal to expel and permit the arrest of the deputies who had allegedly participated in the Ozol affair.

The Ozol affair involved the discovery on May 5 of some documents in the apartment of I. P. Ozol, Duma deputy and member of the Social Democratic party. The government contended that this was evidence of Social Democratic plans to incite insurrection in the army.[44] On June 1 Stolypin requested that the Duma approve the arrest of sixteen Social Democratic deputies and suspend thirty-nine others.

Kokovtsov believed that Stolypin and the Tsar had decided that dissolution was necessary as early as April 17 after the Armenian Social Democratic deputy Zurabov stated that the Russian army was not always victorious.[45] The British observer Sir Bernard Pares considered the Ozol affair merely a pretext for dissolution; the Duma was dissolved, in his opinion, not only because of past conflict with the government, but also in order to avoid future conflict. However, he believed dissolution had been forced upon Stolypin by reactionaries.[46] Sir Arthur Nicolson, on the other hand, accepted the Ozol affair as genuine.[47] The historian George Tokmakoff theorizes that Stolypin did not definitively decide upon dissolution until the night of June 2, when, meeting with the Kadets, he came to understand that they would not support the government demand for arrest and expulsion of the Social Democratic deputies. The dissolution decree had been signed June 1, however, and Tokmakoff admits that

Stolypin might have dissolved the Duma even if the Kadets had acquiesced.[48] Most probably, the decision to dissolve the Duma was made by June 1 and Stolypin met with the Kadet leaders in order to put the onus of dissolution on their shoulders.

In any case, Stolypin waited as long as he did to dissolve the Duma for two reasons. The first was to finish a new electoral law. The ministry had discussed the possibility of a new electoral law as early as the dissolution of the First Duma and had begun working on the law during the winter of 1906-1907. The new law was to be promulgated with the notice of dissolution.[49] Stolypin's second motive was revealed in his letter to the Tsar of April 9. He wanted to give the Duma ample opportunity to discredit itself before the country at large, for if the Duma had been dissolved prematurely, the left would have been able to "create the legend that the Duma would have been wonderful, but the government stifled it and disturbed all."[50]

Stolypin's avowed purpose in issuing the new electoral law, as was his purpose in the reorganization of local self-government which he was formulating at the same time, was to secure representation "of the 'best classes' of the country, those in fact, who had material interests at stake, and who were well educated and men of experience and of business." He believed landowners had been poorly represented in the last two Dumas and manufacturers not at all, with the result that "two stable elements had ˙hitherto had practically no weight or part in the legislation of the Empire." He claimed that he did not desire a "landlords' Duma," but he rejected the notion that the landlords as a class were reactionary. Rather, he stressed that this class contained many Octobrists, Kadets, and other liberals, who he hoped would be elected. The same could be said of urban electors. He emphasized that he did not wish to "exclude the Kadets, whom he considered as possessing some of the best brains in the Empire." What he hoped for was a Duma with a middle-class mentality. He anticipated that the new Duma would be in opposition to the government, but it would be a sensible and moderate opposition, with whom the government could work.[51]

To achieve this kind of Duma the new electoral law reduced the representation of the peasantry from 42 percent to 24½ percent. The percentage allotted to landowners, on the other hand, was increased from 31 percent to 51½ percent. In addition, voters were placed in special categories. In the countryside they were divided into first- and second-class townsmen. Townsmen of the first class consisted of property owners. Those of the second class were nearly all professional people and were likely to vote for the Kadets. In these curiae, landowners and first-class townsmen received artificial majorities. The Law of June 3 also incorporated a Senate decision which disenfranchised about 9 million peasant voters—those employed in towns and those not heads of families. As a result of the Law of June 3 one elector represented 250 landowners, 1,000 bourgeoisie, 15,000 urban lower class, 60,000 peasants, and 125,000 industrial workers.

The law also reduced the representation of national minorities. Central Asian peoples were almost excluded. Siberian representation, which had been strongly Kadet, and Caucasian representation, which had been largely Menshevik, were narrowed. The delegation of Poles from Poland was reduced from thirty-four to fourteen, and two Polish deputies were to be chosen by Russians living in Poland, thus reducing Polish opportunities for vociferousness or obstructionism in the next Duma. The Law of June 3 also permitted the Minister of Internal Affairs to distribute seats.

An average of one-third of the voters were eliminated by the provisions of the June 3 law. In St. Petersburg there was a reduction of nearly 40,000 voters. Only 87,981 persons were qualified to vote under the new electoral law as against 126,389 persons under the old. In thirty-four out of fifty-one provinces the gentry received an absolute majority of electors. Usually not more than one-tenth of the smaller landowners received representation.[52]

In addition to criticizing the content of the Law of June 3, contemporary jurists believed that it had been issued in an unconstitutional manner. According to the Fundamental Laws of 1906, the electoral law could not be changed without consent of the Duma and the State Council. However, the Law of June 3 had been issued in the form of an imperial ukase.[53]

But Stolypin had tackled the problem of achieving a sensible Third Duma with his customary practicality. He conceded that the law might have been issued in an irregular manner (although there is no certainty that he really believed this), but believed it was the only thing which could be done under the circumstances. It was impossible to have a Third Duma composed of elements similar to the First or the Second. Since the Duma would not have approved a new electoral law, it might have been formulated by a national convention of zemstvo bodies meeting especially for this purpose or by the State Council. However, the method which he had taken, though "perhaps, a coup d'etat . . . was the simplest and most direct course."[54]

This is not to say that Stolypin had made his decision lightly or that his political realism had not saved the parliament from a worse fate. According to Kokovtsov, Stolypin had become convinced of the necessity of changing the electoral law only after much soul-searching. Kokovtsov, in fact, believed that the idea had originated with someone other than Stolypin in the Ministry of Internal Affairs.[55] Stolypin also apparently had tempered more extreme versions of the law; it was alleged that the Tsar had not wanted any members of the Second Duma to participate in the Third.[56] Furthermore, Stolypin had been criticized by the reactionary press for postponing dissolution in order to promulgate the new electoral law with the notice of dissolution. British dispatches to the Foreign Office claimed that he almost resigned because his position was so difficult.[57]

Thus, although the June electoral law was an example of Stolypin's matter-of-fact political style, his tendency to eliminate expendable encumbrances with or without adhering to legal niceties, it also illustrated his willingness to experiment with a third Duma, provided it was capable and moderate. The first two Dumas had proved to be unsettling experiences for both government and moderate opposition groups. The Third Duma was to be the real test of the viability of a parliament in Russia.

The Third Duma

The Third Duma was to be a decisive indicator of whether a national, representative legislature could effectively participate in the formulation of state policy, could share in the governance of Russia. As we shall see, Stolypin was sympathetic to the Third Duma and he and the Octobrist party cooperated on many occasions. Nevertheless, Stolypin's relationship with the Duma had to fit within the framework of the political situation which existed in Russia. This meant, first, that his relationship with the Duma always was subordinate to his relationship with the Tsar, whose good will was indispensible for maintaining his position and implementing his policies. Second, Russia had to be kept on an even, moderate course. Thus, to a lesser extent, Stolypin was concerned about keeping crucial sectors under the control of the administration, particularly under his control. These two considerations were to result in two major crises and several minor conflicts and ultimately to lead to a breach between Stolypin and the Duma.

The June 3 electoral law produced its intended effect. The Third

Duma began its first session on November 7, 1907, with an auspicious composition. The Octobrists were the majority party, with 154 seats. They also dominated the most important committees, finance and defense.[58] The parties of the right had 127 seats. The Kadets had only 54 and the leftist parties 33, 17 of which belonged to the Social Democrats. The average age of the deputies was higher (there were few under thirty) and they were better educated that those of the Second Duma.

During almost its entire first session the Duma worked harmoniously with the government. In February 1908, for example, the Kadets condemned terror as a means of carrying on the political struggle.[59] In May the Duma passed the government bill on compulsory primary education, which had also been introduced to the Second Duma.

Stolypin, for his part, showed himself eager to work with the Duma. On November 9, 1907, the Tsar informed Stolypin that he would not receive a delegation from the Duma since it had not yet proved itself willing to cooperate with the government.[60] Stolypin begged Nicholas to retract his refusal, and told him that he was rewording the Tsar's message so that it would not appear that the Tsar had repudiated the Duma. He assured Nicholas that the Duma was "loyal to the Tsar," wished "genuinely and passionately to see him," and looked upon him with "kind attention."[61] In January 1908 the Council of Ministers, including Stolypin, confirmed, in answer to the Minister of Ways and Communications, that ministers and department heads were subject to interpellation by the Duma and its committees and subcommittees, on all reasonable matters.[62] At the same time, the Minister of Ways and Communications was granted conditional credits for the department budget because the state budget had not yet been approved by the Duma and the need was urgent. However, the minister was not given the amount requested because the ministry considered it higher than the budget rules permitted, a fact which might have prejudiced the Duma in considering the budget for 1908.[63]

In March 1908 Stolypin annouced happily to Nicolson that the Third Duma was very different from the first two. Duma members "now showed a sincere desire to work and were assiduous in the Committees. . . . His relations with many members of the Duma were frequent and cordial." In general, he was "fairly satisfied" with the Duma.[64] Stolypin attended Duma committee meetings and there were numerous meetings outside the Duma between the deputies and Stolypin or other ministers, particularly on matters of state defense.[65]

It was with Stolypin's sanction that Guchkov criticized General Roediger, Minister of War and the Grand Duke Nicholas Nikolaevich, chairman of the Council of State Defense, in May and June 1908.[66] In fact, Stolypin maintained particularly close connections with Guchkov and the latter often conferred with Stolypin prior to bringing up business in the Duma.[67] In June 1908 Stolypin proposed that Duma deputies be granted a fixed annual salary of 4,500 rubles, instead of the eight-month allowance of 2,400 rubles they then received. Insufficient remuneration, he told his fellow ministers, was a hardship for the deputies and caused many to refuse Duma membership.[68] In December 1908, despite his first confrontation with the Duma in June (discussed below), he suggested to the Council of Ministers a procedure for "simplifying intercourse between Duma committees and governmental institutions."[69]

There were, of course, points of friction. In March 1908 Stolypin reprimanded the Duma for not having approved the budget and reminded them that June 1 was the last possible date for them to do this.[70] According to A. A. Polivanov, Assistant Minister of War, Stolypin was disturbed when *Novoe vremya,* the paper for which his brother wrote, criticized one minister. He asked the Council of Ministers whether a refutation ought to be written or whether the editor of the paper ought to be fined.[71] Stolypin also supported Minister of Finance Kokovtsov in the so-called no-parliament crisis. On April 24, 1908, during debate over the Duma's right to appoint a commission for investigation of the railroads, Kokovtsov exclaimed: "Thank God we have no parliament yet!" The following day, Duma president N. A. Khomyakov stopped Duma discussion on Kokovtsov's remark, but termed it "unfortunate." Kokovtsov tendered his resignation. Attempting to liquidate the crisis, Stolypin met with Khomyakov and threatened to resign himself unless satisfaction were made to the finance minister. Octobrist member of the Third Duma Prince A. D. Golitsyn recalled that Stolypin stated that it was inadmissible for Duma members, particularly the Duma president, to criticize ministers' speeches: "Today they are characterized 'unfortunate,' tomorrow 'stupid.' If this is not stopped, who knows what will be addressed to the ministry in the Duma."[72] According to Polivanov, Stolypin's reaction was more temperate: "Members of the government cannot argue against the President of the State Duma, and therefore the words of a minister cannot be qualified."[73]

Stolypin's major altercation with the Duma during its first session did not come until June 1908, and in that episode Stolypin made it clear that the government would not be bullied and that his relationship with the Tsar must be considered before his relationship with the Duma. The cause of the conflict was the Duma's refusal to sanction credits for four dreadnoughts being built by the naval ministry until the ministry was reorganized and a general scheme of national defense and naval construction was submitted to the Duma. Both Stolypin and Kokovtsov, in a meeting of the Council of Ministers on February 1, had criticized Grand Duke Nicholas Nikolaevich, head of the Council of State Defense, and the Naval and War ministers for causing difficulty between the government and the Duma by excessive budget requests and lack of a rational program of defense.[74] Thus, Stolypin was wholly in agreement with the Duma's criticism and in a speech to the Duma on June 5 he publicly agreed that there were deficiencies in the naval ministry. Nevertheless, he begged the Duma to grant the appropriations because the national safety was at stake.

Despite Stolypin's argument, the Duma rejected the credits for the four battleships by a vote of 194 to 78 on June 5. The whole of the center (mainly Octobrists) and part of the right voted with the opposition, indicating the solidarity of the Duma.[75]

Stolypin vehemently criticized the Duma's action in a speech to the State Council June 13, 1908. One point of opposition was that, in his opinion, the Duma's action would harm state defense, would reduce the naval administration "to chaos." But his chief point of criticism was that the Duma had directly confronted the government, had attempted to force reforms on the government. This was not only intolerable in itself, but might possibly compromise the government in the Tsar's eyes. "The Duma," he warned the State Council, "had entered on a dangerous path . . . they should have adopted the way of interpellation instead of the present course, which formed a most dangerous precedent. In Russia," Stolypin stressed unambiguously, "the government was only responsible to the Tsar and if the legislature placed obstacles in their way they could no longer continue to accept this responsibility."[76] Thus, Stolypin was admitting that he disapproved of a Duma which could countermand government policy and was emphasizing the source of the government's authority and suggesting the result of the Tsar's withdrawing his sanction from the government.[77]

Stolypin made this point again, but in a more dramatic fashion, in the major crisis which erupted in the spring of 1909—the so-called naval general staff crisis. In this case the conflict occurred between the government and some members of the State Council, and did not involve the Duma. But the result was the same—a declaration that Stolypin's first allegiance was to the Tsar and not to the Duma.

The crisis began innocently enough with passage by the Duma in July 1908 of a government bill proposing the organization of a naval general staff and the appropriations necessary for implementing it. As early as 1906 Nicholas had ordered the establishment of a naval general staff separate from the naval staff. However, the reform had never materialized. The Duma had called for such a measure during the discussion concerning allocations for the dreadnoughts. In any case, it passed the section of the bill referring to the naval general staff as well as that concerning the appropriations. The bill was then forwarded to the State Council.

The reactionary contingent in the State Council objected to the Duma's sanction of the bill and rejected it in December 1908 on the grounds that the Duma had encroached upon the Tsar's prerogatives in approving the organization of the naval general staff. They claimed that according to article 96 of the Fundamental State Laws all matters connected with the organization of military and naval forces were within the exclusive jurisdiction of the Tsar and the Duma should have confined itself to voting on the appropriations.[78]

Because of the deadlock, the bill was submitted again to the Duma shortly before the Christmas recess of 1908, was passed again by the Duma, and reappeared in the State Council on March 19, 1909. Here an extreme right bloc attacked it for the same reasons as previously. The leaders of the opposition included P. N. Durnovo and Count Sergei Witte.[79] But worse was yet to come. Stolypin was striken with pneumonia—or nervous collapse—and withdrew to the relative warmth of the Crimea for a short period of recuperation. In his absence, his opponents stepped up their campaign. Although the State Council finally passed the bill, the reactionary bloc convinced the Tsar that he would jeopardize his imperial prerogatives if he approved the bill. Furthermore, they suggested that the government, particularly Stolypin, was responsible for the threat to the imperial power because he had allowed the bill's introduction to the Duma.

Stolypin considered the activity of the extreme right bloc a deliberate and unfounded attack against him. He complained to Nicolson that "during his illness and absence the Extreme Right parties had seized the opportunity over a Bill of trifling importance to endeavor to undermine his position. . . . He considered that the intrigues against him were low and base."[80] British observers in Russia seconded his opinion.[81] Their views were substantiated by the facts: the State

Council had passed fifteen minor bills of a similar nature, without a murmur, and they had been sanctioned by the Tsar.[82] This is not to say that the application of article 96 was totally clear. Twice during 1908 the Council of Ministers had discussed the proper application of this article and noted the need for its clarification. On June 7 the ministry had questioned the use of article 96 for organizational and staff changes when new disbursements were required. Kokovtsov and some other ministers had been opposed to application of the article at such times. As a result, a committee had been formed for discussion of the problem.[83] On August 5, during another ministerial debate on proper use of the article, Kokovtsov again disapproved of its use.[84] In addition, some jurists considered the reactionary bloc technically correct. Their scruples, however, had come quite late in view of the untroubled passage of like bills.

On April 1 Nicolson discussed Stolypin with the Tsar, and although Nicholas spoke with "warmth and good feeling" about the Chairman of the Council of Ministers, Nicolson informed the Foreign Office that he had heard rumors in palace circles that Stolypin's position was shaken and the future uncertain.[85] On April 23 Stolypin returned to St. Petersburg and met with Nicholas. Kokovtsov has asserted in his memoirs that Stolypin insisted that there had been no talk of resignation during his conference with the Tsar.[86] Nicolson, on the contrary, claimed that Stolypin stated that he had told the Tsar he must resign if the latter did not sanction the bill.[87]

Nicholas did not sanction the bill—but Stolypin did not resign—leaving Nicolson to report that "Russia has a considerable distance to travel before she becomes a constitutional State in the Western acceptance of the term."[88] This was quite true. The principle of representative government was only weakly established in Russia; the principle of parliamentary government not at all. On April 28 Nicholas wrote to Stolypin that he would not hear of Stolypin's resignation or any talk of confidence or lack or confidence.[89] This expression of the Tsar's support, as well as the fact that the naval general staff bill was of minor importance, was enough to make him stay in office, Stolypin informed the Japanese and French ambassadors.[90] Nicolson surmised that another reason may have been Stolypin's fear that if he left office a reactionary ministry might be installed.[91]

In any case, it appeared that Stolypin had played his cards correctly for, with settlement of the crisis, he received the privilege, heretofore shared with the chairman of the State Council, of presenting to the Tsar names of candidates for appointed seats in that chamber. This was considered an advantage for Stolypin since the chairman of the State Council, M. G. Akimov, was a member of the extreme right and usually presented candidates of his own political complexion.[92]

In his article on the naval general staff crisis, Edward Chmielewski has theorized that Stolypin became more conservative and apologetic for the autocracy, nationalism, and Orthodoxy as a result of the crisis. He cites as proof of this Stolypin's speech in the spring of 1909 countering the Duma's liberalization of the government's freedom of belief bill, in which he emphasized the existence of the autocracy; Stolypin's interview with the editor of *Volga,* in which he criticized the debate over whether there was a constitution or autocracy in Russia; the proposal to introduce Russian representatives into the Polish delegation to the State Council from the western provinces; and Stolypin's speech on the clarification of article 96 in the spring of 1910.[93]

Fear of affronting the Tsar is very evident in Stolypin's speeches and in his behavior and that of the entire Council of Ministers after the naval general staff crisis. However, there was no radical departure from Stolypin's previous statements or policies. His opposition to the Duma's version of the freedom of belief bill appears to have been caused by a genuine conflict of opinion.[94] His interview with the editor of *Volga* was, after all, almost a replay of his interview of 1907 in which he had stressed that the question of whether or not Russia was a constitutional state needed further study and that the Russian constitution, a unilateral grant of the Tsar, differed from the constitutions of western states. As for nationalism, one of Stolypin's strongest speeches on the necessity of strengthening Russian influence in the borderlands had been made in 1907.

What of the clarification of article 96? In response to the Tsar's rescript of April 27,[95] a committee consisting of representatives from the Chairman of the Council of Ministers, the Ministry of Finance, and the Naval and War ministries, proposed to eliminate the ambiguities in article 96. Kokovtsov presented the preliminary project to the Council of Ministers on May 26, 1909.

The Council of Ministers' statement on the matter clearly indicated that a residue of the autocracy continued to exist in Russia, and that by the term autocracy they did not mean sovereignty as latter-day historians have suggested. All general legislation regarding shipbuilding, defense of the state, and management of the army and navy, the ministry concluded, was under the immediate jurisdiction of the

"Tsar, Lord Emperor, Autocrat, Sovereign, and Commander of the Army and Navy."

The Council of Ministers went on to state that legislation concerning the cossacks, except in civil matters, and all matters related to the Naval and War ministries that did not require new disbursements or the abolition of laws, also were to be regulated in the same manner. Approximations were to be allowed in appropriations requested from the legislature, if the amounts of estimated expenditures could not be exactly fixed. Matters arising in the Naval and War ministries which did not involve the armed strength of the empire, which concerned civil affairs of the cossacks, which necessitated the change or abolition of laws or new appropriations, or entered the jurisdiction of other ministries were to be handled through the Duma and the State Council.[96]

An indication of Stolypin's dilemma in the Duma-Tsar conflict can be seen in his statement, made during the course of this discussion, that it was very difficult to separate civil from military matters or to decide definitively what business properly involved the application of article 96.[97]

Nicholas approved the clarification of article 96 on August 24, 1909. Baron Alexander Meyendorff, Stolypin's cousin, particularly criticized the government's action,[98] and thirty-two deputies interpellated Stolypin in the fall of 1909, accusing the government of perpetrating an illegal act and of lessening the Duma's power.[99]

Stolypin refuted these charges by reminding the Duma of the political facts of life in Russia. There were certain areas over which the Tsar alone had control, and more importantly, both the ministry and the Duma were subject to his authority. The clarification of article 96, Stolypin emphasized, was not the work of the minister being interpellated, but "the work of the imperial authority . . . an expression of the will of the Sovereign Emperor," sanctioned by the Fundamental Laws.[100] The Duma's power had not been lessened by the clarification of article 96, for it never had had the power to approve organization of army and naval staffs. The significance of the clarification was merely interdepartmental—a demarcation of civil and military jurisdiction within the government.

Stolypin tried to sugar coat the clarification by pointing out that the Duma could still participate in state defense by fixing the contingents of recruits, discussing allocations of credits for war needs, and approving or rejecting these credits.[101] However, this argument carried less weight than it might have since Stolypin himself had tried to curtail the Duma's right of appropriation in the dreadnought conflict of the previous year.

Behind the scenes, Stolypin and the ministry tried to prevent undue friction between government and Duma on financial and budget matters and to prevent misuse of article 96. When in June 1909 Kokovtsov admonished the ministers for excessive use of conditional credits both because this practice strained the treasury and because it violated budget rules, the ministry resolved to curtail conditional credits in deference to the Duma.[102] Later in the month, again in response to a Duma request, the ministry resolved that all budget estimates were to be completely itemized.[103] In September 1909 the Council of Ministers, in answer to the query of the War Minister, concluded that the clarified version of article 96 could not be applied retroactively.[104] On November 3, 1909, the Council of Ministers refused to allow the Naval Minister to invoke article 96 in order to procure more shoes for the navy.[105] On November 10 the Naval Minister again submitted the naval appropriations bill to the Council of Ministers (minus the clause about organization of the naval general staff), prior to the bill's introduction to the Duma and the State Council. The ministers noted, however, that the Naval Minister was asking 25,329 rubles more than in the original bill. Although the Naval Minister attempted to justify the increased amount, the Council of Ministers ordered him to lower the credits requested to the amount which had been approved by the Duma before the naval staff crisis. The Council of Ministers also decided that there was no need to include a statement in the new bill alluding to the clarification of article 96, which might offend the sensibilities of the Duma.[106] In December the Council of Ministers forbade the War Minister to invoke article 96 to obtain money from the ten million fund—and bypass the Duma—since his project did not refer to organizational or staff measures.[107]

All this was noble, but in the background lay Stolypin's old preference for efficiency and the spector of the Tsar. As a result, Stolypin and the Council of Ministers made two other decisions in late 1909-early 1910 which neutralized these concessions to the Duma and, in fact, underscored the ministry's lack of interest, as well as its lack of competence, in the question of raising the Duma from its third- or fourth-rate political position.

The first of these decisions involved the ministry's refusal to approve a Duma request for greater control over the state budget. The second concerned the ministry's opposition to Duma control over private railroads.

The first issue was decided in October 1909. At that time the Council of Ministers discussed a petition presented by forty members of the Duma asking for changes in the method of examining the budget. The Duma requested four improvements: 1) the right to freely discuss and change amounts of appropriations for unforeseen, extraordinary expenditures; 2) inclusion under imperial prerogative and exclusion from the jursidiction of the Duma only those items of imperial expenditure declared before April 23, 1906; 3) limitation of extrabudget appropriations, ordered by the Council of Ministers without preliminary decision of the legislative institutions, to appropriations during or for the preparation of war; and 4) legislative initiative in altering or abolishing budget rules.[108] The Council of Ministers admitted that there were defects and lack of clarity in the budget regulations, but it rejected the Duma's request partly for practical reasons and partly to avoid disturbing the Tsar. The ministry declared that allowing the Duma to reduce appropriations for unforeseen expenses would lead to great financial danger, "as many of the extrabudget requests are urgent." Furthermore, the Tsar appropriated funds by his immediate will only when there was no "destruction of lawful interests and civil rights," and some of these funds covered salaries of civil servants. Abolishing this imperial prerogative would lead to "undesirable misunderstanding." Extrabudget allocations could not be limited to wartime or the preparation of war, because there were other calamities such as flood, famine, and city-wide conflagrations which would require funds immediately. Article 87, which would allow the Duma to discuss the appropriations later, could not be used as the Duma suggested because this article was meant to be employed only when the Duma was not in session. The Council of Ministers also voted against giving the Duma legislative initiative in altering or abolishing budget rules. Such initiative could only belong to the government, for budget allocations were so comprehensive they could only be arranged by governmental institutions.[109]

The Council of Ministers intended to discuss further, with the possibility of implementation, only two points of the Duma request: a deadline for presenting conditional credits and the significance of legislative veto once these credits had been issued.[110]

Kokovtsov recalled that at first Stolypin agreed with Foreign Minister A. P. Izvolsky that the Council of Ministers should adopt a tolerant attitude and merely warn the Duma of the consequences of its demands. However, he then accepted the more conservative opinion of the majority of the ministry which held that the government should "bitterly oppose the project from the outset."[111]

The ministry's stand in 1910 on Duma control over private railroads illustrated even more sharply its dual fear that increasing the Duma's financial powers might harm the country's economy and also might be construed as an attempt to lessen the Tsar's authority.

According to laws of 1905 and 1906, the Duma was to supervise railroads supported by the state treasury, and private roads were under the jurisdiction of the Second Department of the State Council. The private railroads were more important than those subsidized by the treasury, and in 1908 and 1909, claiming that there had been irregularities, the Duma attempted to secure authority over them.[112]

Because of the Duma's unanimity in the issue, Stolypin instructed Kokovtsov and the Minister of Ways and Communications to draw up a project which would delineate the jurisdiction of the Duma and administrative agencies regarding railway construction and which would allow the legislative institutions some voice in private railroad building.[113]

Kokovtsov's subsequent scheme was not revolutionary. It provided that matters concerning railroads supported by the treasury or private roads directly aided by treasury funds were to be decided, as formerly, by the Duma and the State Council. Decisions with regard to the building of private roads or those which received loans from the treasury to be paid back out of profits were now relegated to a joint commission, comprising the Second Department of the State Council and five deputies each from the Duma and the elected portion of the State Council, chosen by their respective institutions.[114]

In the report of its discussion of the project in January 1910, the Council of Ministers stated that entrusting the complicated business of private railway building to the Duma, which did not possess "specialized knowledge and experience," would be "too-delaying" and would result in "decisions not corresponding to the needs of the country and the need for healthy economic policy."[115] A handful of carefully selected legislators, on the other hand, would help to satisfy the Duma's desire to control private railroads and would also insure "correct management" of the vital matter of railroad construction.[116]

From this statement, it was clear that the ministry still distrusted the Duma's ability to handle important sectors of the economy ably and efficiently. It also was clear that the ministry had to take great care to insure that it would not appear that any government proposal allowed the Duma to encroach upon the Tsar's jurisdiction. The ministry stressed that the project did not "incorrectly confuse" legislative and administrative power. To make doubly certain of this, Stolypin suggested that the Duma and the State Council members on the joint commission be appointed by the Tsar, rather than elected by the Duma and the State Council as stated in the original project.[117] The ministry also explained in its report to the Tsar that, although the project would be represented (some newspapers were already doing so) as a plan to "increase the power of the legislature" at the expense of the "sacred prerogatives of the Tsar," in fact the project was merely a means of bettering the conditions of railway building. As such, the Council of Ministers asked the Tsar to approve it.[118]

By the spring of 1911 revolutionary turmoil had pretty much subsided. Although most of Stolypin's reform proposals and those of the other ministers were gathering dust, the agrarian reform was plodding along and a project for the establishment of universal primary education had been inaugurated. But the constant need to conciliate the Duma, on the one hand, and to placate the Tsar, on the other, left Stolypin exhausted. Worst of all, the strength and influence of his reactionary opponents had increased. In 1910 his enemies in the State Council denounced his telegram to Prime Minister Asquith on the occasion of Edward VII's death: "He signs himself president [of the Council of Ministers]: is that of a present or future republic?"[119] The State Council further blocked legislation—from major bills like the extension of the agrarian measures to such minor proposals as the improvement of statistics-taking—to the extent that the Duma was considering a "work-stoppage" in protest.[120] A. V. Obolensky, Stolypin's friend in the Ministry of Internal Affairs, Sir Bernard Pares, and British diplomats decried the intrigue in the State Council against Stolypin. There were reports in the early months of 1911 that he was so tired and frustrated that he was considering resignation.[121]

Stolypin felt that the greatest assault on him, and one which he could not afford to pass unchecked, came with the rejection by the State Council of a significant aspect of his zemstvo bill for the western provinces, which has been described in another chapter. Although the Duma finally approved the bill in 1910, objections had been raised to portions of it. While supporting Stolypin's belief that the western zemstvos must be Russian, the Duma committee on local self-government had suggested that the two curiae, Polish and non-Polish, be united in areas where two-thirds of the voters approved. The committee also had rejected as unnecessary a provision establishing a quota of Russians in managerial positions. The committee believed that Russians would naturally predominate in these positions if they predominated in the zemstvo.[122]

In its plenary session the Duma had stressed the benefits of introducing zemstvos in the western provinces and also had agreed that the western zemstvos must be Russian.[123] However, there had been opposition from the peasant leftist groups and from the Kadets and "left" Octobrists. These groups charged that the bill could destroy the unity of the empire, that it permitted too much interference by the central government, and that it did not award the peasants sufficient representation.[124] But the bill finally passed the Duma.

It was introduced to the State Council at the end of January 1911. Principal objections to the bill were two: the nationalistic curiae discriminated against the Poles and would have a divisive effect on the empire; lowering the suffrage qualifications would flood the zemstvos with "uncultured" elements.[125] On March 4 the council rejected article 6, which dealt with the division of voters into Polish and non-Polish curiae, by a vote of ninety-two to sixty-eight.[126] The State Council discussed the bill for two more sittings.

The leading opponent of the bill in the State Council was former Chairman of the Council of Ministers and Finance Minister Sergei Witte. P. N. Durnovo and V. F. Trepov campaigned against the bill behind the scenes. Stolypin sent a deputation from the southwestern provinces to the Tsar in order to display the support of the local populace for the curiae. The Tsar at that time expressed approval of the bill and apparently told the president of the State Council, Akimov, that the right should vote in favor of the curiae, an imperial wish which Akimov duly made known.[127] Meanwhile, Durnovo wrote the Tsar denouncing the deputation as consisting of officials. Trepov had an audience with the Tsar in which he obtained permission for the members of the State Council to vote according to their consciences in the matter of the curiae.[128]

Stolypin's supporters in the Duma rallied to his side. Guchkov argued with the rightist faction in the Duma and 200 deputies, predominantly Octobrists, signed a petition for the bill to be reintroduced in that chamber, thereby assuring Stolypin passage of the bill.

However, Stolypin's anger and frustration at the action of the right in the State Council knew no bounds. He threatened to resign unless Nicholas prorogued the Duma and the State Council in order to permit passage of the bill according to the procedure established by article 87 and unless the Tsar sent Durnovo and Trepov away from the capital for a period of time. He refused to follow the advice of several fellow ministers who urged him to submit the bill to the legislature a second time and find other disciplinary measures for Durnovo and Trepov, stating: "Let those look for compromise who value their positions; as for myself, I prefer to step aside rather than retain my position under such circumstances."[129] Despite Kokovtsov's disapproval of his actions, Stolypin forced Kokovstov to sign the memorandum of Stolypin's terms for remaining in office. Kokovtsov yielded because the alternative was resignation, a step he considered unwise at such a time.[130]

For three days, Stolypin's fate hung in the balance. A. A. Bobrinsky noted in his diary that every three hours news changed. On March 9 a large department store in Moscow displayed a huge portrait of Kokovtsov with the inscription, "Chairman of the Council of Ministers." On March 10 the portrait was down and it was rumored that Stolypin remained "premier."[131] By the evening of March 11, the Tsar capitulated to Stolypin's demands and he remained in office. Stolypin told confidants that Nicholas asked him to stay with tears in his eyes.[132]

Stolypin's conditions were met. The Duma and the State Council were prorogued from March 12 to March 15 and the zemstvo bill was passed under the terms of article 87. Durnovo and Trepov were sent on an extended leave of absence.

Stolypin's method of handling the zemstvo crisis resulted in a wave of criticism. The Kadets and most of the Octobrists in the Duma considered his action unconstitutional and a repudiation of the parliament. Guchkov, who had succeded Khomyakov as president of the Duma in March 1910, resigned. The State Council protested the treatment of Durnovo and Trepov and claimed its rights had been violated.

One American historian has condemned Stolypin, calling his action an example of "his accustomed self-direction, compulsive behavior, unwillingness to consider alternatives, and poorly timed inflexibility."[133] The Soviet historian A. Ya. Avrekh, on the other hand, has emphasized that the objections to the bill on the part of the right in the State Council were really an attack against Stolypin. He believes that members of the right opposed the bill not because of sympathy with the Poles, but because they feared that lower suffrage qualifications would strengthen the smallholders to the detriment of the land-owning class—they also feared these lower qualifications might be introduced in the internal provinces. To prove his thesis Avrekh points out that not one of the opponents of the bill supported a Duma amendment which would have increased Polish representation, namely, that representation be fixed by one criterion (percentage of property held), rather than two (percentage of property held and percentage of the population). On the contrary, Witte, one of the arch opponents of the bill, proposed raising the percentage of representation allotted to the communal peasants, which would have increased the number of Russians, or at least persons not of Polish extraction, and would have also have increased the amount of "uncultured" elements.[134]

Stolypin, convinced that opposition to the bill thinly disguised opposition to himself, felt that he had to prove once and for all whom the Tsar supported—himself or his enemies on the right. As he told Professor Zenkovsky in May 1911, he realized that using article 87 to implement the western zemstvo law was a risky measure, for many in the State Duma and the State Council would feel that he was violating the Fundamental Laws. But "it was not so much a question of urgent execution of the law regarding the western zemstvos, as . . . the extreme necessity of putting a limit to the purely reactionary element in the State Council, who by braking almost any reform were exposing the state to the extremely dangerous situation it experienced in 1905."[135]

On May 1, 1911, he wrote to the Tsar with discernible anguish of "the insuperable obstacles in my path . . . the walls [of] which I cannot surmount. I mean the artificial obstructionism created for me in the State Council. The tireless activity of P. A. Durnovo in that direction continues."[136]

Stolypin's defense of the legality of his action appeared the work of a distraught man, clutching at straws. He maintained that the government could interrupt the legislative session in troubled times for the purpose of applying article 87, or in other words, the condition that the Duma not be in session when article 87 was used could be artificially created by the government if there were sufficient urgency. The government, of course, had the authority to determine what constituted a state of emergency. He claimed that precedents for this course of action could be found in applications of article 63 of the Prussian constitution and article 14 of the Austrian constitution, which were similar to article 87. He even found an example of such procedure in recent English history: Gladstone, he asserted, had once prorogued the English parliament because of conflict with the House of Lords.[137]

Sir James Buchanan, British ambassador to Russia at the time, believed that the question of the legality of Stolypin's action was open to discussion. He cabled the Foreign Office that "had [Stolypin] felt compelled to insist upon resignation, worse might have befallen Russia. He might plead at present that he has done evil only that good might come. It is harder to judge the case because Russia as a constitutional country being still young, constitutional usages are still in such a fluid state that it is impossible to say what situation makes a minister's resignation necessary and what rebuffs he can ignore."[138]

Stolypin tried to pacify the Duma and the State Council by reminding them that under the terms of article 87 they had the power, for a two-month period, to approve or disapprove the zemstvo bill.[139] However, both chambers were hastily shut down for the summer before the two-month period had expired.

The zemstvo crisis was the result of many factors. A five-year, uphill fight to rectify Russia's problems and to restore order, a tremendous work load, and the ceaseless obstructionism of his enemies impaired Stolypin's judgment. In part the crisis was caused by Stolypin's innate authoritarianism which was, ironically, a quality necessary to achieve reform and order. His failure also was due to the political structure which had been erected in 1906. For Stolypin's power base was poorly defined. The Duma's support would aid passage of his proposals but it did not insure him of power, the Tsar's support was crucial for Stolypin but it could not always be relied upon, and both Stolypin and the Duma had ineffectual power vis-a-vis the State Council. The Tsar did not actively interfere with the Duma from 1909 to 1911, but Stolypin and the government had to be careful lest it appear they supported the Duma against the Tsar.[140] In 1909, because his position was dependent upon the Tsar, Stolypin chose the Tsar's support rather than that tendered him by the Duma. In 1911 attempts to compromise with the State Council might have peacefully settled the zemstvo crisis, but then again, given the State Council's record during 1910 and 1911, this procedure might not have been effective. Stolypin's enemies were out to get him and because the Tsar remained the ultimate authority, both Stolypin and his enemies yielded to the temptation of appealing to the Tsar to act as arbitrator in disputes between parliament and government.

Notes

1. See chapter 2, p. 27.
2. See chapter 1, p. 14.
3. Great Britain, Public Record Office, Foreign Office (hereafter cited F.O.) 371, vol. 326, no. 29515, August 16, 1907, p. 2.
4. Out of a total of 524 delegates, the Kadets had 180 seats. In the opinion of

Richard Charques, they could count on support from the 35 to 50 liberals, the 70 Polish deputies, and most of the 200 peasant delegates. The remainder of the Duma consisted of 12 Octobrists (their platform is discussed on pp. 156-57 below) and 18 Mensheviks. Extreme right groups and the Bolsheviks boycotted the elections. *The Twilight of Imperial Russia* (Fair Lawn, N.J.: Essential Books, 1959), pp. 151-52, 154. Elections were delayed in some areas of Siberia, in Russian Central Asia and the Far East so that the Duma actually had only 480 to 500 deputies. Howard D. Mehlinger and John M. Thompson, *Count Witte and the Tsarist Government in the 1905 Revolution* (Bloomington: Indiana University Press, 1972), p. 243.

5. Day by day descriptions of the Duma are contained in British diplomatic dispatches, F. O. 371, vol. 126, no. 23117, June 4, 1906; *ibid.*, no. 23118, June 4-20, 1906; *ibid.*, no. 21893, June 23, 1906; *ibid.*, 21436, June 17, 1906; *ibid.*, no. 21429, June 14, 1906.

6. Vladimir Nikolaevich Kokovtsov, *Iz moego proshlago* (The Hague: Mouton, 1969), vol. 1, pp. 187-89. First ed., 1933.

7. Kokovtsov, *Out of My Past* (Stanford, California: Stanford University Press, 1936), pp. 130, 138, 142, 151.

8. F. O. 371, vol. 126, no. 23110 (no. 415), July 2, 1906, p. 2.

9. D. N. Shipov, *Vospominaniya i dumy o perezhitom* (Moscow: Tipografiya "Pechatnya S. P. Yakovleva," 1918), p. 464.

10. To Sir Donald MacKenzie Wallace, contained in F. O. 371, vol. 127, no. 27544 (no. 509), August 6, 1906, pp. 1-2.

11. To Nicolson, quoted in F. O. 371, vol. 126, no. 23110 (no. 415), July 2, 1906, p. 1.

12. F. O. 371, vol. 126, no. 26834 (no. 480), July 25, 1906, p. 1.

13. To Donald MacKenzie Wallace, F. O. 371, vol. 127, no. 27544 (no. 509), August 6, 1906, pp. 1-2.

14. To Nicolson, quoted in F. O. 371, vol. 126, no. 23110 (no. 415), p. 1.

15. P. N. Miliukov, *Vospominaniya* (New York: Chekhov Publishing House, 1955), vol. 1, pp. 377-84.

16. Stolypin to Sir Donald MacKenzie Wallace, quoted in F. O. 371, vol. 127, no. 27544, p. 2.

17. Miliukov, *Vospominaniya*, vol. 1, pp. 401-416.

18. The article is summarized in F. O. 371, vol. 128, no. 29749, August 30, 1906.

19. Stolypin to Nicolson, quoted in F. O. 371, vol. 126, no. 26843 (no. 480), July 25, p. 1. If a parliamentary government were established and the Kadets failed, Stolypin pointed out, Aladin (a radical Trudovik) would form the cabinet.

21. Neville Henderson, in F. O. 371, vol. 318, no. 26078, August 1, 1907; Sir Bernard Pares, in *ibid.*, vol. 512, no. 30901, September 4, 1908; Nicolson, in *ibid.*, vol. 327, no. 33976, October 7, 1907; Kokovtsov, *Out of My Past*, pp. 324-25, 337.

22. During the last half of 1906, 260 opposition papers were suppressed. In January 1907, 77 papers were suppressed and 60 publishers prosecuted. Adolph Torngren, *L'evolution de la Russie pendant les années 1904-1907* (Paris: Plon-Nourrit, 1914), p. 188. During the elections for the first session of the Third Duma, Kadet papers were almost destroyed by administrative fines. F. O. 371, vol. 512, no. 30901, September 4, 1908 (Pares).

23. Quoted in F. O. 371, vol. 318, no. 578, January 3, 1907.

24. Shipov, *Vospominaniya i dumy o perezhitom*, pp. 465, 470-71.

25. Quoted in F. O. 371, vol. 128, no. 29750 (no. 569), August 30, 1906 (Nicolson).

180   Peter Arkad'evich Stolypin

26. Shipov, *Vospominaniya i dumy o perezhitom,* p. 464.

27. F. O. 371, vol. 127, no. 27544 (no. 509), pp. 2-3.

28. *Ibid.,* p. 3.

29. "O dopolnenii nekotorykh postanovlenii deistvuyushchago zakona, kasayushchik-sya krestyanskago zemlevladeniya i zemlepolozovaniya," *Osobyi zhurnal soveta ministrov* (hereafter cited *Osobyi zhurnal*), 1906, no. 98, October 10, pp. 6-15, 17-19.

30. "Rasporyazhenie otnositelno proizvodstva vyborov novago sostava chlenov v Gosudarstvennuyu Dumu," contained in *Predsedatel' soveta ministrov, Petr Arkad'evich Stolypin,* ed. E. Verpakhovsky (St. Petersburg: Izdanie sostavitelya, 1909), pp. 23-26.

31. Detailed accounts of the arrests and election irregularities are contained in F. O. 371, vol. 318, no. 578, January 3, 1907, and *ibid.,* no. 8615, March 14, 1907. Also, Miliukov, *Vospominaniya,* vol. 1, pp. 414-25.

32. "Ob ogranichenii dolzhnostnykh lits i sluzhashchikh v gosudarstvennykh uchrezhdeniyakh po vol'nomu naimu v prav uchastvovat v politicheskikh partiyakh i soyuzakh i o pregrazhdenii takovym litsam protivopravitel'stvennoi agitatsii," *Osobyi zhurnal,* 1906, no. 38, August 4; "Po voprosu o primenenii tsirkulyara Soveta Ministrov 14 Sentyabrya 1906 godu k sluzhashchim v zemskikh, gorodskikh i soslovnykh uchrezhdeniyakh," *Osobyi zhurnal,* 1906, no. 155, November 28.

33. Pavel Grigorevich Kurlov, *Gibel' imperatorskoi Rossii* (Berlin: Otto Kirchner and Co., 1923), pp. 73-74. See also my chapter 2, p. 32.

34. (New Haven: Yale University Press, 1940).

35. Biweekly reports of the Second Duma are contained in F. O. 371, vols. 318, 322, 324, 326, *passim.*

36. Miliukov's account of his relationship with Stolypin during the Second Duma and Kadet efforts to save the Duma are contained in his *Vospominaniya,* vol. 1, pp. 426-31.

37. Alexandre Iswolsky, *Memoirs* (Paris: Payot, 1923), p. 233.

38. F. A. Golovin, "Zapisky," *Krasnyi arkhiv,* 19 (1926), pp. 133-48. For a detailed discussion of Stolypin's reform proposals see chapter 3, above.

39. Letter of Stolypin to Golovin on the admittance of "foreign" persons to Duma sessions, March 29, 1907, contained in *Predsedatel' soveta ministrov,* pp. 65-66. Stolypin, as Minister of Internal Affairs, was given this right by the Fundamental Laws, *Polnoe sobranie zakonov Rossiiskoi Imperii. Sobranie tretie,* March 1, 1885-December 31, 1913 (St. Petersburg, 1885-1916), 1906, no. 27726, April 17, articles 4, 5, pp. 20-21. Also, F. O. 371, vol. 326, no. 23525, July 9, 1907.

40. *Osobyi zhurnal,* 1906, no. 172, December 8.

41. F. O. 371, vol. 128, no. 31315, September 7, 1907.

42. "Perepiska N. A. Romanova i P. A. Stolypina," *Krasnyi arkhiv,* 5, p. 110.

43. *Ibid.,* p. 111.

44. *Gosudarstvennaya Duma: Stenograficheskie otchety,* Vtoroi sozyv, sessiya II, zasedanie 34, May 7, 1907.

45. Kokovtsov, *Iz moego proshlago,* vol. 1, p. 262.

46. F. O. 371, vol. 326, no. 23525, July 9, 1907.

47. F. O. 371, vol. 324, no. 19791, June 15, 1907; *ibid.,* no. 20722, June 17, 1907. Nicolson believed that the revolutionary parties were bent on revolution. *Ibid.,* no. 20710, June 12, 1907.

48. "P. A. Stolypin and the Second Duma," *The Slavonic and East European Review,* 50, no. 118 (January 1972), pp. 59-61. Tokmakoff, on p. 60 of this article, bases his opinion largely on Stolypin's words to Maklakov: "Only remember what I

have to say: you have just dissolved the Duma." V. A. Maklakov, *Vtoraya gosudarstvennaya Duma* (Paris, 1944), p. 247.

49. Kokovtsov, *Iz moego proshlago,* I, pp. 233-34, 264; Sergei Efimovich Kryzhanovsky, *Vospominaniya* (Berlin: Speer and Schmidt, n.d.), pp. 107-121; Kryzhanovsky, in *Padenie tsarskago rezhima,* ed. P. S. Schegolev (Moscow-Leningrad: Government Publishing Office, 1926), vol. 5, p. 401; V. N. Kokovtsov, in *ibid.,* vol. 7, p. 199.

50. "Perepiska N. A. Romanova i P. A. Stolypina," *Krasnyi arkhiv,* 5, p. 110.

51. Stolypin to Nicolson, in F. O. 371, vol. 324, no. 21209 (no. 340), June 22, 1907.

52. For additional information on the Law of June 3 see Alfred Levin's "The Russian Voter in the Elections to the Third Duma," *Slavic Review,* 21, no. 4 (December 1962), pp. 660-77.

53. N. M. Korkunov, *Russkoe gosudarstvennoe pravo* (St. Petersburg: tipografiya M. M. Stasyulevicha, 1909), vol. 2, pp. 160-61; F. O. 371, vol. 324, no. 20722, June 17, 1907; *ibid.,* no. 20678, June 22, 1907.

54. Contained in F. O. 371, vol. 324, no. 21209 (no. 340), June 22, 1907.

55. Kokovtsov, *Out of my Past,* p. 166.

56. Kryzhanovsky, *Vospominaniya,* p. 108; Sir Bernard Pares, in F. O. 371, vol. 512, no. 30901, September 4, 1908.

57. Claude Russell, in F. O. 371, vol. 318, no. 15487, May 9, 1907; Pares, in *ibid.,* vol. 512, no. 30901, September 4, 1908; *ibid.,* vol. 326, no. 23525; A. P. Izvolsky to Nicolson, *ibid.,* vol. 327, no. 38719.

58. The Kadets were barred from these committees by the Octobrist leader, Guchkov. Miliukov, *Vospominaniya,* vol. 2, pp. 19-20. By 1910-1911, numbers of various parties in the Duma had changed. For these years the figures are: Octobrists, 120; Right Octobrists, 11; Russian Nationalists, 76; Independent Nationalists, 16; Right, 53; Kadets, 52; Progressives, 39; Trudoviks and Social Democrats, each 14; Poles and Polish Lithuanian, 17; Moslems, 9. *Gosudarstvennaya Duma: Stenograficheskie otchety,* Tretii sozyv, sessiya 4, pp. 3-18, as quoted in Hugh Seton-Watson, *The Russian Empire* (Oxford: Clarendon Press, 1967), p. 628.

59. Charles Bentinck, in F. O. 371, vol. 318, no. 27123, November 7, 1907; *ibid.,* vol. 512, no. 7144, February 26, 1908. In the words of one British diplomat in Russia the Third Duma was "hardworking," of "good sense," "moderate," and "able." Hugh O'Beirne, in F. O. 371, vol. 512, no. 25037, July 16, 1908.

60. "Perepiska N. A. Romanova i P. A. Stolypina," *Krasnyi arkhiv,* 5, p. 115.

61. "Iz perepiski P. A. Stolypina s Nikolaem Romanovym," *Krasnyi arkhiv,* 30 (1928), p. 80, November 9, 1907. In February 1908, the Tsar and Tsarina finally received about 300 deputies in their summer palace of Tsarskoe Selo. The deputies were affiliated with the parties of the right, Octobrists, Peaceful Renovators (a branch of the Octobrists), Lithuanian faction, Polish "Kolo," and Muslins. The Kadets and revolutionary parties were absent. F. O. 371, vol. 513, no. 7125, February 26, 1908.

62. *Osobyi zhurnal,* 1908, vol. 3, no. 5, January 4.

63. *Ibid.* The budget rules included the following stipulations: according to article 13 (*Polnoe sobranie zakonov Rossiiskoi Imperii,* ed. 1906, Law. no. 27505, March 8), the previous year's budget remained in force with only those changes made by the legislature, until the new budget was approved. Until the new budget's approval, upon decision of the Council of Ministers and rulings of ministries and special departments, ministers were permitted to receive so-called conditional credits. The totality of these credits for any month was not to exceed one-twelfth of the entire budget. These credits were to be approved by the State Duma and the State Council (article 14*, *ibid.*). The execution,

in the course of the existing State budget, of unforeseen, urgent expenditures, if these could not be covered on the account of special credits for expenditures not foreseen by the budget, for extraordinary needs in the course of the year, or on the account of the expected economy within the limits of allocations for the chief subdivisions of the budget, were allowed, not otherwise than by requesting a decision on them in the order established for the approval of the budget, with the exception of cases enumerated in articles 16 and 17 (article 15, *ibid.*). If requesting a decision on urgent expenditures, in the order established for the approval of the budget, appeared impossible, because of shortness of time, in the course of which the expenditures had to be executed, then the necessary credits to cover such expenditures were to be allotted by resolution of the Council of Ministers. Ministers and Chief Directors of Departments, on the accounts of whom the credits had been issued, were to make special presentation about these appropriations to the State Duma. If the presentation was urgent it was to be made before the end of the session; if not, it was to be made during the first two months of the next session. Deviations from this rule were allowed only if the credits required secrecy. (article 16, *ibid.*). Article 17 dealt with credits for war or special preparation for war, issued in all departments according to the Imperial order of February 26, 1890.

The Council of Ministers's record in regard to observance of the budget rules was good during 1908. The following are some examples: *Osobyi zhurnal,* 1908, vol. 3, no. 9: The Council of Ministers advised the Minister of Communications to request the Duma's approval of extrabudget credit for 30 million rubles; *ibid., no.* 23, January 22: The Council of Ministers followed article 16 of the budget rules in regard to a monetary request of the Minister of Justice; *ibid.,* no. 27, January 29: The Council of Ministers adhered to the budget rules in regard to a monetary request of the Minister of Internal Affairs—part of the request was put on the general account of the Ministry of Internal Affairs, the rest was to be asked of the legislature; *ibid.,* no. 40, February 12: payment was granted to an Archangelsk hospital on the remainder of the zemstvo account for that *guberniya,* with the stipulation that this appropriation be submitted to the legislature with the next budget; *ibid.,* no. 45, February 12: The Council of Ministers decided that the budget request of the Naval Minister opposed article 41 of the budget rules; the budget of two years' past could not be carried over. The Naval Minister was to ask the Duma for additional credits; *ibid.,* no. 90, January 22 and March 11: The Council of Ministers decided there was some lack of clarity in the new budget rules regarding the transfer of unforeseen credits from one division of the account to another and as to whether legislative approval was needed in such a case; *ibid., no.* 115, March 28: The Council of Ministers stated that extrabudget appropriations were extremely undesirable, but since one amount requested by the Minister of Justice was not greatly different from that requested it was to be allowed. The other extrabudget sum requested (amounting to about 5 million rubles), not being urgent, was to be put before the Duma in its autumn session; *ibid.,* no. 240, August 26: The Minister of Finance (Kokovtov) noted that the increase in the budget being proposed was incorrect—changes of regular credits relating to bonuses and grants could be done only in the legislative order. The Council of Ministers decided to leave the credits requested as they had been stipulated in that year's budget. The Council of Ministers also lowered the appropriation being asked for repair of a factory because of budget considerations. One request by the Minister of Ways and Communications for additional credit, in the opinion of Kokovtsov conflicted with budget rules. The Council of Ministers, sympathizing with the Minister of Ways that the request was urgent and that it might not be approved by the Duma decided to study the matter further. *Ibid.,* no. 259, September 9.

On March 11, 1908, the Council of Ministers refused the request of thirty-five members of the Duma of 6 million rubles for school repair, because this appropriation could only be included in the 1909 budget and, if granted, it would throw the finances of the empire into confusion. *Osobyi zhurnal,* 1908, vol. 3, no. 87.

*The numbers of these articles differ according to the edition.

64. F. O. 371, vol. 512, no. 8047 (no. 122), pp. 1-2.

65. Aleksei Andreevich Polivanov, *Iz dnevnikov i vospominanii po dolzhnosti voennogo ministra i ego pomoshchika, 1907-1916* (Moscow: Vyshii voennyi redaktsionnyi sovet, 1924), pp. 34-35, 40, 43-44, 46-47, 98.

66. *Ibid.,* p. 47.

67. On one occasion Stolypin suggested to Guchkov that the reactionary minister, State Comptroller P. Kh. Schwanebach, be replaced with a member of the Third Duma if a suitable person could be found. F. O. 371, vol. 512, no. 30901, September 4, 1908.

68. Stolypin based his idea on practices in the United States and European countries. "O naznachenii chlenam Gosudarstvennoi Dumy ezhegodnago soderzhaniya," *Osobyi zhurnal,* 1908, vol. 1, no. 100, June 3.

69. *Osobyi zhurnal,* 1908, vol. 3, no. 364, December 9.

70. F. O. 371, vol. 512, no. 8955, March 13.

71. Polivanov, *Iz dnevnikov i vospominanii,* p. 47.

72. Prince A. D. Golitsyn, "Vospominaniya," book 10, pp. 247-48; MS, Russian Archive, Columbia University.

73. Polivanov, *Iz dnevnikov i vospominanii,* p. 45.

74. *Osobyi zhurnal,* 1908, vol. 1, no. 26, February 1.

75. F. O. 371, vol. 512, no. 21300, June 18, 1908.

76. *Gosudarstvennyi Sovet. Stenograficheskie otchety 1907-1908 gg.,* Sessiya III, cols. 1706-1709.

77. A very significant statement on the secondary role of the Duma as compared with that of the administrative branch of the government and the relationship of the administration to the Tsar was made in camera by the Council of Ministers during discussion of the revised Kholm province measure, January 13, 1909. (This measure has been discussed in chapter 5). However, Minister of Finance Kokovtsov presided at this meeting and there is no comment by Stolypin or even evidence that he was present. Thus, although he probably agreed with the ministry's theory, we cannot definitely attribute it to him.

The ministry emphasized the following principles: 1) the spheres of influence of the legislative and executive branches had been severely defined by the Fundamental Laws of 1906 and this demarcation line must be observed; 2) the legislature had no right to give orders to the government; 3) the legislature's right of legislative initiative was limited to raising questions on the necessity of the drafting of a new law, and if the relevant minister rejected the drafting of this bill, the legislature might independently work it out. The legislature had no right, however, to impose a specific task upon the representatives of the executive branch of the government. "Po proektu Ministerstva Vnutrennikh Del o vydelenii iz sostava Privislinskago kraya vostochnykh chastei Sedletskoi i Lyublinskoi gubernii, s obrazovaniem iz nikh osoboi Kholmskoi gubernii," *Osobyi zhurnal,* 1908, vol. 3, January 13, 1909, pp. 15-17.

78. F. O. 371, vol. 726, no. 13601, April 7, 1909.

79. *Ibid.;* also, Kokovtsov, *Iz moego proshlago,* vol. I, p. 342.

80. F. O. 371, vol. 729, no. 18277 (no. 292), May 7, 1909.

81. *Ibid.,* no. 13989, April 14, 1909; *ibid.,* no. 14478, April 19; *ibid.,* no. 16363,

April 30; Kokovtsov, in *ibid.*, no. 17571, May 1; Nicolson, in *ibid.*, no. 17906, May 11; Spring-Rice in *ibid.*, vol. 726, no. 15542, April 22, 1909; *ibid.*, vol. 976, no. 159, December 1909 (1910).

82. Nicolson, in F. O. 371, vol. 729, no. 18277 (no. 292), May 7, 1909, p. 2.

83. *Osobyi zhurnal,* 1908, vol. 3, no. 184, Kokovtsov, p. 2.

84. *Osobyi zhurnal,* 1908, vol. 3, no. 214.

85. F. O. 371, vol. 729, no. 15520.

86. Kokovtsov, *Iz moego proshlago,* I, pp. 344-45. This claim was noted by Edward Chmielewski, "Stolypin and the Russian Ministerial Crisis of 1909," *California Slavic Studies,* 4 (1967), pp. 26-27.

87. F. O. 371, vol. 729, no. 17374 (no. 240); *ibid.*, no. 18227 (no. 292). Polivanov claimed that the other ministers planned to resign with Stolypin. *Iz dnevnikov i vospominanii,* p. 69.

88. F. O. 371, vol. 729, no. 18284 (no. 300), May 12, 1909.

89. Nicholas' letter to Stolypin, April 25, 1909, is in "Perepiska N. A. Romanova i P. A. Stolypina," *Krasnyi arkhiv,* 5, p. 120.

90. F. O. 371, vol. 729, no. 19347 (no. 313), May 16, 1909.

91. *Ibid.*, no. 18284 (no. 300).

92. *Ibid.*, no. 19347 (no. 313); Kokovtsov, *Iz moego proshlago,* vol. 2, pp. 5-6.

93. Chmielewski, "Stolypin and the Ministerial Crisis of 1909," *California Slavic Studies,* 4 (1967), pp. 27-38.

94. See chapter 3, above, pp. 77-78.

95. The Tsar's rescript appeared in *Pravitel'stvennyi vestnik.* An English translation was contained in F. O. 371, vol. 729, no. 18284 (no. 300).

96. *Osobyi zhurnal,* 1909, vol. 1, no. 79, pp. 10-12; 15, on Stolypin versus the Minister of War.

97. *Ibid.*

98. Ben-Cion Pinchuk, *The Octobrists in the Third Duma* (Seattle: University of Washington Press, 1974), p. 110.

99. *Gosudarstvennaya Duma: Stenograficheskie otchety,* Tretii sozyv, sessiya III, zasedanie 87, col. 2522.

100. *Ibid.*, cols. 2521-30.

101. *Ibid.*

102. *Osobyi zhurnal,* 1909, vol. 1, no. 85, June 9.

103. *Ibid.*, vol. 3, no. 137, June 23.

104. *Ibid.*, no. 235.

105. *Ibid.*, no. 201, September 15.

106. *Ibid.*, no. 234.

107. *Ibid.*, no. 252, December 1. See chapter 2, note 43, for an explantion of the ten million fund.

108. "Po voznikshemu v Gosudarstvennoi Dume zakonodatel' nomu predpolozheniyu ob izmenenii pravil o poryadke razsmotreniya gosudarstvennoi rospisi," *Osobyi zhurnal,* 1909, vol. 2, no. 147, pp. 1-3.

109. *Ibid.*, pp. 3-13.

110. *Ibid.*, p. 11.

111. Kokovtsov, *Out of My Past,* p. 199.

112. "Ob izmenenii poryadka napravleniya del o novykh zheleznykh dorogakh i razsmotreniya voprosov, vytekayushchikh iz ustavov zheleznodorozhnykh obshchestve," *Osobyi zhurnal,* 1910, vol. 1, no. 17, January 26, pp. 1-7, 10-11.

113. *Ibid.*, pp. 7-8.

114. *Ibid.*, pp. 8-9.

115. *Ibid.*, pp. 22-23.

116. *Ibid.*, pp. 23-24.

117. *Ibid.*, pp. 19-21.

118. *Ibid.*, pp. 24-25.

119. F. O. 371, vol. 979, no. 19549, May 28, 1910.

120. F. O. 371, vol. 1217, no. 29095, July 24, 1911 (Pares); Kryzhanovsky, *Vospominaniya*, pp. 140-41.

121. A. V. Obolensky, *Moi vospominaniya i razmyshleniya* (Stockholm: Izdanie zhurnala "Rodnye Perezvony," 1961), p. 82; F. O. 371, vol. 1214, no. 11048, March 23, 1911 (Garnett); *ibid.*, no. 10572, March 22, 1911 (Buchanan); *ibid.*, vol. 1217, no. 29095, July 24, 1911 (Pares).

122. *Gosudarstvennaya Duma: Stenograficheskie otchety*, Tretii sozyv, sessiya III, zasedanie 103, May 7, 1910, cols. 740-47.

123. *Ibid.*, May 7, cols. 744-91; and *ibid.*, May 15, cols. 1391-93.

124. Speeches of the opponents of the zemstvo bill are contained in *Gosudarstvennaya Duma: Stenograficheskie otchety*, Tretii sozyv, sessiya III, zasedaniya May 7, 8, 11, 12, 15, 17, 18, *passim*.

125. *Gosudarstvennyi Sovet: Stenograficheskie otchety*, Sessiya VI, 1911, January 28, cols. 252-818; February 1 and 4, cols. 824-984; March 4, cols. 1196-1267; March 8 and 11, cols. 1274-1362.

126. *Gosudarstvennyi Sovet: Stenograficheskie otchety*, Sessiya VI, zasedanie 25, cols. 1255-56.

127. A. A. Bobrinsky, "Dnevnik A. A. Bobrinskogo (1910-1911), *Krasnyi arkhiv*, 26 (1928), p. 144 (6 marta).

128. F. O. 371, vol. 1217, no. 29095, July 24, 1911 (Pares).

129. Kokovtsov, *Out of My Past*, p. 565.

130. Polivanov, *Iz dnevnikov i vospominanii*, p. 103.

131. Bobrinsky, "Dnevnik A. A. Bobrinskogo," *Krasnyi arkhiv*, 26, p. 145 (10 marta).

132. *Ibid.*, p. 146 (11 marta).

133. Edward Chmielewski, "Stolypin's Last Crisis," *California Slavic Studies*, 3 (1964), p. 116.

134. "Vopros o zapadnom zemstve i bankrotstvo Stolypina," *Istoricheskie zapiski*, 70 (1961), pp. 91-109.

135. A. V. Zenkovsky, "Moi dopolnitelnye vospominaniya o P. A. Stolypine," 1953, p. 3; MS, Russian Archive, Columbia University.
Stolypin complained directly to the State Council of the harassment of him by some of its members and their obstruction of government proposals, *Gosudarstvennyi Sovet: Stenograficheskie otchety*, Sessiya VI, zasedanie 36, col. 1793.

136. "Iz perepiski P. A. Stolypina s Nikolaem Romanovym," *Krasnyi arkhiv*, 30, p. 86.

137. Speech to the Duma, April 27, 1911, *Gosudarstvennaya Duma: Stenograficheskie otchety*, Tretii sozyv, sessiya IV, zasedanie 101, cols. 2852, 2853, 2857; Speech to the State Council, April 1, 1911, *Gosudarstvennyi Sovet: Stenograficheskie otchety*, Sessiya VI, zasedanie 36, cols. 1782-86, 1784-85, 1791, 1792.

138. F. O. 371, vol. 1214, no. 12058, March 27, 1911.

139. Speech to the Duma, April 27, 1911, *Gosudarstvennaya Duma: Stenograficheskie otchety*, Tretii sozyv, sessiya IV, zasedanie 101, cols. 2851-52, 2857, 2860.

Stolypin claimed the Duma had wanted the government to use article 87 to implement a law concerning the Old Believers. Speech to the State Council, *Gosudarstvennyi Sovet: Stenograficheskie otchety,* Sessiya VI, zasedanie 36, cols. 1785, 1789-90.

140. In addition to evidence cited on this score, Prince A. V. Obolensky recalled that the Tsar did not like Guchkov, the Octobrist leader in the Third Duma, and this was reflected in the Tsar's relationship with Stolypin, who was close to Guchkov. *Moi vospominaniya i razmyshleniya,* p. 82. Sir Bernard Pares believed that Stolypin took the course he did during the zemstvo crisis because he needed the support of the Tsar rather than the Duma. Pares states that Stolypin used article 87 rather than reintroducing the zemstvo bill to the Duma, as it had been passed by the Duma, because the latter action would have made him appear a champion of the Duma and a supporter of the parliamentary system. In this case, Stolypin would have been opposed, in Pares' opinion, not merely by a majority of the State Council but a majority at court. Pares believed Stolypin wished to appear a "trusted Minister—responsible only to his Sovereign—to put the Tsar definitely on his side against court intriguers." F. O. 371, vol. 1217, no. 29095, July 24, 1911.

Chapter 7:
The End

During the summer following the zemstvo crisis, Stolypin was weary and depressed.[1] At the end of August he went to Kiev with the imperial retinue to dedicate a memorial to Alexander II and to view military maneuvers. In the photographs of Stolypin in Kiev taken August 30, 1911, he appears tall and serious of expression, wearing a white uniform decorated with sash and medals, standing to the right of the Tsar as Nicholas received a deputation from the peasantry.[2]

A few days later, on the evening of September 1, Stolypin and the imperial family were watching a performance of Rimsky-Korsakov's *Tsar Sultan* in the yellow and white Kiev opera house. Maria, Stolypin's eldest daughter, recalled that she had stayed at home with her sister, Olga, who had scarletina, and that Stolypin attended the opera with his wife, Olga Borisovna.[3] During the second intermission, a young man shot Stolypin before the horrified gaze of the audience. Tsar Nicholas wrote his mother that, have just left his box, he heard two sounds like opera glasses being dropped, turned to see the crowd and officers pulling someone along, and then saw Stolypin directly in front of him at his seat. Stolypin turned his face toward the Tsar and made the sign of the cross in the air with his left hand. It was only then, Nicholas wrote, that he realized that Stolypin was pale and that his right hand and uniform were stained with blood.[4]

Stolypin lingered three days, his pain alleviated by morphine, and then died. He was buried in the *Pecherskaya lavra* in Kiev, one of the holiest and most historical places in Russia. Nicholas attempted to see Stolypin on September 3, but Olga Borisovna would not permit him to do so. Maria claimed that no one realized how serious her father's condition was and that is why the Tsar did not come sooner. After Stolypin's death, Nicholas attended a memorial service for him where he was heard to whisper, "Forgive."[5]

Nicholas' own account of the assassination, contained in a letter to his mother written shortly after the event, illustrates the callousness which Gurko attributed to the Tsar. While Nicholas appears to have been distressed by Stolypin's death, he devoted equal space in his letter to the glories of reviewing the troops and the pleasant vacation his family was enjoying, alternating in staccato fashion between these topics:

> Poor Stolypin passed a very bad night and had to have several injections of morphine. The next day, September 2nd, there was a magnificent review of troops at the place where the manoeuvres had ended. . . .
>
> I returned to Kieff in the evening of September 3rd, called at the nursing home where Stolypin was lying, and met his wife who would not let me see him. On the 4th I went to the first school to be founded at Kieff which was celebrating its 100th anniversary. I went with the girls [his daughters] to the Museum of Military History and to the Museum of Peasant Handiwork.
>
> On September 6th at 9 a.m. I returned to Kieff. Here, on the pier, I heard from Kokovtsoff that Stolypin had died. I went at once to the nursing home, and a memorial service was afterward held in my presence. The poor widow stood as though turned to stone and was unable to weep. Her brother and Vasselkina were with her. At 11 o'clock we, i.e. Alix, the children and I, left Kieff, accompanied by a crowd which kept perfect order all the time. I had a complete rest on the train. We arrived at tea time. It was a glorious warm day. It is an immense pleasure to be back on the yacht again.
>
> The next day, September 8th, I reviewed the Black Sea fleet and visited the ships *Panteleimon, Yohann Zlatoust* and *Evstafij.* The last two are brand new. The truly magnificent condition of the ships and hardy faces of the crews filled me with admiration. What a difference between this and what they were quite a short time back! Thank God![6]

The amazing sangfroid displayed in this letter and Nicholas' utterance of the word "Forgive" led historians to theorize that he was implicated in Stolypin's assassination. The commander of the gendarmerie, Kurlov, and other high police officials were tried and dismissed for negligence of duty, with suspicion of complicity. The assassin, Dmitrii Bogrov, a Jewish student and erstwhile member of the Socialist Revolutionary party, was hanged without revealing why he killed Stolypin.[7]

Guchkov, for one, believed that the assassination was tolerated, if not planned, by those in high office as a convenient way of getting rid of Stolypin, who otherwise would have been relegated to the position of Viceroy of Siberia. The Governor General of Kiev, F. F. Trepov, and Colonel Spiridovich, chief of the palace guards, protected only the imperial family, although revolutionary plots always threatened Stolypin. When this particular plot was discovered, Guchkov claimed, these individuals decided not to interfere. In fact, Finnish nationalists also had organized a plot simultaneously.[8]

Kurlov, of course, tried to exonerate himself in his memoirs. He claimed that he had become ill after arriving in Kiev and was confined to his room from August 15 to 25, but did not neglect security preparations. These were entrusted primarily to the Kiev Okhrana, which Kurlov decided to strengthen since it was weaker in numbers than the Kiev gendarmerie.[9] One day, a certain Kulyabko informed Kurlov that a former collaborator of the Kiev Okhrana, Bogrov, had come to him, Kulyabko, telling about a plot against the Tsar. Kurlov apprised Stolypin of this information, but Stolypin thought Kurlov's fears exaggerated. Nevertheless, Kurlov assigned a Captain Essaulov, unknown to the Okhrana, to watch the Tsar, and Bogrov's apartment was kept under surveillance. Kurlov cautioned Stolypin to use no other automobile than that assigned him and strengthened the guard at the governor general's home, where Stolypin was staying. Persons wishing to see Stolypin were to be carefully examined. Stolypin also was warned that he ought to sit in the governor general's box, rather than in his front row seat at the opera, but he refused.[10]

Although Bogrov was to be confined to his apartment, although Kurlov and Colonel Spiridovich ordered tickets for the opera to be scrutinized, and although fifteen officers and ninety-two agents of the palace security guards and of the Kiev Okhrana were appointed to the theater the night of the fateful performance, Bogrov did get into the theater. He talked with Colonel Kulyabko, telling him that the attempt on the Tsar's life had not come off. Kurlov ordered Bogrov out and commanded Captain Essaulov to remain at Stolypin's side.[11] At the second intermission, according to Kurlov, he told Stolypin of Bogrov's presence but Stolypin appeared unworried. Essaulov at that time was in the foyer. Kurlov, according to his own account, went into the corridor, heard shots of a Browning, thought at first the Tsar had been hit, and then discovered it was Stolypin.[12] This was the last time Kurlov saw Stolypin alive.

During the investigation it was discovered that Bogrov had been in intimate connection with one of the spies of the Kiev Okhrana. Kurlov, however, insisted that this piece of evidence was fabricated by Trussevich, under whose chairmanship the investigation took place, in order to retaliate for Kurlov's criticism of the police under Trussevich's command.[13]

The truth of Stolypin's assassination probably will never be known.

Immediately after Stolypin's death, governmental agents sequestered all papers of governmental significance from his desk at Kolnoberzhe and from his office in St. Petersburg so that, as his daughter Maria lamented, not one important or even interesting paper remained in the family.[14] The family moved to the estate of Kolnoberzhe. During the First World War, Olga Petrovna and Alexandra did volunteer work at an infirmary in St. Petersburg. During the civil war they, Olga Borisovna and Natalya Stolypin took refuge with the Shcherbatov family (Elena Stolypin had married Prince Shcherbatov) at their estate in the Ukraine. The Bolsheviks shot Prince Shcherbatov, his mother and Olga Petrovna. Olga Borisovna fled to a convent and then to Paris. Natalya and Alexandra fled to Warsaw.[15] Natalya died of cancer in 1956. Elena Stolypin, Princess Shcherbatov, by her first marriage, and Princess Volkonsky, by her second, is still living, as is Alexandra Stolypin, Countess Keiserling by her marriage. Arkadii Stolypin, who was only seven when his father died, is living in Paris.[16]

Maria, Stolypin's eldest daughter, who was twenty-five at the time of her father's death, married Boris von Bock, a naval officer. They lived in Berlin, where her husband served in the Russian embassy, until the First World War. They retired to Kolnoberzhe and lived there, in what became Lithuania, until 1938, when the Germans took over the estate. The von Bock's life then became an odyssey—they lived in Japan for three years, Boris serving in a Swiss firm, then moved to Berlin for three years. When the Russians entered Eastern Europe, the von Bocks fled to Denmark, to Austria, and finally, in 1948, to the United States. Boris von Bock died in 1955,[17] but Maria, a gracious and intelligent lady, still resides in San Francisco, the possessor of portraits of her father, the imperial family, and many memories.

General Conclusions

From the time he entered the central government in 1906 Stolypin attempted to function within the confused, hybrid political framework recently erected in Russia and to solve Russia's manifold problems with equanimity and common sense. He accepted the fact that he was second in command over Russia's domestic policy in a quasi-autocratic state and worked in comparative harmony with the Tsar, whose ideas did not always coincide with his own. He parried the assaults of his enemies adroitly until late in his administration. Toward the new parliament Stolypin was, partly from instinct, partly from necessity, ambivalent. Alfred Levin's analysis of Stolypin's attitude toward the Duma probably remains most apt. Stolypin faced the twentieth century Russian parliament as a nineteenth century Russian bureaucrat.[18] In part this was due to the conditions in Russia which cried for immediate remedy, to the fact that remedies are faster if administered by a few people from above, and to the ineptitude of the first two Dumas. During the Third Duma, Stolypin's relationship with the Duma was somewhat affected by his attraction to efficiency, but also by the obstructionism of the State Council and the fact that in Russia it was the Tsar and not the Duma whose power was crucial for Stolypin.

The spate of reform proposals which streamed forth from the ministry during the first year of Stolypin's administration were evidence of the government's desire to improve many sectors of Russian life. Most of these proposals had been bandied about for years, but it was Stolypin who got them before the public. The proposals which Stolypin particularly sponsored were realistic, feasible schemes. This is not to say that the land reforms, the proposals on education, changes in *volost'* government, and reform of the *volost'* courts would not have led to momentous changes in peasant life—indeed in the fabric of all Russia. But they were to be realized only over the long term, and, in fact, by Stolypin's death little had been accomplished.[19]

Some of the other reforms particularly identified with Stolypin were quite cautious. The state—the administration—was to dominate local self-government just as it dominated the national representative legislature. The state was to dominate education. Though the position of Old Believers and sectarians was to be improved, the Orthodox Church was to remain the state church. The changes in the local administrative apparatus might have insured greater legality in this sector and in conjunction with the plans for local self-government would have better coordinated the local administration and local self-government. However, the basic structure of the local administrative apparatus remained unaltered, as did the basic position of the Jews in all the proposals dealing with them. Stolypin's emphasis on the attainable probably was due in part to his temperament and in part to his first hand experience with the problems in question. Unfortunately, most of the reform proposals were doomed to languish unimplemented because of the strength of reactionary opposition.

Stolypin's repressive policies were harsh, but probably necessary for the most part if order was to be reestablished and progress achieved. His nationality policies were not farsighted. But they were neither unreasonable, given the thinking of the age, nor intolerable, insofar as the Finns and the Poles in the western Russian provinces were concerned. Stolypin's contention that the Ukrainians were basically Russian was not without foundation.

The obstacles Stolypin faced were enormous. The country was greatly in need of revitalization. His boss was an indecisive individual who at times gave him enormous latitude and confidence, and at other times thwarted him. Intriguers sought constantly to erode the Tsar's support for Stolypin. He had no means of control over his colleagues in the ministry and met their opposition on many of his significant proposals. The police were a government within the government. Subordinates in far-flung provinces were difficult to supervise, and Stolypin seems to have concentrated his energy and attention on critical areas like Finland. His work load was staggering. The difficulties he faced are evidenced by the few accomplishments of his administration as compared with the number planned at the outset. Stolypin was not a philosophical man, but a practical administrator attempting to manage Russia properly, as he saw it. By nature, he was strong-minded. He often insisted upon the implementation of measures which he considered necessary, although he backed down because of the Tsar's disapproval or too great opposition on the part of his fellow ministers. The irritation he suffered from his enemies, the unpredictability of the Tsar, the pressures of his job made Stolypin finally intransigent. The wonder was not that he was uncompromising. In the beginning he was determined to accomplish moderate, constructive measures; in the end he was trying desperately to save his position and whatever authority he still possessed. The wonder was that he managed to operate and to survive as long as he did.

Notes

1. Alexander Ivanovich Guchkov, "Iz vospominaniya," *Poslednie novosti,* nos. 5633 and 6537, August 26 and 30, 1936, quoted in Vladimir Iosifovich Gurko, *Features and Figures of the Past,* trans. Laura Matveev (Stanford, California: Stanford University Press, 1939), p. 723; Maria Petrovna von Bock, *Vospominaniya o moem ottse, P. A. Stolypine* (New York: Chekhov Publishing House, 1953), p. 335.

2. A. V. Zenkovsky, *Pravda o Stolypine* (New York: Vseslovyanskoe Izdatel'stvo, 1956), cover photograph; Prince A. V. Obolensky, *Moi vospominaniya i razmyshleniya* (Stockholm: Izdanie zhurnala "Rodnye Perezvony," 1961), photographs, pp. 79, 80.

3. Bock, *Vospominaniya o moem ottse, P. A. Stolypine,* pp. 335-44.

4. Nicholas Romanov, *Secret Letters of the Last Tsar,* ed. Edward J. Bing (New York: Longmans, Green and Co., 1938), pp. 264-65.

5. Bock, *Vospominaniya o moem ottse, P. A. Stolypine,* p. 343.

6. Romanov, *Secret Letters of the Last Tsar,* pp. 263-67.

7. P. G. Kurlov, *Gibel' imperatorskoi Rossii* (Berlin: Otto Kirchner and Co., 1923), pp. 121-34; A. Mushin, *Dmitrii Bogrov i ubiistvo Stolypina* (Paris: 1914), *passim;* L. Gan, "Ubiistvo P. A. Stolypina," *Istoricheskii vestnik,* no. 135 (1914), pp. 960-97.

8. Gurko, *Features and Figures of the Past,* pp. 723-24.

According to Kokovtsov, in the spring of 1911, Rasputin and G. P. Sazonov (no relation to Stolypin's brother-in-law, Minister of Foreign Affairs), journeyed to Nizhnii Novgorod to sound out the young governor of that province N. A. Khvostov on the possibility of replacing Stolypin as Minister of Internal Affairs. Sergei Witte was to take over Stolypin's other position as Chairman of the Council of Ministers. Apparently, Khvostov refused, because he did not get along with Witte. Khvostov later served as Minister of Internal Affairs for a short time in 1915 and was shot by the Bolsheviks in 1918. Vladimir Nikolaevich Kokovtsov, *Iz moego proshlago* (Paris, The Hague: Mouton, 1969), vol. 2, pp. 22-23, 110, 133. First edition, 1933.

Grigorii Petrovich Sazonov, a critic of economic affairs, had vague political connections and influences.

L. M. Klyachko, a journalist of the period, gave yet another version of how the Tsar had decided to dispose of Stolypin after the latter had forced Nicholas' hand and precipitated the zemstvo crisis in the spring of 1911. According to Klyachko, the extreme right clique convinced the Tsar that Stolypin had tried to limit the autocracy by his actions in the zemstvo affair, and the Tsar had decided to get Stolypin out of the capital by appointing him Viceroy of the Caucasus. Klyachko also described the enmity between Stolypin and Witte, claiming that this was an additional factor in the Tsar's decision to put Stolypin out of harm's way. Stolypin, according to Klyachko, soon after the zemstvo crisis tried to shake Witte's hand. Witte refused, whereupon Stolypin challenged him to a duel. The Tsar forbade this and decided to send Stolypin to the Caucasus as viceroy. Lev Moiseevich Klyachko, *Povesti proshlogo* (Leningrad: Izdatel'stvo pisatelai, 1920), pp. 38, 77-78.

9. Kurlov, *Gibel' imperatorskoi Rossii,* pp. 123-24.

10. *Ibid.,* pp. 123-27.

11. *Ibid.,* p. 130.

12. *Ibid.,* p. 131.

13. *Ibid.,* pp. 133, 134.

14. Bock, *Vospominaniya o moem ottse, P. A. Stolypine,* pp. 345-46.

15. Alexandra Stolypine, *L'homme du dernier Tsar* (Paris: Redier, Librairie de la Revue Francaise, 1931), pp. 155-246.

16. Maria Petrovna von Bock to the author, March 16, 1976, letter in possession of the author.

Natalya Stolypin's feet were crushed in the Aptekarsky explosion of 1906 and were very nearly amputated. Alexandra Stolypin claimed that they were still crippled in later life. (*L'homme du dernier Tsar*, p. 246). Maria Bock, however, in her letter of March 16, 1976, recalling the details of the explosion, stated that although Natalya's feet were never the same as before, she was able to dance.

17. *Ibid.*

18. Alfred Levin, "Peter Arkad'evich Stolypin: A Political Appraisal," *The Journal of Modern History*, 37, no. 4 (1965), pp. 445-63.

19. I did not think it necessary to go into detail on the course of the land reforms themselves, for three reasons: this had been done with such proficiency by Geroid Tanquary Robinson, the reforms had just gotten under way when Stolypin was assassinated, and finally, I was more concerned about dilineating Stolypin's attitude toward the reforms. However, perhaps it might be satisfying to note the approximate results of the major aspects of the reform—change in the type of peasant tenure—by 1917. According to Robinson, in 1917, of the thirteen or fourteen millions of peasant allotments, some five millions of holdings remained in unchanged repartitional tenure, over one million holdings were covered by the new dissolution stipulations of 1910, but their status had not yet been changed, over one and one-half million holdings had been affected by the regulations of 1910, but the changes had not been fully recorded, there were over four million holdings in hereditary title, but still existing in scattered strips, and finally, only about 1,300,000 holdings existed under hereditary title and in consolidated form. *Rural Russia Under the Old Regime* (New York: Macmillan, 1961), pp. 226-27.

Bibliography

Primary Sources

Books

von Bock, Maria Petrovna. *Vospominaniya o moem ottse, P. A. Stolypine.* New York: Chekhov Publishing House, 1953.

    Maria Bock was twenty-one when Stolypin became Minister of Internal Affairs and Chairman of the Council of Ministers. Her account is useful for its information on Stolypin's personal life and career before his entrance into the central government. Mrs. Bock knew little about her father's career after 1906.

Guchkov, Alexander Ivanovich. "Iz vospominaniya," *Poslednie novosti,* nos. 5633 and 6537, August 26 and 30, 1936, quoted in Vladimir Iosifovich Gurko, *Features and Figures of the Past,* pp. 721-724. (The full citation of Gurko is given below.)

    Guchkov was leader of the Octobrist fraction and President of the Third Duma, after 1910. Though sparse, the three pages of Guchkov's vignette of Stolypin cited in Gurko are valuable for their presentation of Stolypin's views on the large landowners and on the western zemstvo crisis of 1911.

Guerassimov, General Alexandre Vasilevich. *Tsarisme et terrorisme.* Paris: Librairie Plon—Plon et Nourrit, 1934.

    Gerassimov was Chief of the Petersburg Okhrana during the early years of Stolypin's tenure. His memoirs portray the internecine rivalry among the police authorities, and give information on Stolypin's relationship with the Okhrana and with reactionary groups.

Gurko, Vladimir Iosifovich. *Features and Figures of the Past.* trans. by Laura Matveev. California: Stanford University Press, 1939.

    Gurko was Assistant Minister of Internal Affairs under Stolypin only until December, 1906. His memoirs are completely inaccurate with regard to Stolypin's ideas on the commune. However, Gurko gives helpful information on the work of Stolypin's predecessors in the Ministry of Internal Affairs and on Stolypin's appointment.

Iswolsky, Alexandre. *Memoires.* Paris: Payot, 1923.

    Izvolsky, Minister of Foreign Affairs from 1906-1910, gives no new insights into Stolypin's policies.

Karpov, N. I. *Agrarnaya politika Stolypina.* Leningrad: Rabochee Izdatel'stvo "Priboi," 1925.

Karpov is invaluable for the inclusion of two letters: that of Stolypin to the Minister of Internal Affairs Durnovo, January, 1906 (pp. 172-174) and that of S. Belsky to Stolypin, 1909 (pp. 174-175). The latter has comments by Stolypin.

Klyachko, Lev Moiseevich. *Povesti proshlogo.* Leningrad: Izdatel'stvo pisatelei, 1929.

Klyachko, a journalist of the period, gives some interesting anecdotes regarding Stolypin and Witte's relationship, but the work is sensationalistic and unreliable.

Kokovtsov, Count Vladimir Nikolaevich. *Out of My Past.* trans. by Laura Matveev. California: Stanford University Press, 1935.

Kokovtsov, Minister of Finance during Stolypin's entire administration, describes the workings of the Council of Ministers and the chief episodes of Stolypin's political career. Kokovtsov seems fairly reliable.

_____ *Iz moego proshlago.* 1933. Reprinted in Paris-The Hague: Mouton, 1969 (2 vols.).

Kryzhanovsky, Sergei Efimovich. *Vospominaniya.* Berlin: Speer and Schmidt, n.d.

Kryzhanovsky, who served as Assistant Minister of Internal Affairs under Stolypin presents interesting information regarding the composition of the Electoral Law of June 3 and disbursement of funds to reactionary groups.

Kurlov, General Pavel Grigorevich. *Gibel' imperatorskoi Rossii.* Berlin: Otto Kirchner and Co., 1923.

Kurlov was commander of the Gendarmerie, 1909-1911, and in charge of security in Kiev at the time of Stolypin's assassination. Kurlov's account of his relationship with Stolypin is contradicted by every other writer of the period. However, his memoirs contain one of the most detailed records of Stolypin's assassination.

Miliukov, Pavel Nikolaevich. *Vospominaniya.* New York: Chekhov Publishing House, 1955. (2 vols.)

The description of the Kadet program and activity of the Kadet leader Miliukov is necessary for an understanding of Stolypin's attitude toward the Kadets. Miliukov also gives the fullest account of the negotiations for the Kadet Cabinet.

Naumov, A. N. *Iz utselevshikh vospominanii.* New York: Izdanie A. K. Naumovia i O. A. Kusevitskoi, 1955. (2 vols.)

Naumov, an official in Samara *guberniya* government adjoining Saratov, gives some details on the revolution of 1905 and Stolypin's command of the situation in Saratov.

Obolensky, A. V. *Moi vospominaniya i razmyshleniya.* Stockholm: Izdanie zhurnala "Rodnye Perezvony," Brussels, 1961.

Obolensky served in the *guberniya* chancellery when Stolypin was Governor of Grodno and later held a post in the Ministry of Internal Affairs. The few pages of the book devoted to Stolypin contain information on Stolypin's appointment as Governor of Grodno and the intrigue at the court of Nicholas II.

Oznobishin, A. A. *Vospominaniya.* Paris: Sklad i izdatelstvo E. Siyalskoi, 1927.

The author found nothing useful in this book by a former Marshal of the Nobility and Assistant Governor of Grodno.

Polivanov, Aleksei Andreevich. *Iz dnevnikov i vospominanii po dolzhnosti voennogo ministra i ego pomoshchika, 1907-1916.* Moscow: Vysshii voennyi redaktsionnyi sovet, 1924.

Polivanov was Assistant Minister of War during Stolypin's term of office. His journal of the meetings of the Council of Ministers gives vivid descriptions of the ministers, their relationships, the attitude of the State Council toward Stolypin, the relations between the ministry and the Duma, and gives insight into Stolypin's attitude toward the Duma, the Tsar, and repression.

Radziwill, Count Paul Vasilii. *Behind the Veil at the Russian Court.* New York: John Lane, Co., 1914.

This gossipy book contains a few apparently accurate pieces of information on how the Tsar spent his leisure time and on Stolypin's father, Arkadii Dmitrievich.

Romanov, Nicholas. *Archives secretes de L'Empereur Nicolas II.* trans. by Vladimir Lazarevski. Paris: Payot, 1928.

_____ *Secret Letters of the Last Tsar.* ed. Edward J. Bing. New York: Longmans, Green and Co., 1938.

Nicholas' correspondence provides remarkable insight into his general mentality, and his attitude toward the Duma and certain governmental personages. There are few references to Stolypin in the two books whose collections of letters overlap and complement each other.

Sazonov, Sergei Dmitrievich. *Vospominaniya.* Paris: Knigoizdatelstvo E. Siyalskoi, 1927.

Stolypin's brother-in-law and Minister of Foreign Affairs from 1910-1916, Sazonov says little about Stolypin except that the latter had nothing to do with Sazonov's appointment.

Shipov, D. N. *Vospominaniya i dumy o perezhitom.* Moscow: Tipografiya "Pechatnaya S. P. Yakovleva," 1918.

Shipov, leader of the Moscow *guberniya* zemstvo, ex-Kadet, member of the Octobrist and later the Party of Peaceful Reconstruction, is helpful for better understanding Stolypin's attitude toward the Kadets and presents the fullest account of the Cabinet of Public Men episode.

Skripitsyn, V. A. *Bogatyr mysli, slova i dela.* St. Petersburg: Gorodskaya Tipografiya, 1911.

Skripitsyn was editor of a Saratov newspaper while Stolypin was Governor. His pamphlet contains a few anecdotes on Stolypin's activity as Governor.

Stolypine, Alexandra. *L'homme du dernier Tsar.* Paris: Alex Redier, Editeur Librairie de la Revue Française, 1931.

Alexandra Stolypine is useful for information on Stolypin's personal life after his entrance into the central government, supplementing the account of her sister Maria. Alexandra also gives fascinating descriptions of the family after Stolypin's death, particularly during the revolutions of 1917.

Stolypin, Arkadii Petrovich. *P. A. Stolypin.* Paris: Imp. Scientifique et Commerciale, 1927.

Arkadii Stolypin was only seven when his father died. His tribute to his father is merely a brief compilation of existing information.

Sukhomlinov, Vladimir Aleksandrovich. *Vospominaniya.* Berlin: Russkoe universalnoe izdatelstvo, 1924.

Sukhomlinov, Minister of War from 1909 until after Stolypin's death, gives a meager and thoroughly unreliable account of his relationship with Stolypin.

Trufanoff, Sergei Michailovich. *The Mad Monk of Russia, Iliodor.* New York: Century, 1918.

Trufanoff was the given name of the monk Iliodor. His book, a diatribe against the government and Stolypin in particular, is useful as a revelation of Iliodor's mentality.

Vasiliev, Aleksei Tikhonovich. *The Ochrana, The Russian Secret Police.* London: George G. Harrap and Co., 1930.

Vasiliev was a police chief during the latter years of the empire. His book is interesting for its information on the workings of the Okhrana, and the incredible blundering and myopic mentality of the Okhrana chiefs.

Verpakhovsky, E., ed. *Predsedatel' soveta ministrov Petr Arkad'evich Stolypin.* St. Petersburg: Izdanie sostavitelya, 1909.

A compilation of Stolypin's speeches and interviews, and articles about him, 1906-1909.

——— *Gosudarstvennaya deyatel'nost' predsedatelya soveta ministrov, stats sekretarya, Petra Arkad'evicha Stolypina.* St. Petersburg: Izdanie sostavitelya, 1911.

A compilation of Stolypin's speeches and interviews, and articles about him, 1909-1911.

Viroubova, Anna. *Memories of the Russia Court.* New York: The Macmillan Co., 1923.

Vyrubova seems to be accurate in her descriptions of the Imperial family's daily domestic routine.

Zavarzin, Pavel Pavlovich. *Rabota tainoi politsii.* Paris: Izdanie avtora—tipografiya "Franco-Russkaya Pechat," 1924.

——— *Souveniers d'un chef de l'Okhrana.* Paris: Payot, 1930.

Zavarzin, a police official, gives particularly useful information on the so-called black cabinets and double agents. The books contain almost identical information.

Articles

Fedyushin, K. "Petr Arkadevich Stolypin i studenty," *Istoricheskii vestnik,* no. 5 (May, 1914), pp. 531-537.

A student's account of Stolypin's relationship with Petersburg students and of political currents among the students of Petersburg and Odessa, 1907-1911.

Krasnyi arkhiv:

Bobrinsky, A. A. "Dnevnik A. A. Bobrinskogo," vol. 26 (1928), pp. 127-50.

Bobrinsky was very critical of Stolypin and, thus, he provides a very biased, but eyewitness account of some major episodes in Stolypin's career, notably the zemstvo crisis, during 1910 and 1911.

Golovin, F. A. "Zapiski," vol. 19 (1926), pp. 133-48.

This brief account of the Second Duma by its President relates Stolypin's treatment of the Duma and his relationship with Golovin himself.

"Iz perepiski P. A. Stolypina s Nikolaem Romanovyn," vol. 30 (1928), pp. 80-88.

"Perepiska N. A. Romanova i P. A. Stolypina," vol. 5 (1924), pp. 102-28.

The letters from Stolypin to Nicholas in volume 30 as well as those between Nicholas and Stolypin in volume 5 present Stolypin's views on several major governmental issues and give insight into Stolypin's attitude toward the Duma and his relationship with the Tsar.

"Pisma P. A. Stolypina na imya kn. Nikolaya Nikolaevicha [Gazenkampf] ot 27 yanvarya, 10 fevralya, 1908 g.," vol. 19 (1926), pp. 215-21.

An enlightening, but obviously not all-inclusive statement of Stolypin's views on the necessity of repressing disorder in 1908.

"Pismo predsedatelya Soveta Ministrov i ministra vnutr. del P. A. Stolypina na imya namestnika na Kavkaze gr. I. I. Vorontsova-Dashkova ot 11 aprelya (st. st.) 1908 g. No. 64885, Bor'ba s revolyutsionnym dvizheniem na Kavkaze v epokhu stolypinshchinu," vol. 34 (1929), pp. 187-202.

"Tsirkulyar predsedatelya soveta ministrov P. A. Stolypina ot 15 sentyabrya 1906 g. general-gubernatoram, gubernatoram i gradonachalnikam," vol. 32 (1929), pp. 162-81.

A long circular expressing Stolypin's views on repression in 1906.

"Vsepoddanneishii otchet saratovskogo gubernatora P. Stolypina za 1904 god," vol. 17 (1926), pp. 81-87.

The report is valuable as the second earliest verbatim record of Stolypin's ideas on the agrarian problem and the earliest statement of his views on revolution, the liberal groups, and the Duma.

Legras, Jules. "Souvenirs sur P. A. Stolypine," *Vie des peuples* vol. 7 (Paris, 1922), pp. 1003-1020.

Legras' brief account of two interviews which he had with Stolypin, the first in Saratov in 1903, the second in 1909. Both give insight into Stolypin's political philosophy.

Lvov, L. "Perepiska grafa S. Yu. Witte i P. A. Stolypina," *Russkaya mysl,* no. 3 (Mowcow, 1915), pp. 134-53.

The irate letters between Witte and Stolypin, regarding the attempt on Witte's life in 1910, are peripheral to the subject of this book.

"Perepiska Tolstoga s A. A. Stolypinym," pub. by N. Guseva, *Literaturnoe nasledstvo,* Moscow, vols. 37-38 (1939), pp. 324-29.

The résumés of Tolstoy's letters to Stolypin and the quotation of correspondence between Alexander Stolypin and Tolstoy are interesting as expressions of Tolstoy's critique of Stolypin's agrarian and repressive policies, and Stolypin's attitude toward and relationship with the grand old man of Russian letters.

Tverskoi, P. A. "K istoricheskim materialam o pokoinom P. A. Stolypine," *Vestnik Evropy,* no. 4 (April, 1912), pp. 183-201.

A record of an interview with Stolypin by an American (former Russian) journalist early in 1907 regarding the state of affairs in Russia. The article consists almost entirely of direct quotations.

Documents

Great Britain. Public Record Office. British Diplomatic Correspondence, 1906-1911, Foreign Office 371, vols. 100-1217.

The dispatches of the British diplomats and observers in Russia are valuable for the many interviews with Stolypin which they record and for their eye-witness accounts and judicious analysis of events.

Gosudarstvennaya Duma: Stenograficheskie otchety, 1906-1911.

Gosudarstvennyi Sovet: Stenograficheskie otchety, 1911.

The stenographic reports of the Duma contain records of several government bills otherwise unavailable, as well as popular opinion on Stolypin's policies. Stolypin's speeches to both chambers must be used with caution, but several seem to be forthright statements of his political philosophy.

Knizhnaya letopis. St. Petersburg: Glavnago upravleniya po delam pechati, 1907-1911.

A bi-weekly compilation of books and journal articles published, useful for an analysis of "freedom of the press," as well as the tenor of the times.

Materialy: Vysochaishe uchrezhdennoe osoboe soveshchanie o nuzhdakh sel'-skokhozyaistvennoi promyshlennosti. St. Petersburg, 1904.

This summary of the reports of the *guberniya* and *uezd* Committees on the Needs of Local Agricultural Industry, 1902-1903, is useful as an indication of the views of the country at large toward the commune.

Ministerstvo vnutrennikh del:

Department politsii. Proekty i predpolozheniya. Bill no. 56956, November 1, 1907; "Ob assignovanii v rasporyazhenie Ministra Vnutrennikh Del na 1910, 250,000 r. na vydachu posobii chinam politsii obshchei politsii i otdelnago korpusa zhandarmov," no. 54246, August 8, 1909.

Glavnoe upravlenie po delam mestnago khozyaistva kantselyariya, "Ob ustanovlenii glavnykh osnovanii preobrazovaniya zemskikh i gorodskikh uchrezhdenii," No. 17, February 7, 1907.

Zemskii otdel, "Polozhenie o poselkovom upravlenii," no. 29489, October, 1908 and no. 34012, December, 1908.

Department obshchikh del, Bill on the extension of the terms of representatives from the western provinces to the State Council, no. 14521, May 8, 1909.

All four bills are in the Hoover Library, Stanford, California. The projects are valuable for the expression of Stolypin's views on local self-government and nationalism.

Sovet po delam mestnago khozyaistva. Zhurnal komissii po proektu preobrazovaniya uchrezhdenii gubernskago upravleniya, March 1909.

Osobyi zhurnal soveta ministrov. St. Petersburg: Gosudarstvennaya Tipografiya, 1906-1911, after 1907, three vols. annually.

The confidential summaries of the discussions of the meetings of the Council of Ministers are one of the most valuable sources for an analysis of Stolypin's policies and political philosophy. The journals present majority and minority opinions, but unfortunately discussions on some major issues, notably the Law of June 3, 1907, are omitted.

Pervaya vseobshchaya perepis naseleniya Rossiiskoi imperii, 1897: Obshchii svod po imperii, rezultatov razrabotki. ed. N. A. Troinitskii. St. Petersburg: Ministerstvo Vnutrennikh Del, 1905.

The census of 1897 gives useful background information.

Polnoe sobranie zakonov Rossiiskoi imperii. Sobranie tretie, March 1, 1881-December 31, 1913. St. Petersburg, 1885-1916, 33 vols.

A complete collection of the laws of the Russian Empire, third collection is contained in the Hoover Library, Stanford, California.

Padenie Tsarskogo rezhima. ed. P. S. Shchegolev. Moscow-Leningrad: Gosudarstvennoe Izdatel'stvo, 1926, 7 vols. (Records of the Provisional Government Investigating Committee Hearings, 1917.)

This testimony, given under duress, must be used with caution.

Trudy mestnykh komitetov o nuzhdakh sel'skokhozyaistvennoi promyshlennosti, vol. 11, Grodnenskaya Guberniya. St. Petersburg: Tipografiya Izadora Gol'dberga, 1903.

The stenographic record of the Grodno Committee proceedings is valuable as the earliest verbatim record of Stolypin's views on the agrarian problem, the industrial laborer and education.

Finland, Valtionarkisto (National Archives). KKK (Fund of the Governor General of Finland), 1906-1911. VSV (Fund of the State Secretary for Finnish Affairs), 1906-1911.

These two funds include copies of the *Osobyi zhurnal Soveta Ministrov* on Finnish topics, reports of the Vysochaishe uchrezhdennago osobago soveshchaniya po delam Velikago Knyazhestva Finlyandskago, reports of Duma commissions, petitions and statements from the Finnish Diet and Senate, laws regarding Finland, correspondence between Stolypin and the governors general of Finland and the Minister State Secretary for Finnish Affairs and are, thus, a rich mine of information on Finnish-Russian relationships from 1906-1911.

Zhurnal': mezhduvedomstvennoi komissii po preobrazovaniyu politsii v Imperii. St. Petersburg: Gosudarstvennaya Tipografiya, 1911, 11 vols. (Hoover Library, Stanford, California).

These volumes describe the condition of the police in Russia and Stolypin's policies with regard to them.

Newspapers

Pravitel'stvennyi vestnik. 1905-1906.

Considered a government organ, this Petersburg newspaper contains vivid reports from Saratov of the revolutionary turmoil there in 1905-1906.

Vozrozhdenie. Paris, 1935. (Hoover Library, Stanford, California)

The 1935 edition of this émigré newspaper contained a series of articles by Maria Bock on her father.

Manuscripts - (Unless specified, manuscripts are in the Russian Archive, Columbia University)

Hessen, I. V. "Reminiscences," Hoover Library, Stanford, California.

Though they contain little original material on Stolypin, Hessen's memoirs are interesting as the opinion of a "liberal" on Stolypin's policies.

Golitsyn, Prince A. D. "Vospominaniya."

Golitsyn, a member of the Kharkov *uezd* zemstvo and Octobrist member of the Budget and Local Self-Government Committees of the Third Duma, gives interesting information on Stolypin's attitude toward and treatment of local self-government, and on Stolypin's relationship with Kokovtsov.

Lyubimov, D. N. "Russkaya smuta snachala devyatisotykh godov, 1902-1906."

Lyubimov, who served as Secretary of the Ministry of Internal Affairs only until June, 1906, recounts only a minute amount about Stolypin as Minister.

Melnikov, N. "19 let na zemskii sluzhbe".

The author found nothing useful in this account by a member of the Kazan Zemstvo.

Mendeleev, Pavel Pavlovich, "Svety i teni v moei zhizni. Obryvki vospominanii".

Mendeleev, who served in the Chancellery of the Council of Ministers, 1906-

1909, and was not favorably disposed to Stolypin, gives brief but interesting accounts of the meetings of the Council and Stolypin's personality.

Meyendorff, Baron Alexander. "A Brief Appreciation of P. Stolypin's Tenure of Office," written 1932-1947.

Baron Meyendorff was Stolypin's cousin and political opponent, an Octobrist member of the Third Duma and a scholar. His incredibly jumbled manuscript has snatches of information on the extent of Stolypin's knowledge of law and on his personal life.

_____ Memoirs. Written in 1942. In possession of Maria von Bock, San Francisco.

Baron Meyendorff lived with Stolypin's parents while a law student at the University of Petersburg, ca. 1888. His brief, handwritten memoirs contain fascinating and otherwise unattainable information on Stolypin's father and Stolypin's university life and early career.

Shlipie, Feodor Vladimirovich. "Memoirs".

Shlipie, head of the land development commission of the Moscow zemstvo presents some interesting details on Stolypin's relationship with zemstvo figures and his interest in the agrarian program.

Troitsky, Konstantin Konstantinovich. "Iz vospominanii chinovnika osobykh poruchenii V kl. pri Ministerstve vnutrennikh del".

Troitsky, who served in the Land Section of the Ministry of Internal Affairs, 1906-1912, gives brief information on Stolypin's plan to increase the authority of local self-government institutions in economic matters.

Zenkovsky, Professor A. V. "Petr Arkadevich Stolypin," composed in 1952.

Zenkovsky, member of the Kiev zemstvo, relates his nineteen meetings with Stolypin between 1906-1911 and gives insight into Stolypin's relationship with zemstvo personages and his attitude toward local self-government.

_____ MS Memoirs, 1952.

A description of Stolypin's Plan for the Transformation of the Russian Government which Zenkovsky claims Stolypin dictated to him in early May, 1911.

_____ "Moi dopolnitelnye vospominaniya o P. A. Stolypine," written 1953.

A fuller description of Stolypin's alleged project which Zenkovsky supposedly rediscovered during 1953.

Letters

von Bock, Boris to Professor A. V. Zenkovsky, 1953 (Russian Archive, Columbia University):

April 24: on the authenticity of Stolypin's alleged Project for the Transformation of the Russian Government.

May 23: on the authenticity of Stolypin's Project.

June 10: quotes Stolypin's remark concerning his irritation at not being able to choose his subordinates.

June 24: on the Tsarina's dislike of Stolypin.

von Bock, Maria Petrovna to Professor Zenkovsky, July 11, 1953 (Russian Archive, Columbia University):

On the Tsarina's dislike of Stolypin, the authenticity of Stolypin's Project, and Stolypin's annoyance with Kokovtsov.

von Bock, Maria Petrovna to the author, 1964 (in possession of the author):

June 3: details on Stolypin's early education, additional information on his relatives in Dresden.

June 7: on the reason Stolypin was born in Dresden; on the cause of his paralyzed right arm.

June 19, 1973: details on the Stolypin family's residence in the Winter Palace. (in possession of the author).

March 16, 1976: history of Stolypin's children from his death in 1911 to the present (in possession of the author).

Shipov, D. N. to his wife Anna, March 4, 1910 (Russian Archive, Columbia University):
The letter criticizes Stolypin's power politics.

Stolypin, Arkadii to the author, July 15, 1964 (in possession of the author):
concerning Stolypin's dissertation on tobacco plantations in southern Russia.

Personal Interviews

Maria von Bock, San Francisco, winter-spring, 1962-1963, three interviews.

Telephone conversation with Mrs. Bock, July 23, 1964.

Prince A. V. Obolensky, Stockholm, July, 1963, two interviews. (Prince Obolensky served in the Chancellery of the Governor of Grodno, while Stolypin was in office there, and in the Ministry of Internal Affairs, while Stolypin was Minister and Chairman of the Council of Ministers.

Secondary Sources

General Reference Works

Entsiklopedicheskii slovar, ed. Brockhaus and Efron. St. Petersburg, 1890-1904, 41 vols.

Russkii biograficheskii slovar. St. Petersburg, 1909.

Books

Antonova, S. I. *Vliyanie Stolypinskoi agrarnoi reformy na izmeneniya v sostave rabochego klassa.* Moscow: Izdatel'stvo Moscovskogo universiteta, 1951.
A study of the effects of the agrarian legislation on industrialization in Moscow *Guberniya,* 1906-1913, the work was too specialized for this book.

Atsarkin, A. N. *Lektsiya Stolypinskaya reaktsiya. Bor'ba V. I. Lenina za teoreticheskie osnovy marksistskoi partii.* Moscow: Izdatel'stvo Moscovskogo universiteta, 1956.
The book contains only a superficial account of Stolypin's policies.

Avrekh, A. Ya. *Stolypin i Tret'ya Duma.* Moscow: Izdatel'stvo "Nauka", 1968.
Avrekh's work concentrates more on the Third Duma than on Stolypin.

Blinov, I. *Gubernatory.* St. Petersburg: Tipografiya K. L. Tsenkovskago, 1905.

Bogrov, Vladimir Grigor'evich. *Dmitrii Bogrov i ubiistvo Stolypina.* Razoblachenie "deistvitel'nykh i mnimykh tain!" Berlin: Knigoisdatel'stvo "Strela," 1931.

A sympathetic, but objective description of Stolypin's assassin, by his brother, a man of non-revolutionary political persuasion.

Charques, Richard. *The Twilight of Imperial Russia.* Fair Lawn, New Jersey: Essential Books, 1959.

This standard text is helpful for a background of the period.

Chmieleweski, Edward. *The Polish Question in the Russian State Duma.* Knoxville: University of Tennessee Press, 1970.

Dobb, Maurice. *Soviet Economic Development since 1917.* New York: International Publishers, 1948.

Dobb is helpful for information on the pre-Soviet Russian economy.

Dubrovskii, S. M. *Stolypinskaya zemel'naya reforma.* Moscow: Akademiya nauk SSSR, Institut istorii, 1963.

One of the most thorough studies of the so-called Stolypin agrarian legislation. The book gives much valuable information, but some of the statistics in its innumerable charts are distorted.

Gribovskii, V. M. *Gosudarstvennoi ustroistvo i upravlenie Rossiiskoi imperii.* Odessa: Tipografiya Teknik, 1912.

Hare, Richard. *Portraits of Russian Personalities.* London: Oxford University Press, 1959.

Hare presents only a superficial sketch of Stolypin.

Hosking, Geoffrey A. *The Russian Constitutional Experiment: Government and Duma, 1907-1914.* New York, London: Cambridge University Press, 1973.

This book is a thoughtful and thorough description of Duma-government relations during the Third Duma and the first part of the Fourth Duma.

Izgoev, A. S. *P. A. Stolypin.* Moscow, 1912.

A tiny, but perceptive analysis of Stolypin's policies and political philosophy by a contemporary liberal journalist.

————— *Russkoe obshchestvo i revolyutsiya.* Moscow: Izdanie zhurnala "Russkaya mysl," Tovarishchestvo tipografii A. I. Mamontova, 1910.

A collection of articles analyzing the situation in Russia and Stolypin's policies.

Korkunov, N. M. *Russkoe gosudarstvennoe pravo.* St. Petersburg: Tipografiya M. M. Stasiulevicha, 1905; 1909.

A monumental history and analysis of Russian governmental institutions by one of Russia's foremost legal scholars. The 1905 edition, treating Russia prior to the October Manifesto, is helpful for an understanding of the Russian governmental apparatus and political theory. The 1909 edition is interesting for its critique of the legality of certain of Stolypin's policies, such as the Law of June 3, 1907.

Kornilov, A. *Iz istorii voprosa ob izbiratel'nom prave v zemstve.* St. Petersburg, 1906.

Laporte, Maurice. *Histoire de l'Okhrana.* Paris: Payot, 1923.

An enlightening study of the political police based on archival materials.

Lazarevskii, N. I. *Lektsii po Russkomu gosudarstvennomu pravu.* St. Petersburg: Tipografiya "Slovo", 1910, II, Administrativnoe pravo.

Levin, Alfred. *The Second Duma.* New Haven: Yale University Press, 1940.

An analysis of the stenographic reports of the Second Duma; the book gives a comprehensive and vivid description of that body.

Liashchenko, Peter Ivanovich. *History of the National Economy of Russian to the 1917 Revolution.* New York: Macmillan, 1949.

A creditable, Soviet economics text.

Maevskii, Vladimir. *Borets za blago Rossii.* Madrid: Izdanie pochitatelei gosudarstvennoi deyatel'nosti P. A. Stolypina, 1962.

A substantial, but undocumented review of Stolypin's political policies.

Mehlinger, Howard D. and Thompson, John M. *Count Witte and the Tsarist Government in the 1905 Revolution.* Bloomington: Indiana University Press, 1972.

Mirsky, Prince D. S. *Contemporary Russian Literature, 1881-1925.* New York: Alfred A. Knopf, 1926.

The author consulted Mirsky for information on the poet, A. N. Apukhtin.

Monas, Sidney. *The Third Section.* Cambridge: Harvard University Press, 1961.

An interesting analysis of the predecessor of the Okhrana.

Mushin, A. *Dmitrii Bogrov i ubiistvo Stolypina.* Paris, 1914.

A comprehensive account of Stolypin's assassination.

Nikolaevsky, Boris Ivanovich. *Istoriya odnogo predatelya.* Berlin: Petropolis-Verlag, 1932.

An undocumented, journalistic account of the so-called Azef affair.

Pinchuk, Ben-Cion. *The Octobrists in the Third Duma, 1907-1912.* Seattle: Washington University Press, 1974.

Professor Pinchuk presents an enlightening account of Octobrist policy and activity during the Third Duma.

Polner, Tikhon J., Obolensky, Prince Vladimir, and Turpin, Sergius P. *Russian Local Government During the War and the Union of Zemstvos.* New Haven: Yale University Press, 1930.

The study includes statistics on zemstvo work in the early twentieth century.

Prokof'yev, M. *O sovremennom polozhenii zemstve* (*Vestnik Novgorodskago Zemstva,* no. 16). Novgorod, 1906.

Robinson, Geroid T. *Rural Russia Under the Old Regime.* New York: Macmillan Co., 1961, 3rd edition.

One of the foremost studies on the peasant question and the agrarian legislation enacted by Stolypin.

Schwartz, Harry. *Russia's Soviet Economy.* Engelwood Cliffs, New Jersey: Prentice Hall, Inc., 1960, 4th edition.

The author consulted the book for statistics on the pre-Soviet economy.

Seton-Watson, Hugh. *The Decline of Imperial Russia.* New York: Frederick Praeger, 1960.

Another standard text of the period.

_____ *The Russian Empire, 1801-1917.* Oxford: The Clarendon Press, 1967.

Skalon, V. Yu. *Po zemskim voprosam.* St. Petersburg, 1905.

Smith, Edward Ellis. *"The Okhrana," The Russian Department of Police.* Stanford: The Hoover Institution on War, Revolution and Peace, 1967.

A highly useful, annotated bibliography on the Okhrana.

Starr, S. Frederick. *Decentralization and Self-Government in Russia, 1830-1870.* Princeton, New Jersey: Princeton University Press, 1972.

An informative and well-written description of the provincial administrative apparatus during the nineteenth century and governmental proposals for reform of the local administration and the establishment of self-government.

Torngren, Adolph. *L'evolution de la Russie pendant les annees 1904-1907.* trans. from the Swedish by Mlle. Frederique Pluche. Paris: Plon Nourrit, 1914.

Unsympathetic to Stolypin, Torngren cites interesting information on the status of the press during Stolypin's tenure.

Uchenye zapiski: vypusk istoricheskii posvyaschennyi 50 letyu pervoi Russkoi revolyutsii. vol. 55, Ministerstvo vysshego obrazovaniya SSSR Saratovskii gosudarstvennyi universitet. Saratov: Izdatelstvo "Kommunist," 1956.

This compilation of articles by various Soviet scholars contains interesting information on the condition of the workers and peasants in Saratov *Guberniia,* ca. 1905.

Vasilevskii, E. G. *Ideinaya bor'ba vokrug stolypinskoi agrarnoi reformy.* Moscow: Izdatel'stvo sotsial'no-ekonomicheskoi literatury, 1960.

Vasilevskii contains a brief, but adequate account of the Bolshevik view of Stolypin's agrarian legislation.

Veselovsky, Boris. *Istoriya zemstva.* 4 volumes. St. Petersburg, 1911.

Von Laue, Theodore H. *Sergei Witte and the Industrialization of Russia.* New York: Columbia University Press, 1963.

Von Laue's work on Witte is helpful as a background for Stolypin's tenure of office.

Wolfe, Bertram D. *Three Who Made a Revolution.* Boston: Beacon Press, 1957.

Wolfe includes statistics on Bolshevik activity and an interesting chapter on Lenin's view of Stolypin's agrarian program.

Wuorinen, John H. *A History of Finland.* New York: Columbia University Press, 1965.

Useful as a background to Stolypin's Finnish policy, Wuorinen is highly critical and biased in his account of the Russian government's Finnish policy during Stolypin's tenure.

Yaney, George L. *The Systematization of the Russian Government:* Urbana: University of Illinois Press, 1973.

Professor Yaney provides the fullest description available in English of the internal workings of the chief governmental bodies in Russia during the nineteenth century.

Zenkovsky, A. V. *Pravda o Stolypine.* New York: All-Slavic Publishing House, 1957.

A eulogy to Stolypin which includes a detailed description of Stolypin's controversial project for the Transformation of the Russia Government and the text of the western zemstvo bill of 1911.

Articles

Avrekh, A. Ya. "Stolypinskim bonapartizm i voprosy voennoi politiki v III Dume," *Voprosy istorii,* no. 11 (November, 1956), pp. 17-33.

Although Avrekh is critical of Stolypin, his article is an objective and scholarly examination of the naval general staff crisis of 1909.

"Vopros o zapadnom zemstve i bankrotstvo Stolypina," *Istoricheskie zapiski,* vol. 70 (1961), pp. 61-112.

A thorough and provocative analysis of the zemstvo crisis of 1911 based on archival sources.

Chmielewski, Edward. "Stolypin and the Russian Ministerial Crisis of 1909," *California Slavic Studies,* vol. 4 (1967), pp. 1-38.

———— "Stolypin's Last Crisis," *California Slavic Studies,* vol. 3 (1964), pp. 95-126.

Gan, L. "Ubiistvo P. A. Stolypina," *Istoricheskii vestnik,* no. 135 (1914), pp. 960-997.

A comprehensive description of Stolypin's assassination, interesting for an inclusion of the floor plan of the Kiev opera house in which Stolypin was shot.

Levin, Alfred. "The Russian Voter in the Elections to the Third Duma," *Slavic Review,* vol. 21, no. 4 (December, 1962).

A study of the effect of the Law of June 3 on elections to the Third Duma in 1907.

"Peter Arkad'evich Stolypin: A Political Appraisal," *The Journal of Modern History,* vol. 37, no. 4 (1965), pp. 445-63.

A very apt analysis of Stolypin.

Mosse, W. E. "Stolypin's Villages," *The Slavonic and East European Review,* London (June, 1965), pp. 257-74.

Rogger, Hans. "Russian Ministers and the Jewish Question, 1881-1917," *California Slavic Studies,* vol. 8 (1975), pp. 15-76.

Independently of each other and using some different sources, Professor Rogger and I have come to much the same conclusion about Stolypin's Jewish policy. Professor Rogger discusses Stolypin on pp. 52-61 of the above article.

Savickij, Nicolas. "P. A. Stolypine," *Le monde slav,* (November, 1933), pp. 227-63; December, pp. 360-83.

A small, but objective study of Stolypin which includes a few new details on Stolypin's family background.

Snow, George Edward. "The Kokovtsov Commission: An Abortive Attempt at Labor Reform in Russia in 1905," *Slavic Review,* vol. 31, no. 4 (December, 1972), pp. 780-96.

Strakhovsky, Leonid I. "The Statesmanship of Peter Stolypin: A Reappraisal," *Slavonic and East European Review,* vol. 37 (1958-1959), pp. 348-70.

The author found the article eulogistic, but it gave helpful references to primary sources concerning the ante-duma.

Tokmakoff, George. "P. A. Stolypin and the Second Duma," *Slavonic and East European Review,* vol. 50, no. 118 (January, 1972), pp. 49-62.

Unpublished Ph. D. Theses

Yaney, George. "The Imperial Russian Government and the Stolypin Land Reforms," 1962, Princeton University Library.

This Ph.D. thesis is useful for background material on the structure of the Russian government and the preparation and implementation of Stolypin's agrarian legislation, and for its reference to other sources.

Index

on colonial-federal questions, 128, 130
on relationship between government and parliament, 177
on Germany, German institutions and society, 6, 10, 103
on German colonization in the western Russian provinces, 118
on industrial workers
  in Kovno, 6
  in Grodno, 10
on Jews, anti-Semitism, pogroms
  in Saratov, 12-13
  as Minister of Internal Affairs, 30, 48-51, 153, 156
and N. M. Korkunov, 16, 63-64, 126
on Kadets, proto-Kadets,
  in Saratov, 14-16
  as Chairman of the Council of Ministers, 153-55
on local administration, 84 n. 63
  in Grodno, 10
  in Saratov, 54
  as Minister of Internal Affairs
    on *guberniya* administration, 54-57
    on *uezd-volost'* administration, 58-60
on local self-government
  in Grodno, 10
  as Minister of Internal Affairs, 62-63, 72
    guberniya, uezd, municipal levels, 64-67
    volost', settlement levels, 67-69
    on representatives from the provinces as advisers in central government, 69-71
    on education and, 79-80
    on role of Ministry of Internal Affairs in local self-government, 66-67
on peasants, communes, and the agrarian problem, 1-2
  in Kovno, 1889-1902, 5-6
  in Grodno, 1902-1903, 8-9
  in Saratov, 1903-1905, 13-14
  as Minister of Internal Affairs, 45-48
on Poles in Poland, 113
on Poles in the western provinces, 115, 116-17, 119, 121-22
on revolution and socialism, 9-10, 12-13, 46-47, 92-93, 94-95, 97-98, 103
  in Finland, 134-35
on a Russian constitution, 29, 169
on the State Duma (in general), 152, 157, 161-62, 165, 166, 170-71, 172, 173-74, 177-78
  in Saratov, 14
  First, 153
  Second, 159-60
  Third, 164
on *volost'* government
  in Grodno, 10
  as Minister of Internal Affairs, 67-69
on zemstvos in the western Russian provinces
  in Grodno, 10
  as Minister of Internal Affairs, 119-22, 174-77
Stundists, 75